TEN IS THE AGE OF DARKNESS

TEN
IS THE AGE
OF DARKNESS

THE BLACK BILDUNGSROMAN

■   ■

GETA LESEUR

University of Missouri Press
Columbia and London

Library of Congress Cataloging-in-Publication Data

LeSeur, Geta J.
Ten is the age of darkness : the Black Bildungsroman / Geta LeSeur.
   p. cm.
   Includes bibliographical references (p. 207) and index.
   ISBN 0-8262-1011-2 (alk. paper)
   1. American fiction—Afro-American authors—History and criticism.
2. West Indian Fiction (English)—Black authors—History and criticism.
3. Afro-American children in literature.   4. Afro-American youth in
literature.   5. Children, Black, in literature.   6. Afro-Americans in
literature.   7. Youth, Black, in literature.   8. West Indies—In
literature.   9. Blacks in literature.   10. Bildungsroman.   I. Title.
PS374.N4L47   1995
813.009'352054'08996073—dc20   95-7717
                                                               CIP

Text design: Rhonda Miller
Jacket design: Kristie Lee
Typesetter: BOOKCOMP
Printer and binder: Thomson-Shore, Inc.
Typefaces: Lithos and New Century Schoolbook

For credits, see page 233.

For
Arabella Ashley—my grandmother,
   who mothered us;
Loleta Viola Ashley—my mother,
   who also fathered me;
Che Arabella LeSeur—great-granddaughter,
   granddaughter, and my daughter—wiser
   because of all of us.

CONTENTS

PREFACE

I came to this project as a neophyte to the literature of my people. Having been born of West Indian parents in Jamaica, I gained all of my early wisdom from my parents, family "relations," community, friends, and colonial schoolteachers and headmasters of the Caribbean and Europe, primarily England. I read all of the "great literature" of the British, memorizing without error pages and pages of poetry and Shakespeare and the key characters of British lore. So, African American literature was new to me, as was the literature of the Caribbean region—my home. I had completed with high marks a private school education, an undergraduate degree from a Black college, and a master's degree from an Ivy League university and had not read much beyond the "masterpieces" of Western civilization—being Western and civilized meant White in all its glory. At this moment in many places, texts from that tradition are still being taught in lieu of other ethnic literatures despite the encroachment of a more multicultural, multiracial world. It's as if no one else lived or wrote in this sphere except White writers, often male, who often did not depict women realistically, if at all.

As I think back, I wonder why, as a student at a Black college, I did not read about, have courses on, or learn of writers from communities of color. Even today, as I visit some traditionally Black colleges, their courses are surprisingly devoid of much of the great body of writing done by our people over the past four hundred years—and before that. Although many scholars are researching and gathering these authors and voices, they appear to have little place or relevancy in the curriculum of some of our most prestigious institutions of learning.

It is a tragedy, to me, that generations of students have passed on and will pass on without having experienced Frederick Douglass's voice, Richard Wright's and James Baldwin's anger, Margaret Walker's dignity, Ralph Ellison's uniqueness, Gwendolyn Brooks's eclectic forms, Zora Neale Hurston's gravitation to folk roots, Toni

Morrison's genius, Alice Childress's experimentation, Alice Walker's protests, Ishmael Reed's and Ntozake Shange's language acrobatics, Derek Walcott's transcendence, Michelle Cliff's awareness, V. S. Naipaul's universality, Paule Marshall's artistic vision, George Lamming's adroitness, and the many renaissances of literature during this century. All of the works since the 1980s, for example, have burst forth as if they are spit from cannons spewing out new themes and ideas, new voices, new forms, new rhythms.

I began to see, read, and hear some of these authors only as a graduate student at Indiana University in Bloomington. Yes—that late! It was the classes of Professor John McCluskey Jr. on the Black novel and the Harlem Renaissance that began the process of my enlightenment. Others who contributed to my awakening were Professor Emile Snyder, who gave me a taste of Mother Africa's words; Professor Erlene Stetson, who introduced me to the African American woman's canon, especially poetry; and Professor Albert Wertheim, who although a twentieth-century drama scholar, saw Anglophone literatures (excluding British and American) as exciting and special. So, there I was in the right place at the right time ready to connect with these wonderful scholars. Thus began my prolonged relationship with African American, African, Australian, East Indian, New Zealandian, Canadian, and, naturally, Caribbean literatures.

All of these people and their courses created for me a place of happiness, awe, and excitement, and there I have stayed. It was also in John McCluskey's class that I first learned the term *bildungsroman*. I believe we were discussing Baldwin's *Go Tell It on the Mountain* at the time that he casually suggested the term and genre as an interesting form for approaching some specialized texts. My ears perked up, and thus began my second journey into another kind of knowledge—understanding the bildungsroman as an old and continuing genre and the ways in which many Black works belonged in it.

I began by reading anything I found pertaining to the Caribbean. Among my materials were primary works, fiction, poetry, essays, journals, sociological texts, reviews—everything. The wonderful and colorful names of authors representing the complexity of racial mixtures in the Caribbean gave me a connection to my Arawak Indian and maroon "cousins." At that point, I felt a little like James Baldwin, who in an interview said that he read every book in the New York Public Library (Harlem Branch) once he discovered that world. So in the Indiana University Library, I, too, discovered myself in George Lamming and Austin Clarke, who made me laugh and cry, in Michael Anthony's honest voice, in Merle Hodge's class and caste consciousness, in Sylvia Wynter's exploration of the psyche, in Zee Edgell's attention to the young girl, in Roger Mais's nation consciousness, in Edward Braithwaite's African pride, the strength of Nanny of the Maroons and Nancy Prince, and many, many more. My thirst was never satisfied. I could have read on and on forever but realized that I had to do something with this information, so I guarded it and kept it in a safe place—in my corner of this new world.

When I looked at the materials from the United States, it was Claude McKay, Toni Morrison, and Paule Marshall with whom I first felt the most in common. McKay and Marshall are connected to the Caribbean by parentage and are, to me, "newmericans." When I first read Marshall's *Brown Girl, Brownstones*, the story of ten-year-old bicultural Selina Boyce struck me deeply. Born in America of Barbadian parents, Selina was trying to belong to both spheres in the throes of a developing consciousness and puberty. In ten-year-old Selina I saw some similarities with my own daughter, Che, also ten, with an American-born father and a Caribbean mother. How will she handle this mixed heritage? Will she answer to one more than the other? Will she blend them successfully? Will she "defect" to one as Selina does? Thus Marshall's novel was absorbing for me and remains a centerpiece in my thoughts as I watch other family offspring struggle with their dual identities, attempting to settle into a space, body, and head "of their own."

It also seemed prophetic that Che came home from school one day, close to Halloween, with terror in her eyes. She told me that a woman had come up to her in the library and said in a penetrating voice, "ten is the age of darkness." I loved the poetic sound of it, but, of course, she did not think it was funny or poetic. However, to this day she can repeat the complete circumstance of this woman's utterance, vividly. Interestingly also, most of the protagonists of the bildungsroman fall between the ages of nine and thirteen, with ten becoming a significant marker. It is Che, therefore, who "gave" me the title of this book. So my thanks to you, dear child, for that!

Other people I would like to acknowledge as having an impact on my life are Drs. Joseph Russell and Ken Gros Louis, who saw my potential for scholarly work many years ago, and Barbara Christian and Opal Palmer Adisa, who during my postdoctoral years at Berkeley encouraged me to become one of a handful of people doing this work. The various people—Marvin Lewis, Tom Quirk, Daryl Dance, and others far and wide—who read and commented on the manuscript were very helpful in my editing at various stages, as was Marilynn Keil, who spent long hours typing it.

Finally, it is difficult for me to express in a public arena, like this, my gratitude and love for those closest to me. However, I must mention first my mother, Loleta, the greatest booster, optimist, and believer one could have. Second, I thank my aunts, brother, friends, and students, who have all been curious about "what it is that Geta does," but applauding all the time. Third is my husband, Ed, who has been outstanding, providing support and empathy when I became dismayed, tired, and frustrated with this process. It is his and their positive attitude and pride in me that got me to this place.

TEN IS THE AGE OF DARKNESS

INTRODUCTION

"OUT OF MANY, ONE"
A CASE OF MULTIPLE CHILDHOODS

Verandahs, where the pages of the sea
are a book left open by an absent master
in the middle of another life—
I begin here again,
begin until this ocean's
a shut book, and, like a bulb
the white moon's filaments wane.
                    Derek Walcott, *Another Life*

Novels of childhood are not new to any particular culture, nationality, or ethnic group. Yet each child's experience is unique because of factors within that child's culture. Do an African American child and a West Indian child share a similar history, or do they share just the experience of growing up in a transplanted culture? The slaves who were taken to the West Indies and the southern United States came almost entirely from West Africa, so James Baldwin, a Harlem Black, and George Lamming, a racially mixed West Indian from Barbados, share an ancestry with Camara Laye from West Africa.

A comparison of African American and West Indian novels of childhood reveals that the West Indian novelist writes a bildungsroman to recall childhood roots and to discover the truth about self and home, while the African American novelist tends to use personal experience in order to make a viable protest that is almost always about race, slave history, and the White establishment.[1] The West

---

1. The bildungsroman is a novelistic form of German origin. Goethe's *Wilhelm Meisters Lehrjahre,* published in 1795, served as a model for the form as it was later seen in France, England, other parts of the European continent, and

Indian writer's concern is for the child who is born into an isolated community and grows up in a world influenced by European administrators. What happens to these children is the very subtle protest the authors project in their novels. Recent history can be seen through these records of childhood, and history is written into everyone's life. The impact of change, the clash of cultures, and the molding of communities are felt through these fictions, and the result is a learning about ourselves, our parents, and our children. Some writers live through multiple childhoods, their own and those of their protagonists.

The Black experience in the United States or the West Indies cannot be limited or defined by parochial frames of reference and value that are derived from traditions (White and European) from which Black people have been largely excluded. Contemporary Black writers have therefore turned their attention inward, seeking to identify the traditions of their race by defining people individually, thus capturing a collective experience that is unique in terms of its circumstances of history and geography. They do not seek an entrée into the mainstream of European or American writing, but wish to explore the indigenous currents of those experiences—to communicate, often to educate, interpret, and reveal the varied experiences of four hundred years of suffering. This new movement in Black writing was referred to in the 1960s and 1970s as Black aesthetics, Black arts, Black consciousness, or cultural nationalism. This "new" Black literature was distinguished from the older literary works in that it was centered around a growing conversation among Black people about heritage and culture. The bildungsroman as a form has been adapted to serve part of that purpose. A society that produces writers and artists of ability and imagination provides its authors with the "real material" for their art. The reader can then appreciate the common humanity of the artist's creation, even though there are many shades of meaning. The focus of this study is on African

---

the United States. The form has been defined in various ways: the novel of development, novel of education (the literal translation of *bildungsroman*), "apprenticeship" novel, autobiographical novel, novel of childhood and adolescence, and the novel of initiation. The word came into use in the late nineteenth century outside Germany and became popular in England in the early Victorian era.

West Indian authors and African American authors whose works are various, rich, and representative of a "new" tradition.[2]

In reading selected childhood novels from the West Indies and the United States, one develops the impression that West Indian children remain "childlike" longer and that childhood can be a wonderful time, no matter how poor one is. The fact that the child is nurtured by the community and village may account for this, although the impression is refuted in several texts, as we learn of the bitter personal circumstances of some of these children, circumstances that are certainly believable and realistic. The natural setting, which all the West Indian writers use liberally in their novels, but do not take for granted, gives a healthy aspect to their protagonists' lives. The African American novel that most closely parallels the West Indian bildungsroman is Langston Hughes's *Not Without Laughter,* in which the boy, Sandy, has the support of an extended "complete" family unit in rural Kansas. The West Indian novel of youth also celebrates life through the use of local color and events. The use of dialect, the names given to characters, and the realism of the depicted scenes enhance the portrayal of the joy and pain of being a child. Despite the terror of the flogging of G by his mother in George Lamming's *In the Castle of My Skin,* for example, there is laughing through tears when they remember an earlier incident in the village; so they share that moment, on two levels. Childhood in the West Indies is not always idyllic by any means, but that "season of youth" is sharply delineated and imprinted on the child's consciousness forever; these texts written in retrospect by mature authors bear that out.

By contrast, the African American bildungsromane do not seem to celebrate life as much. One feels sadness and sorrow for the characters. It almost seems a tragedy to have been born in the first place. Even in Ralph Ellison's *Invisible Man,* which the author said is satire, the humor is lost because of the demeaning circumstances and strong political overtones. There are snatches of humor in particular scenes, but life is "serious business." Black children do not remain childlike for long in the United States, but are initiated into the

2. References made to pieces by White or Creole (White West Indian) writers like Jean Rhys or Geoffrey Drayton are used to compare what the coincidences of setting, time, place, and events do to the text or the development of new themes.

larger problems and cruder side of life very early. They are not as isolated from the rigors of adulthood as the West Indian child, but are given constant reminders of the more negative aspects of Black history as it affects their lives. The setting and American lifestyle do not permit childhood to linger, as the child very quickly experiences a loss of innocence. When young John Grimes, in Baldwin's *Go Tell It on the Mountain,* goes down the hill in Central Park he recognizes the gulf between himself and the old White man instantly; at the young age of nine, he already knows that the White world represents oppression and recognizes the cultural schism between two separate Americas, one Black, one White. The old man is "the other America." Maud Martha, in Gwendolyn Brooks's novel of the same name, knows that despite her intellect, entry into society will be difficult if not futile because of her race, color, and gender; and Selina Boyce, in Paule Marshall's *Brown Girl, Brownstones,* learns that grown Black women are still called "girls." Childhood as presented in the African American bildungsroman is depressing, like America's Black history. It is interesting how literature often confirms, validates, or rejects the findings of sociology.

How do the novels about boys growing up differ from those about girls? Since most of the novels about girls are written by women, the immediate assumption is that they are biased to their authors' points of view. As Paule Marshall has said, "women need to catch up anyway." She further adds that girls seem to have a "fear of growing up, and of other people, and of life, and ultimately retreat into their own worlds."[3] Pecola Breedlove in Toni Morrison's *The Bluest Eye* retreats into a world of madness, Sula Peace in Morrison's *Sula* into her silence and secrecy, Indigo in Ntozake Shange's *Sassafrass, Cypress, and Indigo* into her dolls, and Maud Martha into her books. They predicate their success as women on looks and beauty rather than on intellect. They are alienated from their mothers' community and from society in general. Their initiations are painful. Selina Boyce, whose roots include two cultures, West Indian and American, seems to have the most hope, but she has to return to her parents' homeland, Barbados, to experience rebirth.

3. "Shaping the World of My Art," 110.

Annie John, in Jamaica Kincaid's novel by the same name, has had, in West Indian terms, a charmed and idyllic childhood—a secure home, love from parents, success in school—yet she feels apart from her locus. The reality she shares with us as we read her story is not sadness but the experience of separation from her mother and the selfhood into which she is growing. Thus, the beginning of her second bildungsroman beckons. The "second bildungsroman" usually finds the protagonist entering puberty as well as relocating to a metropolitan sphere for work or further education, leaving home for a new growing experience different from the early or first one.

The girls in the West Indian novels, and that number has increased since the late 1940s and 1950s, are not as concerned with looks as they are with coalescing the twin cultures in which they find themselves. They seem more ambitious, aggressive, and passionate than their African American sisters, but, like them, they learn early about the problems of gender, color, men, and motherhood and community. They also share equal educational advantages with men if they show special intellect or are favored by a sponsor, often a teacher. The blending of maleness and femaleness begins early, even in play, where girls and boys participate in the same games, such as marbles or cricket, and girls have "girlfriends." Despite this superficial equality, there is a code of conduct prescribed for a girl by the family and the "village," so she must at all times remain "feminine." Because of the customary "wandering" nature of men and boys, girls still have a special place in the hearts of their mothers. Interestingly, some of the female protagonists in the novels to be discussed have no mothers in the traditional sense, yet the need to bond forms a significant part of their relationships. Bita Plant in Lamming's *Season of Adventure* and Tee in Merle Hodge's *Crick Crack, Monkey* are orphans, and Fola Piggott in Claude McKay's *Banana Bottom* rejects her mother, yet all of them become educated and attain upward mobility despite that loss, and do well despite their mothers' or fathers' absences or alienated roles. Often these girls, being neither girl nor woman, become neglected.

Boys in the African American and West Indian novels, by contrast, are largely the concern of their mothers, since there is a pervasive and literal absence of fathers in their lives. Many stories point out this fact. Most of the discipline is left to the mother, who, in addition, has all the burdens of providing a livelihood for her children. There is no real abuse, but boys receive strong discipline despite the still current cliché that "mothers love sons and raise daughters," suggesting a stricter hand with girls than with boys. In the West Indies, for example, the boy is often beaten more than once for the same offense: by his teacher, his mother, another family member, and a community elder. The cycle of reciprocal dependence is part of the social pattern of the mother–child relationship, impressed on the child by the mother and the larger society or community pattern of behavior. Previous generations of that family may have functioned in the same way. On the other hand, the boy receives little or no education about his duty as a prospective father. He accepts from his elders the authoritative saying that children are a woman's concern and that there need be no avoidance of procreation until he is in a position to fulfill the obligations of husband and father. Very little in his own experience, society, or the familial situation has enabled him to learn what those obligations might be. Most of the male protagonists, in all settings, West Indian and American, share these experiences. Boys in the West Indies also appear to behave more like "Black colonials" the older they become, the more exposed they are to the imported cosmopolitan culture. Later, having felt inferior for so long, they present themselves as "new massas." Some of their Black brothers in the United States, on the other hand, become self-sufficient and unmasked if they survive their often difficult childhoods, while others carry a lifelong hostility to the point of being dangerous to the larger society. Some, like James Baldwin, Langston Hughes, Richard Wright, and Gordon Parks, become artists. Childhood for Black boys is still full of pain and little joy; manhood seems no better.

The declaration of paternity in the African American novels is peripherally unimportant because of a welfare system that destroys the nuclear family and supports the idea of the absentee father. In the West Indies paternity is not a major issue because it is common and socially accepted in some classes for there to be no marital bonds, as illustrated in Austin Clarke's *Amongst Thistles and Thorns*. A growing number of strong male characters conform to an evolving bildungsroman model in West Indian literature of boys who take on "femaleness." This model may also be attributable to the growing inventiveness of Caribbean writers who are experimenting and redefining the genre on their own terms. In novels by Michael Anthony and Austin Clarke, Francis and Milton, respectively, are the best examples of this duality, but Wilby in Sybil Seaforth's *Growing Up with Miss Milly* appears to resist this designation. The girls in Jamaica Kincaid's works are unique, representing female heroes of a sort rarely seen before. The relationships with family members, especially in the case of the female characters, show similarities in all the West Indian novels. In them girls seem to be closer to their fathers and alienated from their mothers. On the other hand, boys who are "fatherless" seem closer to their mothers. Two conclusions can be drawn—one, that gender roles are somewhat androgynous, and, second, that this is more acceptable in the West Indian culture than some others.

The theme of the child assuming adulthood recurs in all literatures, but it does so with significant regularity in West Indian literature. Novels devoted entirely to the process of the child growing up include V. S. Naipaul's *Miguel Street,* Peter Kempadoo's *Guyana Boy,* Namba Roy's *Black Albino,* Andrew Salkey's series of stories including *Hurricane* (1964), Ian MacDonald's *The Hummingbird Tree* (1969), and Wilson Harris's trilogy of childhood fables, *The Sleepers of Roraima* (1970). Alice Durie's *One Jamaica Gal* (1939) is the earliest novel that sets up the West Indian theme of initiation. The female protagonists of Creole writers Herbert De Lisser and Edward Mittelholzer, although romanticized dark West Indian "daughters," do, in a broad definition, have their personal bildungsromane.[4] De Lisser's *Jane's Career,* for example, follows a naive Black girl from a rural village in Jamaica to Kingston, the capital city, where she makes mistakes and has hostile experiences, mostly at the hands of men. Although interesting, these protagonists lack the reality of characters depicted in novels written after 1950. They are, however, only part of a much wider literature in which initiation into adulthood forms an important part. This may also reflect the importance

---

4. *Creole* as I use the term here refers to White or mulatto authors who, early on, depicted characters in a picaresque and romantic manner. Their journeys or initiations echoed those of the English poor, in Caribbean settings.

of children in Caribbean communities. Children, numerically, make up a large proportion of the population; in Guyana, for instance, one-third of the population is under the age of twenty-one. Further, in part because children have to assume some of the responsibilities of an adult while young, and because of close family ties in the indigenous populations, there has tended to be less cultural division between adult and child than exists in many Western societies. It is still true to say that in the Caribbean the child's point of view has a natural acceptance that can be distinguished from both the stress on maturity and the more self-conscious and intellectualized romantic cult of childhood in the European tradition.

Children can play a part in emergent world literatures, because in cultures seeking independence, children enjoy a natural, if precarious, enfranchisement. They provide a fresh point of view as Gullivers without fantasy, sojourners of the present, exploring the islands of manhood and womanhood, remaking the maps. Mark Twain's novel of boyhood, *Huckleberry Finn* (1855), holds a crucial position in another literature for some of the same reasons. At the same time this natural joy of childhood holds tragic implications, for it invests children with values that, in adulthood, by definition, they must lose.

It is possible to examine most bildungsromane from places where children of color are born and grow up, such as Africa, New Zealand, Oceania, and Australia, to see how those cultures and lifestyles act upon the developing mind of a child. How does growing up in Black Africa differ from growing up as an aborigine in Australia or as a Maori in New Zealand? What effect does living in two worlds have on the development of second-generation children of the West Indians in Britain or Canada? Or on Hispanics in the American Southwest? Or on Puerto Ricans in New York City? Marshall's *Brown Girl, Brownstones* gives us one aspect of that experience; Maxine Hong Kingston's *The Woman Warrior* gives us another.[5]

One could learn much of value from comparative studies of the various literatures and cultures. Samuel Selvon's Londoners and Austin Clarke's Canadians carry their West Indianness with them but soon

5. Kingston's moving book is written from the perspective of a young Chinese American girl who tries desperately to make connections with the old and new of her birthright and culture.

find that, despite their nostalgia for home, and even though their newly created communities cannot completely fulfill their needs, they cannot truly go home again. James Ngugi's *Weep Not Child* has close affinities with Lamming's *In the Castle of My Skin,* since in both novels the boys' growing years take place against the backdrop of a village undergoing social and political change. Peter Abraham's *Mine Boy* explores themes of journey and initiation into manhood and blackness, similar to those of Ralph Ellison's *Invisible Man.* The education Xuma, in Peter Abrahams's *Mine Boy,* receives about his people and his country is invaluable as it provides him with a good sense of his culture, identity, and history. No school learning could equal that experience. Alex La Guma's *A Walk in the Night* and Nkem Nwankwo's *Danda* tell us more about growing up in Africa than most anthropological studies can. The lives they portray are vivid, truthful, functional, and instructional because the omniscient authorial convention of the bildungsroman makes this possible. All of these authors tell us who we are and that a shared culture, custom, and economic common sense are often greater factors for unity than political ideas. This appears to be true as well in the countries and peoples that remain to be written about.

There appear to be a number of similarities between growing up in the West Indies and the United States and growing up in Africa. In African tales and novels like Camara Laye's *The African Child* and Ferdinand Oyono's *House Boy,* for example, the points of view on childhood, village life, family, and events are understandable to readers in the African diaspora. In *Growing Up,* by Deborah Manley, for example, the speaker says:

We do not play with our father, just bowed and greeted him politely . . . I was greatly in awe of him . . .

. . . My earliest world was my mother. . . . Until six years old, a tribal boy's conduct is the concern of his family. Then comes a day when he is to realize that what he does is the concern of the community . . .

What one learns lives in the head. . . . The teacher is in charge of the African boy's total education . . .

As soon as he learned to speak fairly well, a boy is sent on minor domestic errands . . .

Traditional stories are told at night . . .

There is usually some acute discomfort connected with the discovery of
who you are which helps in remembering it.[6]

These lines read like a guidebook on boyhood and girlhood for the
Afro-World child. Any of these statements could have been uttered
by Francis, Milton, G, Sandy, Pecola, Selina, or, perhaps, a Zulu child
from South Africa. It seems, therefore, that these occurrences could
be applicable to other childhoods in other Third World countries. This
is not to say that the Anglo child does not experience the torments
and anguish of childhood, it is simply that, lacking the encumbrances
of race and color, he has less to complicate his voyage into adulthood
than do these children.

Additional questions need to be asked and answered, therefore, in
discussing the novels of youth in the United States and those in the
West Indies: What difference does setting have on the life of the characters? Are Black children in the United States or the West Indies
constricted by society's roles? How do race, color, gender, and class
affect development? Often, children try to negate their blackness
since it robs them of a recognizable history and a sense of who they
are, and because they are conditioned by a society that denies them
recognition as individuals. The first shock comes in childhood. They
envision themselves as leaders or successful human beings, but the
painful "rites of passage" introduce them to their roles in society, and
they are required to perform meaningless rituals that negate their
individual freedoms. One of the tasks of the novelist, therefore, is to
reduce human experience to manageable proportions, and one of the
most effective ways to do so has been to explore the growing process
by writing a novel of childhood.

The perceptions of childhood are indispensable to any complete
understanding of a community and its people, not only because any
child is more honest than the most truthful adult, but also because
children are so often the forgotten camera in the corner. Things are
said and done in their presence, secrets are revealed, gestures are
made that would be concealed from other adults. Everything is new

6. Deborah Manley, *Growing Up*, 13–35.

and huge to children. They have not had time to learn boredom. They do not have to protect themselves against new experience, as adults frequently must when their sensibilities are carrying all the load they can bear. Much of what adults think they see is simply a projection onto some event or some person of what they are, or simply an attempt to find confirmation of their own understandings and prejudices. The adult novelist is no exception. When an adult writes, in retrospect, it is difficult to be objective about specific events that remain vivid and inescapable. By re-inventing or re-creating situations, the novelist can reveal in a person what in life may be hidden and latent. The inventions of the form indicate, in fact, a general principle of the novel, which is that our existence is based on the experiences of life, which in turn are based on particular and identifiable origins of character and incident.

How does belonging to an ethnic group influence one's life? What does it all mean? To many, these questions may have a ring of seriousness, of commitment, of ties to a cultural heritage that certainly makes them "different" and sets them aside from others. Children, if given the chance and a sympathetic audience, have good insights into their conditions and can separate the illusions from the realities of their home and environment. Those who have unhappy or happy memories associated with their cultural lifestyles are given the opportunity to express them freely through the voices of their authors. One hopes that boys and girls will be able to tell their painful or joyful experiences as they search for a unique identity and as they explore the world beyond their communities. Children should never feel that their cultural past is imprisoned in the Anglos' history or that their future is as invisible swimmers in the European mainstream.

This study's purpose is threefold. First, it illustrates the linkages among the disparate experiences of a people who shared a common slave history after dispersal from Africa while maintaining a sense of family, community, and customs. Second, it emphasizes the importance of the formative years of young Black children's lives and shows how they differ from their White peers and from each other because of cultural and colonial differences. Third, it demonstrates the Black writers' ability to use and adapt a traditional form, the European bildungsroman, to create lively, wonderful, and artistically sound novels that can instruct us.

In chapter I, " 'The Ending Up Is the Starting Out': The Bildungsroman Re/formed," I discuss the origins and definition of the form from Goethe to the present. Its development is traced from the 1700s to the 1900s in England, citing selected Victorian models as examples, such as Charles Dickens's *Great Expectations.* The discussion then moves from England to the United States, where the form becomes social documentary, beginning with Mark Twain's *Huckleberry Finn.* Some twentieth-century American examples are noted, including J. D. Salinger's *Catcher in the Rye* and some of William Faulkner's works. For their pertinence to this study, it is critical to consider American history, time periods, and cultural markers. Among the latter are the slave narratives by such writers as Frederick Douglass (*Narrative of the Life*), Harriet Wilson (*Our Nig*), and Harriet Jacobs (*Incidents in the Life of a Slave Girl*). All of these Black works have detailed autobiographical components and may be considered to have laid the groundwork for the African American bildungsroman as we know it.

The discussion then continues to twentieth-century versions of the African American form, such as Richard Wright's *Black Boy,* James Baldwin's *Go Tell It on the Mountain,* and Toni Morrison's *The Bluest Eye.* In novels like George Lamming's *In the Castle of My Skin* and Austin Clarke's *Amongst Thistles and Thorns* it is noted that the West Indian bildungsroman comes closer to the European model, perhaps because of a long history of colonial presence in the Caribbean, where independence did not come to the larger West Indian islands until the 1960s. Also, from Emancipation until the most recent times, education was predominantly British and/or European based. It is only with the new crop of writers (mostly women) from the 1970s and 1980s that the genre has been reshaped to accommodate contemporary stories of male and female development.

In chapter II, " 'Behold the Great Image of Authority': African West Indian Male Initiation," the boys' stories are examined in terms of how the novels depict elements of British colonialism and education, the slave experience, African connections, and the scars of growing up. *In the Castle of My Skin* and *Amongst Thistles and Thorns* both have in their plots British-trained, ruthless, cruel headmasters who are the "great images of authority." In addition, each author has used the original bildungsroman model well; Lamming gives the reader an endearing, poetic look at West Indian childhood, while Clarke presents a harsh yet realistic look at boyhood when one is fatherless and penniless. The latter raises many social and political issues bordering on the African American protest works that are discussed next. Clarke, a Barbadian, is also the first West Indian writer since McKay to emigrate to the United States during the Black civil rights movement of the 1960s and may have been influenced by that era and its militancy.

Chapter III, " 'His Great Struggle Beginning': African American Male Initiation," addresses what is probably one of the most various and complex aspects of the subject because the novels are so politically charged and historically anchored. The slave experience is inherent in them, be it urban or rural, North or South. Not only are the novels examined in this chapter Black boys' initiation stories, but they are also very much in the protest tradition, so that the themes and incidents in *Black Boy* and *Go Tell It on the Mountain,* for example, are fully recognizable for those who have lived through the Black American experience and its harshness. Wright's and Ellison's novels also move the main characters from boyhood to adolescence, which is a clear indication that the Black bildungsroman has no distinct age markers. The protagonists of the African American novels about boys growing up seek experience in a conscious attempt to cultivate inner powers. They must, however, question whatever values prevail in society and construct a morality and philosophy of life from the bottom up. "The goal is not only the harmonious development of the whole personality but the reconciliation of the transferred self with political and social contradictions in society."[7] When this end has been reached, the bildungsroman concludes on an affirmative note; what we see, however, is that these endings are uncommon in the case of the Black boys. Langston Hughes's *Not Without Laughter* is seen as the closest parallel to the West Indian novel of development because the life of the main character, Sandy, is not as politically charged and

7. Barbara White, *Growing Up Female: Adolescent Girlhood in American Fiction,* xii.

is a bit more harmonious than are those of other African American protagonists. This is not to say that Hughes does not present social issues worth exploring. The style of presentation veils, to some extent, the cycle of joblessness and desperation that faces one such Black family trying to raise a sensitive boy in the early part of the twentieth century.

Chapter IV, "Womanish Girls: African American Female Initiation," asks whether a Black girl develops similarly to a Black boy given similar social, cultural, racial, and historical circumstances. In this chapter, I examine Brooks's *Maud Martha,* Morrison's *The Bluest Eye,* and Shange's two novels, *Sassafrass, Cypress, and Indigo* and *Betsey Brown,* as well as Paule Marshall's *Brown Girl, Brownstones* as a bicultural piece.

These stories are very different from the boys' stories discussed in chapter III, mainly because of gender differences. The study of Black female development is crucial, because critics prior to the contemporary surge in critical studies of Black women's writing tended to universalize the experiences of boys, usually White males, while negating female childhood experiences and, even more so, Black female experiences, which are very vague and different from the White girls' experience. Black girls find out very early that the culture's emphasis on physical beauty, color, class, and gender is something to overcome and that it somehow places them at a disadvantage. Maud Martha and Pecola suffer because they are "ugly." Pecola also goes "mad" after being sexually abused by her father. These themes were not explored, put in books, or critiqued before Black women writers like Alice Walker and Morrison broached them. Shange's characters, on the other hand, despite negative encounters with men, are entrenched in Black culture. With their mothers' and Black women's culture as their milieus, they often gain some sense of wholeness by the novels' end. This further emphasizes the importance of women in the raising of their "little women," and what that presence means.

Marshall's *Brown Girl, Brownstones* anchors the chapter because Marshall's place in both African American and West Indian literature is critical to the Black woman writer's renaissance in both spheres. Her main character, Selina Boyce, whose *Bildung* the novel is, exhibits confusion about cultural identity. Eventually she acquires new knowledge about her worlds, which enables her to change as she launches into adolescence. Marshall's text, therefore, is as much about cultural dualism as about the first West Indian migration of the 1920s. During that era, West Indian immigrants were despised by American Blacks, often more so than European immigrants during the same period.

No examination of the work of Black women writers can ignore the portrayal of the Black mother, therefore part of the discussion focuses on her contribution to her daughter's development. The images that surface usually represent historical types like the matriarch, mammy, and madonna, but mostly these images are reformed so that the mothers become, like their daughters, "new" women. Both African American and West Indian mothers are discussed in relationship to their cultural contexts and to their children's lives.

Chapter V, "Journeys to Selfhood: African West Indian Female Initiation," explores a variety of young women's struggles for entrée into their cultures and communities. Bita Plant and Fola Piggott are female heroines in novels by male writers—Claude McKay's *Banana Bottom* and George Lamming's *Season of Adventure,* respectively. These writers' works are used because my reading of Black West Indian male writers has indicated that they present a more rounded and realistic depiction of women than do Black American male writers. McKay's Bita, although a bit romanticized, is recognizable to West Indian readers because of her circumstance of guardianship and patronage by a White family. One must remember that McKay was influenced by the nineteenth-century Romantics and came to the United States early in the twentieth century as a poet rather than a fiction writer,[8] so that he wrote from a foreign and exiled vantage point. Bita's earthiness is similar to that of Janie in *Their Eyes Were Watching God* by Zora Neale Hurston, a Harlem Renaissance contemporary of McKay's. Fola Piggott, as portrayed by Lamming, lives her bildungsroman through political, social, and cultural occurrences. She is atypical of many protagonists in this study, yet

8. Jamaican-born McKay's earliest works were books of poetry, the first being published in 1912. Having established himself as a good poet, he became an active participant in the Harlem Renaissance (1920s and 1930s). His fiction was written after his travels to Russia, England, and Africa. *Banana Bottom* was his first novel.

her initiatory experiences and path to knowledge are memorable. One distinct feature of her journey is the recalling of African rituals, customs, and icons. Her mother in this text warrants some discussion as she, too, is very puzzling as a West Indian mother.[9] Fola is an early West Indian heroine in a novel by a Black writer; other early ones are by White male writers.

Other books, such as Merle Hodge's *Crick Crack, Monkey,* give a fairly traditional and realistic look at a West Indian girl's development from poor circumstances, in a manner that seemingly continues the tradition of seeking educational opportunities that McKay wrote about earlier. Jamaica Kincaid's *Annie John* lifts the spirit because of its many poignant scenes of the pain of growing up female and of the relationships between mother and daughter. Kincaid, being one of the newer voices in West Indian literature, points the way to other women writers in this genre. Zee Edgell, Marlene Nourbouse Philip, Jean Riley, and Sybil Seaforth have all added to this aspect of the Caribbean Black women's canon.

Most of the novels written in the bildungsroman tradition are in various studies referred to as "autobiographical fiction" or "fictive autobiography." Sandra Pouchet Paquet's wonderful essay "West Indian Autobiography" cites several books that can be classified as disguised autobiographies. Some examples are C. L. R. James's *Beyond a Boundary,* written when James was sixty-two years old; Derek Walcott's *Another Life;* and Naipaul's *Finding the Center: Two Narratives.* In all of these, Paquet suggests, there are "portraits of the artist" becoming the artist, and "the autobiography unfolds as a quest for the familial and ethnic roots of his creativity."[10] This entire topic is worthy of a separate study.

This study will show how literature written by West Indian and African American writers describes the thematic parallels of the bildungsroman that mark the literary contemporaneity of each culture. It examines some of the ways in which selected writers used their

---

9. See Edith Clarke, *My Mother Who Fathered Me,* a study of female-headed households in the Caribbean, where this condition is pervasive. Also Leota Lawrence's essay "Mother-Child Relationships in British Caribbean Literature," which discusses *A Year in San Fernando, In the Castle of My Skin,* and *Season of Adventure.*

10. Sandra Pouchet Paquet, "West Indian Autobiography," 197.

cultures' preoccupations to construct separate yet multiple worlds. While this separateness reflects their sometimes sharp, sometimes clouded insights into both their own and their society's distinctiveness, it demonstrates their unrelenting awareness of the distance between themselves as a Black people and the traditional White ways of life. They are conscious, always, of trying to make sense out of chaos, a chaos that their own local histories seem to intensify.

I

"THE ENDING UP IS THE STARTING OUT"
THE BILDUNGSROMAN RE/FORMED

Well, son, I'll tell you:
Life for me ain't been no crystal stair.
. . . .
But all the time
I'se been a-climbin' on,
And reachin' landin's,
And turnin' corners,
And sometimes goin' in the dark
Where there ain't been no light.
So boy, don't you turn back.
Don't you set down on the steps
'Cause you finds it's kinder hard.
Don't you fall now—
Langston Hughes, "Mother to Son"

Within the canon of African American literature, the bildungsroman has no distinct prototype equivalent to that created by White European writers. As a form it tends to be highly autobiographical, and the hero, often a male, tends to be gifted or extraordinarily sensitive. In the traditional Black form, the hero rejects the constraints of home and sets out on a journey through the world, obtaining guides who represent different worldviews, including "a philosophy of darkness."[1] The protagonists in these stories meet with many setbacks before choosing a proper philosophy, mate, and vocation. In early Black literature, the form had as its precursors early autobiographies like Olaudah Equiano's *The Interesting Narrative of the Life of Olaudah Equiano, or Gustavas Vassa, the African, Written*

---

1. White, *Growing Up Female,* 3.

18

by Himself (1789) and Frederick Douglass's *Narrative of the Life of Frederick Douglass, an American Slave, Written by Himself* (1845). Langston Hughes's *Not Without Laughter,* Richard Wright's *Black Boy,* Gwendolyn Brooks's *Maud Martha,* and Claude Brown's *Manchild in the Promised Land* are early twentieth-century examples of the Black bildungsroman.

The term *Black bildungsroman* is being used here to suggest a difference between those stories written by White (that is, American or European) writers and those written by African, African American, and African West Indian writers. Protagonists within both forms may share gender, age, "provinciality," surrogate parentage, and education. They may also leave home, experience isolation, experience debasing or exulting sexual experiences, move to the city or enlightened place, change and transform, experience paranoia, have conflicts with "parents," then "leave" childhood and place only to begin a new phase of the journey to adulthood, the so-called second phase of their development. Yet, for Black children the *incidents* and subsequent *responses* are different from those of White children, perhaps because the authors (Black/White) use different styles of presentation. During the 1950s the trend toward portraiture and individualization saw Blacks exploring their identities. Several characters like the nameless protagonist in Ellison's *Invisible Man,* Cross Damon in *The Outsider* by Richard Wright, and John Grimes in *Go Tell It on the Mountain* by James Baldwin all experience growing-up crises as young Black men.

In writing about childhood, the motion is always back to the place of origin. Mark Twain is the premier American author of the nineteenth century who used this movement in his fiction. *Huckleberry Finn* ends with Huck pointing to the West, ready to light out for the territory in search of the freedom he sought with the slave Jim, but which eluded him. The motion toward childhood was for Twain a motion toward the South where he was born.[2] But we must consider also that Douglass and Black women writers Harriet Jacobs and Harriet Wilson were even earlier writing a form for exploring their version of what slavery was doing to Black people. So we have on the one hand the Huck/Jim story and on the other the experiences

2. Seymour Gross, *Images of Blacks in American Literature,* 62.

of Jacobs's and Wilson's characters Frado and Linda Brent set in the same time period, even though the levels of complexity vary depending on the reader's perspective.

The White "new novel" of the 1920s in England, as written by James Joyce and Virginia Woolf, turned away from the content as well as the form of the original bildungsroman. In America, by the 1930s Thomas Wolfe's *Look Homeward, Angel* (1929) and the Studs Lonigan trilogy by James T. Farrell, with an insistence on the social and economic determinants of character, represented the major mode. The "angry young men" of the 1950s created assertive characters in social jungles, and the conventional bildungsroman appears in their fictions thusly: The hero alienated from his parents, dissatisfied with middle-class education, declares his independence, achieves his sexual initiation, serves a vocational apprenticeship, grubs for money, faces up to the burdens of self-interest and problems of success, and in the end wonders, Is it worth it? Fictions from the 1950s to the 1970s share these concerns. John Wain's *Strike the Father Dead* (1962) is a prototype of this modern form, and J. D. Salinger's *Catcher in the Rye* (1958) is a chronicle of self-discovery and often of the sad state of modern life.

Heroes or heroines, whatever their accomplishments, share something of the imaginative energy of their authors. Authors turn to the bildungsroman to assess their own development and growth. As the hero or heroine reaches maturity, each will typically feel bondage, the multiple constraints of living, often represented by the pressures of the cruel city. The creative vision, however, restores freedom, and the child's questioning sense of outward things is parent of the understanding child; the quickened imagination outlives the troubled "season of youth."[3]

Several of Faulkner's characters go back in time to their childhoods, for example in *The Sound and the Fury* (1929), *Light in August* (1932), *Absalom, Absalom!* (1936), *The Unvanquished* (1938), and *Go Down, Moses* (1942). Some characters give us glimpses of boyhood friendships between Black and White boys, such as that of Bayard and Ringo in *The Unvanquished*. The pioneer spirit of innocence is

---

3. Jerome Buckley, *Season of Youth: The Bildungsroman from Dickens to Golding,* 18.

inherent in the young character and symbolizes freedom from racial and economic barriers. This reaching back seems synonymous with the White man's longing for a vision of a "lost fraternity."

Black novels of childhood, although having some of the characteristics of the European or White bildungsroman, cannot be grouped with any of these novels. They are very distinct in their content and presentation because of a different set of sociological and historical contexts. If only because of the facts of Black history alone, the trappings of class and color, and the general circumstances of home, family, and community, Black children have not flourished like White children. With Emancipation, in the United States and the Caribbean, the newly independent nations, and the African nations' revolutions of the 1960s, a new kind of literature had to be written as an affirmation of those emancipations.

The bildungsroman is a model some Black writers adapted, consciously or unconsciously, to tell their stories; their plots exhibit some parallels with the European model, because some of them seem to have read Goethe's *Wilhelm Meister* or perhaps have used it subconsciously. British-educated George Lamming and Austin Clarke acknowledge their debt to the Europeans. The works of Americans like James Baldwin, Paule Marshall, and Ralph Ellison show it also. This is not to say that their works are not original; actually, their work is much more exciting than the older pieces. One of the first things the reader or researcher of these novels notices, though, is that almost all of these works from Europe or the United States prior to the 1930s were written by males with male protagonists, who were usually fictionalized personae of the authors. Black male writers entered this established tradition later but repeated this same pattern by telling boys' stories. European White female writers did not for the most part use the form, as one finds only a few novels by women in the genre.[4] Clearly, then, male writers, regardless of color or nationality, dominated the tradition early.

West Indian and African American novels of childhood and adolescence share with the European novels the use of provincial and restrictive settings, "fatherlessness," and alienation. Tee in *Crick*

---

4. Olive Schreiner's *The Story of an African Farm* (1883) is an early female bildungsroman.

Crack, Monkey, Fola in *Season of Adventure,* Richard in *Black Boy,* and countless others in both literatures share the same woes with characters like Dickens's David Copperfield and Pip. Alienation from the mother is balanced with dependence on the mother. In novels about West Indian boys growing up—Milton Sobers in *Amongst Thistles and Thorns* and G in *In the Castle of My Skin,* for example—the close mother–son relationship is integral to the plot and the boys' development, whereas in *Season of Adventure* and *Brown Girl, Brownstones* the relationships between mothers and daughters are almost adversarial. Another distinctive trait that the White European and the Black writer share is the journey theme. In the European novels, the protagonist/hero almost always drifts toward the city. For Dickens's David Copperfield and Lawrence's Paul Morel, the movement is toward "the faintly humming town" where the hero must make his way. Although their movement is more localized, Francis in *The Year in San Fernando,* G and Trumper in *In the Castle of My Skin,* John Grimes in *Go Tell It on the Mountain,* and Ellison's nameless protagonist in *Invisible Man* all, notably, do likewise.

The bildungsroman is almost always a "novel of education," and the education may be either formal or informal; in some novels the definition of education is used broadly. Dickens's *Great Expectations,* for example, pays little attention to formal instruction but stresses the educative results of an emotional experience. Pip's trauma and education are quite structured, whereas Black children learn in structured and unstructured ways by observing and listening to others in their community, school, and church. Good examples are John Grimes's life in the Pentecostal churches of Harlem, Pecola's camaraderie with the three prostitutes, and the scenes and stories Selina experiences with West Indian women in her mother's kitchen.

The informal type of education the West Indian child gets is from the village or "yard." The rearing of children is a shared responsibility. They become everybody's as soon as they are old enough to venture out. They learn by partaking in the sights and scenes of life around them. Everything about one's life is also in the public domain. The scene of G in *In the Castle of My Skin* being bathed by his mother and the ensuing confusion, ridicule, and punishment, for example, provide a poignant illustration of how the West Indian community participates in rearing its children.

The "community" or "village" idea is present on another level in the African American novels if we consider the brownstone house in which Selina's family lives in Brooklyn as being a community. Part of Selina's education comes from the various tenants in the building, who advise her just as any family member would. What the Black writer does is to make community an extremely important part of the novel's plot. For Morrison and Marshall, communities take on broader dimensions, and so have lives of their own, just as do the characters.

Education also comes from other sources, and the idea of leaving home adds another dimension to the educative process. Movement or going away from the provincial place is considered an advantage and a blessing in the West Indies and is viewed as education also. When characters go to England to school (like Tee or Bita Plant) or to Trinidad (like G) or from country to town (like Francis), they are seen as being favored by Fortune. Even when Francis goes from his Black rural home to a White urban one, he is considered fortunate, as this scene from *The Year in San Fernando* illustrates:

> Ma rushed home from work one evening, very excited. Usually she'd walk out into the main road . . .
> "You know what happen?" she said, almost out of breath.
> "You know what happen?"
> We waited in suspense to hear, and brother Fred said,
> "What happen, Ma?"
> "Hush up," she said, "I talking. Listen to me!" . . .
> "You all know what happen?" she said.
> We said nothing.
> "Francis going to live in San Fernando." . . .
> There was shock all round and all eyes turned on me. I was flabbergasted. . . . Ma said I was the lucky one because Mr. Chandles could have hundreds of little boys to go but he had asked for me, specially. She thanked God that I had come into such good fortune.[5]

The sending of young boys or girls to live in town with another family is not uncommon in the West Indies. In *Banana Bottom,* for example, Bita Plant's living with the Craigs as an "adopted child" is seen as an advantage for her. Francis's and Bita's social status is

---

5. Michael Anthony, *The Year in San Fernando,* 3–4.

immediately improved, and their class and status change abruptly. From that moment on they will become "been tos." Having "gone to" a new and better place they are viewed differently, with awe and respect, by their friends and relatives. Subsequently, they are expected to behave differently by taking on more urbane and European modes of conduct and performance.

African Americans after Emancipation moved around in the South, as evidenced in Wright's *Black Boy.* But more often the journey is from the rural to the urban, or from South to North. Although the reasons for leaving may be to find a better lifestyle or to "make it big," the urban Black in America as well as the West Indian in London or Toronto usually finds that the city does not often offer the good life. The city becomes a hostile place, a place of dashed hopes. Baldwin's protagonist, Gabriel, finds this to be so, as does Marshall's Deighton Boyce, who migrates from Barbados to Brooklyn. Often, when young Blacks go to a White household it is to work, to do menial labor, and to endure economic and other abuses during their tenure there. One sees this when Francis enters the household in San Fernando and when Richard gets a job with a White woman and other situations in Arkansas, Mississippi, and Tennessee. The move does not represent a step up, so the master–slave relationship and the plantation story are replayed in a harsher key. This is also the scenario in Richard Wright's *Native Son,* in which Bigger Thomas's family lives through a northern plantation story in Chicago. It has been suggested that for the Black man, the city is anti-bildungsroman, and when one looks at how differently and cruelly the city functions in these novels, that statement seems valid.

Formal education is suggested but not explored to any great extent in the African American novels to be studied, even though the reader is aware that John, Richard, Maud, and Selina usually are good students and get noticed by their teachers. The reader is aware that children do go to school, but school is inconsequential to plot and theme because that is not the story to be discussed or explored. In the West Indian novels, however, both formal and informal education merge to form an integral part of the plot. Formal education in these works is the traditional, structured formula sent over from England and in the early novels administered by cruel, merciless headmasters. That foreign education given to children seemed irrelevant and out of place to the average child in the islands, but did prepare many for going "abroad" and for upward social and economic mobility. The West Indians, however, survived the educational process to which they had been subjected. George Lamming survived the school he describes in *In the Castle of My Skin,* as did Austin Clarke in *Amongst Thistles and Thorns* and in his autobiography, *Growing Up Stupid under the Union Jack.* Most writers and their protagonists triumphantly outlived nine or ten years of the deadening ferocity of a harsh and authoritarian discipline. Punishment by flogging as part of the educative process in the West Indies shows another brutal aspect of that education. It is supposed, for example, that the child cannot learn or become an initiate into formal learning without the merciless floggings first introduced by "colonial" headmasters and perpetuated by their Black counterparts.

In Europe and the African diaspora, the bildungsroman has "rites and rituals" as part of its structure. This could mean prescribed action, routine, or pattern in the initiation process. For example, sex, used broadly, is a part of each child's initiation into adulthood. It takes many forms depending on the novel; it may be explicit, natural, or symbolic. For Stephen Dedalus in Joyce's *Portrait of the Artist as a Young Man,* it is a natural pleasurable function; for Francis it is symbolic or implied; but for McKay's Bita Plant and Morrison's Pecola it is explicit, taking the form of rape. Many initiation novels have explored this aspect, but it cannot be negated as important in the typical bildungsroman. Other rituals may be an established routine, such as Francis watering the plants or going to market for Mrs. Chandles; or Milton running errands or reading the Bible for his mother; or G's mother ceremonially fixing food and thus creating a special time for mother and son. In addition there are the more formal cultural initiation rites of Bita Plant at Banana Bottom or Fola at the "tonelle."[6]

Most protagonists usually have a quick and aesthetic sensibility, a dedication to art. All of these Black writers, one supposes, have this sensibility, since the fruits of their creation are their novels. In

6. A "tonelle" is a place where a voodoo ceremony is held. Part of the ceremonial preparation is the creation of visible marks that designate it as a "holy" place.

terms of their life, work, styles, and biographies, George Lamming's, James Baldwin's, and Paule Marshall's works come closest to being the Black New World counterpart of the form and are therefore singularly significant to the genre. Although Paule Marshall's and Jamaica Kincaid's works are considered aesthetic and "arty," their works are actually closer to the *Kunstlerroman*.[7]

The autobiographical component of the bildungsroman cannot be overlooked. Because of a seemingly vast amount of autobiographical experience in these novels, the question must be asked as to whether they are a type of autobiography. The answer is that they are novels of initiation, childhood, youth, education, and the various other definitions used for the bildungsroman, with autobiographical components.[8] Some have more than others, and one can only know this by consulting the biographies and statements made by these authors or such companion pieces as are available in the case of Austin Clarke, James Baldwin, and Richard Wright. The heroes and heroines of these novels are not concerned with what is specific to them as artists, but with something more generally shared in the human experience. The artist is concerned with inward problems and struggles, with emotive experiences, moral values, and imaginative ideals. The writers/artists differ from many autobiographers in that they single out a central issue of character or a distinctive feature and develop that in fictive ways. Baldwin's *Go Tell It on the Mountain* is an excellent example of this, as is Lamming's *In the Castle of My Skin*. Both novels are based to some extent on the authors' personal and impersonal experiences, with some universality of theme, plot, and issue—again, what Pacquet calls fictive autobiography.

While acknowledging the similarities between the Black and European novels of childhood, one needs to understand as well how

7. The *Kunstlerroman* is similar to the bildungsroman except that the protagonist often is a developing artist or is in the process of forming an artistic sensibility. An entire body of work, such as those of Richard Wright, James Baldwin, Paule Marshall, Jamaica Kincaid, or Ntozake Shange, could qualify as *Kunstlerromane*.

8. William L. Andrews, ed., *African American Autobiography: A Collection of Critical Essays*. In the introductory essay Andrews cites classic examples—Ida B. Wells's *Crusade for Justice*, Frederick Douglass's *My Bondage and My Freedom*, and Richard Wright's *Black Boy*—as being distinct forms not like the European versions.

Black writers both in the West Indies and in the United States have remolded or adapted the traditional form to suit their needs and how their novels are distinct from the traditional bildungsroman. Most West Indian writers, especially the early ones, did their writing and publishing from abroad because of a lack of financial support and "sensitivity" to their art in their individual islands. Living abroad, the "exiled" writer almost inevitably returns to a childhood scenario in his first novels in order to discover a "lost domain." This is because the world of childhood retains the freshest images and the most deeply imprinted experiences of a native landscape and sensibility. The need to look back, to reassess one's childhood from the vantage point of maturity, is related to the writer's wish to establish an authentic basis of experience, that is, to repossess or reinterpret a past that to the adult seems broken and fragmentary.

African American writers experience a different kind of exile. They are exiles in their "own" country, and their motive for writing a bildungsroman is not to rediscover a "lost domain" or recapture an "experience," but to expose those conditions that robbed the writer of a memorable and happy childhood. While the West Indian writer's bildungsroman operates more out of the child's consciousness, the Black American writer's becomes a frequent platform for protest.

The novel of childhood for the West Indian has an additional special meaning besides being the record of youth, since, in essence, the novel of the West Indies has no ancestors—this is to say, no true national identity, no background and tradition as do the American or European forms. The West Indian character or person always has to ask, Who am I? This was also true of the African American writer, especially those who wrote before the 1920s. This question is not asked as frequently in European novels because of the literal presence of *the* tradition. Caribbean writers start from having little on which to base new approaches to the novel while considering new subject matter and ethnicity. Theirs, therefore, was a neophyte beginning as they sought to start a tradition.

Sandra Pouchet Paquet has said,

In West Indian literature, *In the Castle of My Skin* has emerged as a paradigm for any number of themes and literary constructs, among these,

the use of childhood and adolescence, the quest for selfhood and perspective, and spiritual reconnection with the poor and oppressed as the
definitive posture of the West Indian writer in relation to the regional
community. Finally, it was *In the Castle of My Skin* that established
certain ground rules for the fictionalizing of the self and the construction
of the autobiographical self in literary discourse.[9]

Lamming's *Castle* demonstrates the reformation of a tradition into
a meaningful historical, cultural, and regional space for an audience
that can recognize itself. It speaks directly to the specific yet diasporic
experience of childhoods. We do enter into the action, landscape, and
psyche of all of these texts because of the individual authors' gifts
and voices. The contrast between the West Indian and the European
is vast. Pip, for example, in *Great Expectations,* has hope, as does
Huck in *Huckleberry Finn.* Despite everything, both are victorious.
This is not often true of those protagonists in Black novels of the
diaspora.

Racial issues have always been a part of the African American
protest, as color and class are for the West Indian writer. However,
novelists George Lamming and Austin Clarke do confront the issue
of race in their first novels, *In the Castle of My Skin* and *Amongst
Thistles and Thorns.* In Lamming's novel a young Barbadian named
Trumper asserts that *Negro* describes a state of being, an act of
identification. In grasping that the term must be distinguished from
the political or national connotations of *American* or *British,* a Black
man can achieve the only kind of self-knowledge that can enable him
to survive spiritually in the milieu of White culture and tradition.
Without such discovery, he remains degraded and self-depreciatory:
"You ain't a thing till you know it, an' that's why you an' none o'
you on this island is a Negro yet." In Lamming's later novel *Season
of Adventure,* a character describes the problem in more universal
terms: "Man is a question the beast ask itself."[10]

Lamming's statements are comparable to the major theme of the
African American revolution. The recurrent thesis of *Malcolm X
Speaks* (1965) is the contention that the Black man ceases to be a

9. Paquet, "West Indian Autobiography," 199.
10. *In the Castle of My Skin,* 37; *Season of Adventure,* 15.

human being when he accepts the cultural and emotional negation of his Blackness by a White society. Similarly, in a speech in Watts, Trinidad-born Stokely Carmichael repeatedly declared, "Every 'Negro' is a potential Blackman."[11] Despite the rejection of *Negro* as a gratuitous euphemism, Carmichael's link with Lamming's Trumper is clear, as is the parallel between the Barbadian novelist and the former Black Power leader.

Trumper's role as an emigrant is analogous to the creative experience of the novelist. Migration or "exile" is a kind of emotional catalyst for both the artist and his characters. Moreover, there is a strong emphasis, throughout most of the novels, on the theme of exile or expatriation from Africa to the Caribbean, from the West Indies to Europe and America, from Black peasant villages to multiracial middle-class society. Any one of these movements heightens our consciousness of the others. Expatriation from the West Indies, for example, increases one's awareness of being an African "exile" in the West. Deighton Boyce in Marshall's *Brown Girl, Brownstones* is a metaphor for this heartbreaking experience.

Like contemporary African Americans, then, the West Indian novelist has gradually become more involved with the cultural symbols of his Black heritage and simultaneously more detached from some Western institutions and values. For the last five decades the West Indian writer has been progressively alienated from the culture of the British Commonwealth. Lamming's *In the Castle of My Skin* views the Commonwealth as a hollow artifice that perpetuates old relationships in new, hypocritical forms; a character says, "One day before time changed to eternity, 'Little England' (Barbados) and Big England, God's anointed on the earth, might hand in hand rule this earth."[12] Austin Clarke's biting satire on "Britannia Land" in *Amongst Thistles and Thorns* emphasizes the complete break by 1965 with the postwar optimism of Jamaican novelist Vic Reid's *New*

---

11. Stokely Carmichael, born in Trinidad, became a revolutionary during the 1960s. In his early speeches he spoke harshly of the Black bourgeoisie. Much of the politics of the era was meant to transform the race, demonstrate reverence for African origins, and execute direct political action to achieve those goals. This quote comes from a speech made in 1967.

12. *In the Castle of My Skin,* 37.

Day (1949), which asserts that the people's culture is more important than the "imposed European standards" presented in the Caribbean.

Popular studies have consistently maintained that the formation of the self in the Black child presents a major problem because of the great influence of oppression. The thesis of Black self-hatred or negative self-image has been very common. These writers draw on the slave narrative tradition and autobiographies that have been popular from the nineteenth century. Paule Marshall mentions that she reads the slave narratives for sustenance, especially Equiano's narrative of his life.[13] Some of their characters embrace White role models and subsequently experience a total rejection of self. It is impossible for Black children who are born into a society that makes a strong distinction between White and Black (and even light and dark skin shades within the race) to grow up without, at some point, entertaining feelings of inferiority because they are not members of the privileged group, which has attached a high premium to white skin. Morrison, like Baldwin and Ellison, in her novel *The Bluest Eye* has as her main theme the idea of the wrong color and race as a detriment to acceptance in American society.

The European bildungsroman in the nineteenth and twentieth centuries concerned itself with the development of a single male protagonist whose growth to maturity was the result of both formal and informal education, the latter acquired largely through his relationship with various women, for example, Pip's with Miss Havisham and Estella in *Great Expectations*. The shift of focus from the English form is symptomatic of a more general shift in the use of the form among postcolonial writers, particularly Black writers of the United States and the British Caribbean, to enunciate their special condition.

---

13. The narrative by Olaudah Equiano, who wrote under the pseudonym Gustavas Vassa, is a combination autobiography/sermon/slave narrative/adventure story. This narrative was the first African American biography to become a bestseller internationally. Stylistically, it is very ambitious; it is also an important work for its time and deserves its place in the canon of Black American literature. The first-person omniscient voice is one of its outstanding characteristics.

II

"BEHOLD THE GREAT IMAGE OF AUTHORITY"
AFRICAN WEST INDIAN MALE INITIATION

> Cut his arse going and coming! Give him the best arse I ever administer
> in forty years teaching school.
>> Austin Clarke, *Amongst Thistles and Thorns*

Caribbean/West Indian writers provide a special and much needed voice in the canon of diasporic literatures. Playing a crucial role by virtue of history, geography, language, race, and cultural heritage, they have a distinct advantage and disadvantage due to their regions' position as the second anchor in the triangular trade route of slavery. Because emancipation came to the British islands earlier than the American states, that literature has a good deal to say about several heritages—African, Caribbean, European, native, and personal. The literature is replete with these images and symbols.

No first novel by a West Indian writer won wider and more enthusiastic acclaim than *In the Castle of My Skin* by George Lamming; it was mainly on the strength of this work that the writer's early reputation rested, although he has written several other worthy novels since then. Lamming was born toward the end of the 1920s in a little village in Barbados, a village that may be the model for Creighton in *In the Castle of My Skin*. He became interested in translations of classic works quite early, and at the age of seventeen he read Goethe's *Wilhelm Meister*. Much of this early exposure to classic literature, along with his early experience in political discussions and memories of the riots of the 1930s, is put into this novel.

The assertion of a rooted, indigenous life merges with the theme of a lost, rural innocence to suggest comparison with other classic childhood novels, such as James Joyce's *A Portrait of the Artist as a Young Man,* in which Stephen Dedalus's love-hate relationship with his native Ireland ends in voluntary exile, or Mark Twain's *Adventures of Huckleberry Finn,* which offers an early declaration of American literary independence, native wit, and lost innocence. Both *Huckleberry Finn,* and *A Portrait of the Artist,* in different ways, are the prototype of a national experience, but in Lamming's novel there is no such celebration. In it no sense of a national consciousness emerges. To Lamming's young hero, G, Stephen Dedalus's vow "to forge in the smithy of my soul the uncreated conscience of my race"[1] would have sounded remarkably like arrogance; Huck Finn's confident existential "Americanness" would have seemed impossibly precocious. G's ninth birthday, with which the book opens, is a sad reminder of his own shaky sense of identity when he says, "My birth began with an almost total absence of family relations . . . and loneliness from which had subsequently grown the consolation of freedom was the legacy with which my first year opened."[2] The consciousness that develops is that of the private individual within the framework of his own little village community. Even other village communities remain largely outside the young G's focus. His is a gradual, often painful growth toward a personal view of the immediate community. *Castle* seems close to Joyce's *Portrait* because of its main theme, which is the development and growth of the young narrator, his sensitive awareness in a repressive island community, and his inevitable drift toward alienation and exile. Both novels also define and examine the passage of the sensitive and developing artist into the professional writer, a passage that can also be seen in *Black Boy* and *Go Tell It on the Mountain.* It is finally G's growing conviction of his uniqueness, of "some infinitely gentle, infinitely suffering thing" within, needing protection, that isolates him from others. Near the end of the novel, as he prepares to leave the island, he like Stephen writes in his diary,

1. James Joyce, *A Portrait of the Artist as a Young Man,* 3. Stephen, poised for flight from his island, also records his thoughts in a diary.
    2. Lamming, *In the Castle of My Skin,* 5. Further references to this work will be made parenthetically in the text.

"Tomorrow I leave. The likenesses will meet and make merry, but they won't know you, the you that's hidden somewhere in the castle of your skin" (261).

Lamming tends to use place and time symbolically, incorporating the West Indian world, experience, and landscape; in *Season of Adventure,* for example, the place-names used are from at least six islands. Therefore, Creighton, the locale in *Castle,* could be anyplace in the West Indies. The poetic quality of the novel is attributed to Lamming's early and continued interest in and writing of poetry. Although it is also his most autobiographical work, *Castle* is no mere autobiography because Lamming gives the reader not just a portrait of himself, not just the story of his movement toward manhood, but the psychological landscape of an emergent society in the growing pains of its evolution and development. As an initiation novel, its themes are growth and change, isolation and exile.

The narrator is G, the protagonist, which is not uncommon in the bildungsroman. The other boys closest to his experiences and his world are Trumper, Boy Blue, Bob, and Po Ping. The pertinent experiences are a group experience; the narrator's voice becomes the group voice. The novel reflects different social levels in the West Indies, and its unique style sets it apart from the other novels to be examined here, *The Year in San Fernando* and *Amongst Thistles and Thorns.* Stylistically it comes closest to Geoffrey Drayton's *Christopher* because of the narrator's poetic voice. Christopher is a White West Indian boy, as is the author, which makes this comparison interesting at many levels.

Interwoven with G's story is that of the village, which also undergoes dramatic changes during the course of the novel. From the outset, G's sensibility is distinct from that of the other villagers. His birthday coincides with a flood that threatens to wash Creighton's village into the sea. The villagers' resistance to the flood is signified by a song taken up from house to house until "the whole village shook with song on its foundation" (4). But the song has a second purpose; it is started by G's mother to suppress the boy's inquiry into his past—this "always happened when I tried to remember" (3). His attempt to find out who he is by prodding into his family's history poses another threat to the village, since the past, with its story of slavery and oppression, has been buried. Even teachers at the village school know nothing of it. Barbados, the villagers believe, has always been a junior partner of England, "Little England—not a subservient colony. . . . No one was ever a slave, the teacher said. It was in another part of the world that those things happened. Not in Little England. The little boy didn't like the sound of it" (51–52).

The opening scene of the novel with G and his mother is symbolic in that it points to isolation, a sensitive initiatory familial experience, and the change and exile that will come later. It is also interesting that Lamming begins and ends the novel with G and his mother in intimate, natural conversations. The silent communication and sparse conversation are beautiful and symbolic of the bonding be-tween mother and son. G learns about the village, his family history, and his mother's life. The mother–son relationship is a bonding one of the sort Edith Clarke talks about in some detail in her book *My Mother Who Fathered Me,* the title of which is taken from a statement G makes in *Castle:* "And what did I remember? My father who had only fathered the idea of me had left me the sole liability of my mother who really fathered me" (3). Clarke argues that the failure to establish a paternal relationship, and excessive reliance on the mother, has its effect on a young man when he grows up, and that the mother often impresses upon the young son that it is his duty to repay her for the hardship she endured as his principal support. Although G's mother "grumbles" and complains a lot, she does a fantastic job of raising him. There are several scenes in which even while punishing him by "flogging," they are laughing through tears. G remembers: "and I felt the sting of the belt tight on my leg, and cried again louder than ever. 'Hard ears you won' hear, hard ears you must feel.' She raised the belt again, but I couldn't resist the switch-over that took place in my head. The laughter burst through my tears" (112). Communication was never lacking in their relationship. In the West Indies, in all aspects of home training, the mother is the principal actor. Later on, like G, adult men tell stories of their mothers flogging them while in the same breath enlarging upon their devotion to them. One reason for this is that the mother was often the only continuing stable relationship in the child's life, which for various reasons is not an uncommon aspect of Black life in the Caribbean, the United States, and other segments of society.

From the outset, G is shown discovering his essential difference from others in his age group and his aloneness within the village community. An early episode, in which he stands naked in the yard, obscured by the neighbors' children while his mother bathes him, manages to be both a celebration of community life in the "yards"[3] and an illustration of G's sense of loneliness within that community. The accidentally damaged pumpkin vine, the anger of Bob's mother, the laughter of the children peeping over the fence all contribute to a sense of a tightly knit community. But G, temporarily forgotten in the general hubbub, is left vulnerable: "On all sides the fences had been weighed down with people, boys and girls and grown-ups. The girls were laughing and looking across to where I stood on the pool of pebbles, naked, waiting" (10–11). To his eyes, home life and village life still present a whole, if not fully comprehensible, pattern. The apparent order of Creighton's village—with its benevolent Great House on the hill and its feudal system of landlord, overseer, villager, and serf, in which "the obedient lived in the hope that the great might not be offended" (21)—is deceptive, concealing the germ of discontent and violence. The boys, placing their nails on the railway line to be flattened by the train's iron wheels, unknowingly mirror this darker aspect of the tidy pattern of village life. On the other hand, life in the village does have its distinctive character, its shared, communal rituals, like the customary weekly gathering at the crossroads for black pudding and souse.

The boys' education is largely a matter of irrelevant colonial knowledge, as illustrated when Trumper, Boy Blue, and Bob "test" the words of King Canute to the sea from the Michael John history book— "the book wid B.C. 55 and the Battle of Hastin's" (26)—and find them entirely ineffectual in real life. Their education also involves impressive but empty rituals, as when G's school celebrates Empire Day with full paraphernalia of Union Jacks, paramilitary parades, and a patriotic address by the White Inspector, who says, "We're all

3. Yards in the Caribbean are created after the African model. Several houses in close proximity usually share a common water standpipe or cooking hearth. A convivial spirit of sharing and openness is common.

subjects and partakers in the great design, the British Empire, and your loyalty to the Empire can be seen in the splendid performance which your school decorations and the discipline of these squads represent" (38). The passage on King Canute from the Michael John book is an attack on the senseless educational system that forces West Indian schoolboys to learn irrelevant and useless information, but the attempt of the boys to connect this obscure gentleman with their lives is a triumph of the spirit of boyhood.

The Black headmaster's beating of the boy who had giggled during his speech about Queen Victoria's wisdom is not, as the other boys instinctively recognize, "what you would call a natural beating" (37). His fury represents an equal and opposite displacement of angst, for his public behavior is the result of private frustrations. His status as a Black colonial gentleman is precarious. But the beating is particularly savage because he recognizes the boy as the son of his cook, who has been a witness to his own humiliation by his wife.

The boys' experience and tentative discussion of such events lead, especially in G's case, to a gradual development of a critical awareness and to the need to make choices. G's mother flogs him for playing on the corner frequented by "low" types in an attempt to dissuade him from the wrong choice of friends. The policeman, a Black symbol of White authority, breaks up a village fight with the words, "Why all you can't live like the people in Belleville?" (105). Even the book's natural imagery underlines social and class distinctions:

> Only the doves seemed to have found some peace in these surroundings. . . . Neither the sparrows nor the black birds making their noise from the trees flew down to join them, and suddenly it occurred to me that in the village the sparrows and the blackbirds which were the commonest victims of our snares had seldom been joined by the doves. (109)

Belleville, where the White people live, is the home of doves; lowly sparrows and blackbirds live in the village. But the widening pattern of G's experience makes a choice of sides more and more difficult.

The recurring image of the crabs in the novel is a constant reminder of a need to protect identity. To G the crabs appear puzzling, self-contained, their delicate stalklike eyes acting as independent agents of the creature hidden away within its shell. The schoolboy jingle, "a b ab catch a crab" (113) gains in significance when we discover that crab catching is, for the boys, a means of self-expression, a personal accomplishment. These crabs are not the large, clumsy (though edible) ones that blunder into the village after heavy rain, but the small, "decorous" beach-crabs: "like cups and saucers which my mother bought and put away, . . . Boy Blue didn't really want to eat one of these. He wanted to catch them as a kind of triumph" (150).

G soon learns that the inner "you" is fragile, unknown, and complex. His growth is not only a hesitant, crablike movement toward awareness, toward real freedom of choice, but also a process hedged about with dangers against which the inner self must be protected, like the tender crab within its "castle" of shell. The pebble he finds one day on the top of a pile of others, "as though it stood out from the others and asked to be taken away" (218), soon takes on a symbolic meaning for him. It is no longer a pebble, but the "lapis" of his inner self, his individuality; his first impulse is to protect it, to hide it from others. Its subsequent, mysterious disappearance crystallizes G's growing sense of loss, of alienation from home and village; it represents the beginning of exile.

G has the questing, sensitive awareness of the creative artist. In his development the natural, undifferentiated world of the village and the private world of literature and art are inevitably drawing apart. His overriding concern becomes a need to preserve this new sense of integrity as a private individual in a society that can no longer nourish or contain him. But if G—a high school graduate now—can no longer find acceptance with the village, it is also true that he cannot relate meaningfully to his new status. He observes, "If I asserted myself they made it clear that I didn't belong just as Bob, Trumper and Boy Blue later insisted that I was no longer one of the boys" (224). Yet he recognizes that the reason for his sense of alienation is something more than the experience of high school. It is that sensitive, inner thing within the castle of his skin that has made the difference.

At the level of personal initiation, the story has wider implications. The boys speak with terror of the thing that goes

"Pop Pop" in one's head, "an' you's a different man. You ain't the same sort of person you wus, an' the next thing you hear, you ain't the same sort of person everybody is. You start to feel you different from everybody else, an' if that sort of thing go on you'll feel that there's nobody like you." (143)

The process of growing into individuality is menacing, for it is also the growth away from community. Further, the inner pattern of the child's growth is interwoven with the wider scene of a village community in transition from the old ways of life toward a new and fragmented culture.

G's school is regimented, dominated by the British flag and the image of a Barbados that, it was rumored, telegrammed England at the beginning of the war, "Go brave Big England for Little England is Behind You" (223). Even the early scene where his mother scurries about the house trying to keep her provisions and supplies out of the rain is blended with the picture of the village eroded by floods and houses being swept out to sea. Above all, the boy's relationship to his mother is set against that of the figures of Ma and Pa to the village, who as the parental consciousness of the community, also see their children becoming estranged from them. Potentially, they are a part of a cycle. As Boy Blue declares, "they say that after a certain age you start to get a child again, like Ma and Pa for instance" (120). There can be no renewed identity between the old and new generations, and Pa, widowed, is bundled off to the anonymity of an almshouse, while the land is taken over by a new generation of Black entrepreneurs. Unable to accept the simplified vision of politics, G retreats into a stance of self-protection and isolation, and he too knows he has mentally said "farewell" to his village.

Castle ends with the protagonist leaving Barbados to take a job in Trinidad, and to begin his adult and perhaps lonely journey through the world. His decision to leave Barbados is a deliberate but painful one. His going marks not only a momentous turning point in his own life, a culmination of the process of personal growth that the novel traces, but also an epochal point in the history of the island, and more particularly the community of which he has been a part. The momentousness of the departure and the ominousness and uncertainty with which it is invested are emphasized by the fact that our last image of him is of a young man walking alone into the night. The darkness suggests all the danger and uncertainty ahead, the beckoning terror of the unknown, as well as the darkness of his ignorance, which he must discover: "The earth where I walked was a marvel of blackness and I knew in a sense more deep than simple departure I had said farewell, farewell to the land" (303).

The last scenes of the novel are carefully placed to complement one another in developing the meaning of G's departure and in deepening the emotional resonance of the novel's close. The very last scene, in which he bids good-bye to Pa, is one that conveys the most sustained straightforward pathos and poignancy, and the most direct sense of an ending. The old man, the last relic and repository of the old ways of the village, is himself about to go on a journey, to the almshouse, to await the final darkness. The farewell blessing he bestows on G neatly imparts the idea of an old order changing, yielding place to the new, as well as the idea of the passing down of community traditions from one generation to the next, even though not all of the traditions are admirable. G's departure also signifies, to a certain extent, the breakup of the community and its traditions.

Just before the scene with Pa, there is G's conversation with Trumper, his former schoolmate, who had emigrated to the United States. His return to Barbados on a visit, just when G is about to leave, and his assertion of a newfound sense of purpose as a result of his American experience serve as reassuring auguries for G's departure. But there is something glib and possibly naive about the new Trumper, which highlights by contrast the greater complexity of G's personal quest and anguish.

More elaborate and complex than either the scene with Pa or the one with Trumper is the long scene between G and his mother. In terms of the story of G's development, this passage is the emotional climax of the novel. Rich in nuance, it provides us with our most extended view of the deep and intricate relationship between mother and child, a relationship that is central to the novel and a microcosm of his relationship with the community of the island as a whole.

The occasion of this final scene between G and his mother is a meal, the last she prepares for him. The dish she serves is a Barbadian specialty—flying fish and cuckoo. This section of the narrative, which is particularly intriguing, gives a detailed account of the mother's preparation of the meal, especially the cuckoo. It is as though Lamming has interrupted the narrative, and his portrayal of the relationship between boy and mother, to describe in detail how the mother made the cuckoo. The meal that G's mother prepares for him is clearly a ceremony of love, one that shows the deep and sustaining bond between them. Lamming's awareness of the social and cultural significance of food is expressed not only in what the reader can see underneath the account of the meal, but also in the author's own observations as well as in comments by other characters elsewhere in the novel. This account of the preparation embodies and brings into sharp focus vital concerns of the novel. It symbolizes the importance of values attached to the concepts of tradition, community, self-respect, creativity, and work and signifies the lack of them or the possibility of them in the kind of society that the novel depicts, as well as the importance of them in human life generally. It symbolizes, in effect, a vision of life and society and, consequently, criticizes actual conditions of life and society as depicted in the novel.

The story is not just G's bildungsroman; it is also the story of his four best friends emerging from a very simple and complacent society and facing the dawn of an infinitely more complicated one. It is a picture of boundless captured energy about to explode as the match of inevitable change ignites the fuse. The reader of this *Bildungs/Kunstler* becomes a spectator to a drama of human life as it struggles against and for the inevitable forces of change. The reader sees the impact of these forces through the naive yet prescient minds and expressions of young people—principally G, Boy Blue, and Trumper. A similar technique is eminently effective in *Black Boy,* where the reader sees Black culture through adolescent eyes and "where literature authenticates experience and becomes an outlet for it."[4] Thus *Castle,* written from the first-person point of view, creates an atmosphere of autobiographical authenticity as it slowly unfolds the checkered career of Creighton's village from the eviction of its residents by the flood to their eviction by new owners of the land. It also documents the childhood togetherness of G and his friends, and the inevitable separation of these friends as their interests,

4. John Reilly, "Afterword" to Richard Wright's *Black Boy,* 288.

talents, and ambitions develop in different directions. In addition, it poignantly describes the unhappiness, misunderstanding, distrust, and frustration on this small island. The boys, to find sanctuary in tenacity and subjectivity, all escape, like the crabs on the beach, into their skin's castle. One wonderful aspect of this novel is that there is no preoccupation with race or color, or passionate protests, but a richness in the contemplation of life despite a wariness with it. "Also, the absence of the father and ever-present proximity of the mother make for the development of a binding relationship between mother and son."[5] Because boys also gain status by relinquishing attachment to the mother, G's journey to Trinidad and his antecedent experience will serve him well as he begins the second stage of his development.

■   ■

Trinidadian Michael Anthony's major intent in *The Year in San Fernando* is hardly to convey social or political messages. He should not, therefore, be compared at one level to other West Indian writers like George Lamming or Austin Clarke whose bildungsromane do infer social and political ideas. Neither should he be compared to African Americans James Baldwin and Ralph Ellison, whose works are packed social canvases. Concentrating on a careful re-creating of the humble, ordinary life of the rural and semi-rural Trinidad of his youth, Anthony refreshes our awareness of the significance of the ordinary and of how, in its simplest homeliest motions, the heart can touch so much that is at once elemental and complex. His memory shapes evocations of a particular place and time, by being true to time and place. He captures, naturally, some of the realities and nuances of West Indian social relationships, without interposing the zeal of anger, protest, or ridicule. His novel is, in part, an autobiographical recollection of childhood in which the central figure attempts to adjust to a new environment; in this case it is the city of San Fernando.

In a limited way, Anthony affirms the presence of his folk as persons, rather than using his novels as political arguments for their presence and personality. So whereas a novel such as *Castle* is of

5. Lawrence, "Mother–Child Relationships," 11.

far greater scope and depth than Anthony's novels, the latter's boy protagonists are more real than imagined; they are more complete in their own right and less complicated. The boys' persona and consciousness in Anthony's novels remain childlike longer. This is also true in his other books, *The Games Were Coming* (1963), *Green Days by the River* (1967), *Cricket in the Road* (1973), and *All That Glitters* (1980), all of which seem to be set in Mayaro, Anthony's hometown in Trinidad. His gift for capturing the voice of youth is one of his major accomplishments, and his fame has rested mostly on the writing of West Indian boyhood novels.

Against a background of change and growth in nature, represented by the seasonal cycles and their effect on agriculture, Anthony traces in *The Year in San Fernando* the physical and psychological development of the twelve-year-old Francis as he enters into early adolescence. There are clear indications throughout the narrative of increasing maturity of both body and mind, although Francis cannot be said to have achieved adolescence by the end of the novel nor the second stage of his bildungsroman.

The exposure to the "more complicated" life of urban San Fernando, however, compared to rural Mayaro, leaves him with a greater awareness of the inconsistencies of life, and the compassion that grows in him shows a deepening understanding of the human condition. Anthony's use of a first-person narrator creates a point of view that is in some ways limited. Nonetheless, the question of reliability can be misleading, because the surface action is not the major concern of the novel. The value of the novel lies deeper, in its success at conveying the evolving state of young Francis's mind and his movement toward maturity, as he tries to make sense of the experiences he gains in both environments. At the end of the book Francis speaks of the way people can be "genuine to you." The initiation of the West Indian child to adult responsibility can be both hard and frustrating. Francis's exposure to the colonial White world of San Fernando is as a servile young man in a White "colonial" household. The experience almost emasculates him, yet by the end of the novel he is transformed by the adult household in which he works for one year.

Kenneth Ramchand says of the formation of *The Year in San Fernando,* "Anthony is very careful to make the reader conscious of the time process. It determines the title; it determines the structure; it determines the dominant patterns of imagery: birth, growth, death, regeneration, the fundamental movements of nature, all fit neatly into Anthony's year. In other words, cyclical time patterns are super-imposed on a clearly defined linear sequence of twelve months, and the events of these months are thereby, to a considerable extent, parallel with universal time and seasons."[6] The novel, therefore, is rhythmically plotted by moods and seasons and reminds us of Toni Morrison's *Bluest Eye,* which begins with autumn and ends with summer. Like Morrison, Anthony takes the reader through the seasons by the mention of the elements—rain, fire, growth, flowers, colors, and so on.

The ability to see clearly but never to quite understand stays with Francis throughout the novel, and it gives him an engaging humility. As a twelve year old, Francis has a certain nonchalance about him, of course, but this should not be allowed to obscure the fact that Francis, like everything else, undergoes changes in the course of the year. He grows physically and psychologically, and this makes for a gradual transformation of the narrative. This is not to say that Francis has become any more "reliable" as a narrator by the end of the novel or that he has completely lost his innocence and immaturity. He is still puzzled by many things as the bus takes him back to Mayaro, but he has moved many steps toward an eventual understanding of his San Fernando experience. He is certainly more aware at the end about such matters as human greed, hate, and sexuality than he was at the beginning. Even if only in a very general and half-realized way, and even if the city has not been as hostile for him as London, for example, is for Pip or Memphis is for Richard, he does discover that life is more complicated than it had appeared before in simple, almost idyllic Mayaro. In San Fernando he "felt like a prisoner in this giddy town."[7]

There is ample evidence of Francis's physical growth in the novel. Very early in the book he sees himself as one of "hundreds of little

6. See Ramchand's *The West Indian Novel and Its Background,* 205–22, and the "Introduction" to *The Year in San Fernando,* written with Paul Edwards.

7. Anthony, *The Year in San Fernando,* 67. Further references to this work will be made parenthetically in the text.

boys" (11), and his "smallness" stands in marked contrast to all that is "big" around him: Mr. Chandles's "big job" with the "Great Asphalt Company"; Mr. Chandles's "big house" in the "great town" of San Fernando (which seems to dwarf Francis as he enters it); the "big mirror" before which he stands feeling small and awkward before going to the market with Brinetta. At the end of the novel Francis sees that he too has become "big." As he hurriedly prepares to leave on the bus to return to Mayaro, he finds that he can scarcely button his shirt because he is now a "big" boy. With careful artistry Anthony sets him before the mirror once again: "I went to see myself in the glass now. I looked so different standing there with brown pants and sky-blue shirt. It almost didn't look like me. It was strange and very good" (182). Here Francis clearly sees the results of a year's physical growth in himself. He does not quite know what to make of what is so plainly before him, but he is pleased, nonetheless.

This awareness of himself as a physical being gradually builds up in the course of the year as others become aware of his growing and draw his attention to it. Brinetta, from the start, calls him a man, and it doesn't take him long after this to realize that he is "already twelve" (49). He is no longer a "little boy," and his physical development inevitably has sexual repercussions. Julia's sister, Enid, is attracted to him, but the literal interpretation of her comment— "Enid say you getting big man now" (148)—makes a more immediate impact on him than the sexuality behind it. The innocence of this country boy is real.

Growth to the young Francis means simply physical growth. At first, he feels awkward, as when Julia goes on about it, but he comes ultimately to be happy about it. Thus while he has grown old enough to appreciate surface changes, he is still too young to understand what is happening to him sexually and, in a wider and deeper sense, psychologically. But this happens calmly. The author never allows it to become the central concern of the novel, but he nonetheless provides broad hints throughout the narrative so that the reader, unlike Francis, is made fully aware of it. Francis's inability to catch all the sexual innuendos that float around and within him is never allowed to become unsympathetic or condescending. As the months go by in San Fernando, it becomes increasingly clear that Francis is actually undergoing puberty. His first description of Julia indicates that he is sensitive to the attractions of the opposite sex and hence past the stage of ignoring girls: "She was so slim and delicate that her dress seemed to drape around her, but she had a nice face, and her hair was combed up in the 'rose' style. It made her look—not glamorous—but extremely comely" (27).

A short time later (under the house, feeling a hatred for Mr. Chandles and his mother, who are quarreling upstairs), he recalls this first encounter with Julia and feels "cheered." He recalls the eyes, the eyebrows, the hair. He now compares her to his sister, Anna, who is back in Mayaro. Both girls (he still calls Julia a girl, not a woman) comb their hair the same way. But Julia is different somehow, "more beautiful than ever" (70). A few lines later he is even imagining asking her to marry him if he were grown up. The passage, ending with an unconsciously understated "I liked her" (71), convincingly traces the movement of the mind of the adolescent Francis—the attraction to facial beauty; the comparison to the sister and the differentiation between female sibling and female nonsibling; the naive fantasizing about marriage and the concluding declaration of puppy love. Though Francis is still young, his feelings toward Julia as a member of the opposite sex have already grown more intimate since their first meeting. This infatuation grows, reaching a climax on Easter Day when, for the second time, he comes upon her and Chandles embracing in the dark. His fear that Chandles saw him is accompanied by anger at Julia. He experiences a fit of jealousy described in unmistakably sexual terms: "I turned from one side to the other and I felt as if there was a heat on my face. I said to myself, 'She's pretty but she's only a tramp.' I turned and removed the wet bedclothes from under my cheek. And I lay in pain for some time" (85).

Francis's heated condition is attributable to both fear and sexual excitement. He is also confused about what is happening to him. He never completely forgets Julia, and he dreams of her the night before leaving to return to Mayaro. In the dream she says: "'Little boy like you—before you study your book you studying to love big woman!' Shocked and excited I had awakened from that dream" (179). It is mainly through the relationship with Julia, then, that Anthony expresses the gradual sexual awakening of his young narrator. Anthony is extremely careful to understate, though never to let us forget, his young narrator's developing sexuality. The author parallels the cane fires with the boys' growing, and the heated passion of approaching adolescence and the theme of "sexual growth" have a key role in this bildungsroman.

In *Go Tell It on the Mountain* John Grimes recognizes his awakening sexuality in the opening scenes of the novel, which range from the overt scenes in the alleys of Harlem to his "wet dream" and attraction to Brother Elisha. As with Francis, John doesn't seem to know what is happening, but the narrative suggests clearly what is occurring in both cases. This allows for very subtle effects on the narrative's continuity. If the narrator is changing in the course of the year, the viewpoint he provides should be gradually altered to suit his steadily changing self. Whether or not the boy reports these transformations with increasing accuracy is of secondary importance to the process of change taking place within him.

Very naturally, Francis's mother is the strongest emotional link to his life before San Fernando and hence the hardest to weaken. Because she is a potential threat to his newly forming sense of self, the author prolongs her visit to San Fernando and very carefully follows the changing relationship between mother and son. At first, it seems as if Francis returns to his boyhood state of emotional dependency: "Ma, I cried, running towards her. I absolutely forgot myself" (86). But it soon becomes clear that Francis can now regard his mother with a certain degree of detachment. Anthony purposely keeps mother and son from becoming intimate in the course of the visit by using Mr. Chandles as the agent of discord. Francis does not want to destroy his Ma's illusions about the Chandles family, but implicit in the silence he maintains is no small measure of independence from his mother and Mayaro, the provincial place of his birth. He feels dejected when she departs. But San Fernando has broadened his perspective, indicating his absorption into a world that is much wider and more adult than that which revolved around his community activities and his mother in Mayaro.

Most of Francis's activities in San Fernando revolve around another "mother," an older woman, the sick and unhappy Mrs. Chandles, and in dealing with her he shows a growing maturity. She is the third woman in the young boy's life and the one with whom he has the most direct and prolonged contact. He experiences a range of emotions toward the old woman—timidity, fear, hatred, happiness, affection, sympathy. These follow one after another in sequence as Francis comes gradually to a more considered evaluation of her. True enough, part of his reaction to her might be explained by her treatment of him. Very simply, when she is harsh toward him, he dislikes her, and when she becomes kind, he feels affection. But this would be to oversimplify the situation and do little justice to the more complex psychological process that the author traces in the young boy. The initial timidity and fear that Francis feels around Mrs. Chandles (and her son) reflect his boyish innocence in the face of "big people's business" (104). He cringes before the old woman's harshness and, being "fresh" from Mayaro, feels "unsettled." This fear continues and, as Francis experiences more of her behavior, he feels himself hating her. But in the midst of this early period, as Francis feels intense dislike, he says, "sometimes my thoughts pondered here on this house and on Mr. Chandles and this mother of his, and often I remembered what Brinetta had said, that the old lady wasn't so bad, it was the old age" (52). Francis's response to her behavior here is one of cautious appreciation. He is happy at her affability, but he realizes that it is "strange." The old lady, as Brinetta suggests, may not be so bad after all.

As their relationship becomes established on a new and friendlier plane, Francis displays a remarkable lack of naïveté in assessing the changes taking place. A key passage comes right after his mother has returned to Mayaro. Mrs. Chandles tells Francis that he is "nearly a San Fernando boy now" (98). His reaction is warm but by no means childish. He says, "The fact was, I did feel a little pleasant to hear her say that. There was nothing false in her grin. . . . I believed in her. We smiled broadly" (98). The exchange of smiles, partly spontaneous, partly calculated on Francis's part, heralds the establishment of a new basis for the relationship, one of mutual respect and understanding. The closeness between the old woman and the boy is confirmed by the fact that he learns a lot by observing her many behaviors and that despite his disdain for the "stench of bed clothes" he wonders "how was she feeling inside."

It is Mrs. Chandles's approaching death in the closing chapters of the novel—and the end of Francis's year in San Fernando—that forces him, as never before, to try to cope with the realities of human experience. At first Francis feels helpless at Mrs. Chandles's rapidly deteriorating condition, along with terror at the prospect of death: "I didn't want anybody to die and I was afraid of death in the house. And perhaps I would miss Mrs. Chandles a little" (168). Anthony prolongs the old woman's illness so that the now older Francis is given the chance to come to grips with the fact of death. Proximity to the dying woman (bringing the porridge, propping up the pillows, helping to change the dirty sheets), and his observation of the "elderly lady" who is nursing Mrs. Chandles, brings him gradually to a calmer view of the situation. Francis learns that he too must "wrestle with death" and extend a steady, sympathetic hand to the dying. His final, calm handshake with Mrs. Chandles should be seen in this light. Francis's relationship with this old White woman reminds readers of Pip's relationship with Ms. Havisham in *Great Expectations*—love, hate, fascination with another world and culture. He first hears of her as old and lonely and wanting someone to stay with her; his first experience of her is a remote voice. When he first sees her she is aloof and somewhat frightened: "Mrs. Chandles had stood up for a moment as if inspecting me. She was very old and wrinkled and small. The next moment she hobbled away through the door through which Mr. Chandles had gone." As the novel progresses, Mrs. Chandles emerges as demanding, cunning, and nasty. "I wondered to myself what sort of human being this old lady could be. She hadn't cooked . . . she had left me to starve and like Mr. Chandles she did not care a damn!" (9). What we do discover is that during the course of Francis's year he and Mrs. Chandles develop a relationship. She is dependent on everyone for her care, Francis included, and he, having the lowest stature by age, gender, and race in the household, finds an attachment to her that propels his growing into intimate knowledge of many things.

Francis's relationship with Mr. Chandles, the man responsible for precipitating him into the "heady" world of San Fernando, is nowhere near as interesting or as complex as his relationship with the three important women in the novel. In Mayaro, Francis displays the awe of the young and the unsophisticated in the face of the cosmopolite, Chandles, who is "tidy and elegant" in his coat and tie, appears "aristocratic" to the villagers. In San Fernando, it soon becomes clear to the isolated Francis that Chandles is something less than noble. There is ambivalence in the boy's feelings about Chandles because he represents a link to Mayaro life: "It was not easy to think whether I was glad to see Mr. Chandles, or not. He was the only person in San Fernando I could say I knew" (45).

Chandles's value as an emotional link decreases, however, as tensions in the household become unbearable. Francis finds that he can relax only when Chandles is not around because then there are no quarrels. Chandles's affairs with Marva and Julia are another source of anxiety for Francis, but by keeping Chandles off the scene for much of the book, the author keeps the tension between the two from developing into full-fledged hostility. Absence allows for an eventual fondness between the man and the boy. Three days before Francis leaves for Mayaro, Chandles shows himself to be amiable and frank, talking to Francis like an adult. Francis responds sympathetically: "I was looking outside but there was growing within me a strange, close feeling for him. It was coming home to me that at this late hour we were becoming friends. I could feel it there between us. I could feel it strong and real" (176).

Anthony had ample opportunity to make this bildungsroman a protest piece depicting a Black boy in a "little slave" situation, but he chose instead to use the cultural context wherein Francis's mother sees his being in the Chandles household as an opportunity for education and upward mobility. Francis did grow, he did not stagnate, so even though he has many things to sort out, the experiences of the year were an education. How a child like this might turn out is difficult to forecast because by the novel's end we see him returning to the rural village of Mayaro. If the city has been hostile to Francis, it was not apparent. Despite being in a White household, he was protected, unlike many young boys in similar novels. The situations to which Francis was exposed are definitely those of a mistress–slave boy relationship—the good White person giving the lucky Black boy an opportunity. That he is separated from his family, that formal schooling is not emphasized, and that he is now viewed as "sexless" and voiceless are issues not raised by the author.

Francis's thoughts take the place of action and participation. He can only *think* about the White world, not articulate his opinions. The reader hears those thoughts, but no one else in his sphere views him as a person. The dictum that children are seen and not heard is very much in play here. Will Francis's initiation lead him into a healthy adolescence and manhood? One of the most striking similarities in various accounts of youth is the emphasis on subordination. Childhood as well as adolescence is a journey of diminishing status, and a long period of dependence and low status can lead either to rebellion or to submissiveness. One of the great gifts of *The Year in San Fernando* is the use the author makes of his superior narrative art and fine storytelling. As Paul Edwards and Kenneth Ramchand note, "*The Year in San Fernando* leads us away from the notion of fixed personality or conventional ideas of character formation; and points towards a more liberal view of latent and sporadically realized possibilities."[8]

■   ■

It is interesting to compare the initiations of Black children such as Francis and the title character of St. Lucian Garth St. Omer's *Syrop* with those of White West Indians such as the hero of Geoffrey Drayton's *Christopher* because of the ways in which their passages into adolescence and away from childhood differ. Although both Syrop and White Christopher Stevens share a colonial setting, culture, and language, Christopher, who lives on the other side of the plantation wall, does not face the deprivation, poverty, and crime that Syrop does to prove his manhood. He does experience, nevertheless, the severe strains of a planter's family life. He is financially embarrassed by his father's improvidence, the fall of sugar prices after the war, and the jealousy of the Frasers. The Frasers had risen from a dubious background in the trading boom and, to complicate matters, they envy the Stevens's planter-class status. The insecure and frustrated father focuses on his only son as the embodiment of his wife's family,

8. "Introduction" to *The Year in San Fernando*, xix.

and the affectionate but weak mother can do little to protect him. Being a sensitive boy, Christopher immerses himself in his private world of growing things, centered on his own private fern garden. The coreopsis in this garden are easier to recognize and come to terms with than his father's anger, as are snails grown from the egg in comparison to the terrifying mysteries of sexual passion. Gradually he begins to internalize this world of beauty through his painting. Drayton's passionate dependence on Barbadian nature makes this story, in a different way from Anthony's, a psychological exploration of another life within a specific area of West Indian experience—the colonial Creole class.

As Anthony hints of the importance of Francis's awareness of his mother to the boy's identity and will to live, so Christopher also exhibits a growing personality capable of experience in a relationship. In his case the relationship is not with his mother, but with his Black nurse, Gip. As Mrs. Stevens wistfully realizes, Gip "made the colors of his day, and her life had not left his when she put out the lamp at night."[9] When Christopher is dangerously ill, it is only Gip who can help him through the crisis, nursing him with native infusions and sleeping at the foot of the bed through the night. These scenes are reminiscent of the countless Black women of the servant class who historically have cared for White children. Through Gip, Christopher's world touches that of the Black community that stands continually in the margin of his consciousness, like the drums that sound from the village by night and make him wake up screaming some hours after they have stopped; or the half-understood sexual hieroglyph etched on the spiky agave leaves in the tenantry gully. But Christopher's world is fragmented. He knows the Black religion mainly as "malignant obeah,"[10] and is terrified by it. Yet, through Gip, something from the Black world has given him an essence of his life. The three sections of the book tell of his emancipation first from

9. Drayton, *Christopher,* 189. Further references to this work will be made parenthetically in the text.

10. Louis James, introduction to the paperback edition of *Christopher,* Caribbean Writers Series 7. "Obeah" is the practice of "folk" witchcraft similar to voodoo in Haiti. Obeah men/women enjoy a special status in most communities. It is not a religion per se, but indicates the joining of native rituals, magic, and a strong belief system.

his father, whose rages he comes to understand, and so despise, and then from his mother, when he discovers that his bond of guilt for the supposed death of his stillborn brother is unfounded. But in the third section his release from Gip, by her death, is only partial. As she is dying in the hospital, he wakes up in terror of the moonlight. But "it was alright. She was still there, sitting peacefully in the rocking chair. There was nothing to be afraid of. Turning over on his face, Christopher went back to sleep" (188).

There are many documented accounts of the bonds of Black domestics and nannies with the families for whom they worked for years. In those families Blacks become mothers to children, keepers of secrets, loyal beyond expectation. These matriarchal figures have become the object of study and critical analyses. Despite protests about their significant roles in White households, their place in history and literature cannot be denigrated. They appear more frequently in African American and American literature than in West Indian or African. Faulkner's Dilsey in *The Sound and the Fury* and Margaret Walker's Vyry in *Jubilee* are stereotypical figures of these women. While it is possible that Whites such as Mrs. Chandles or the Frasers bond to their servants, what is more evident are the everlasting connections of Blacks to their patrons and White households. *Christopher* is a very poetic piece and an unusual male bildungsroman from the Caribbean region. Drayton's major contribution here may be the exploration of the psyche of an old and dying planter class and a boy making the transformation to an emancipated era.

■   ■

There seems to be a widely accepted thesis that West Indian novels traditionally seek to discover and define a "West Indian" consciousness, usually in terms of racial and national identity, and that the process of identification is sparked by the novelists' absence from the West Indian scene. Even though some of these writers owe their insights to North American experiences, this catalyst for "exile" has usually been provided by temporary or permanent residence in England and Europe. This fact, together with the postwar phenomenon that transformed the old capitals of empire into the colonial outposts of new artistic movements, ensured that the West Indian novelists' works were studied primarily within a British context.

One of the major historical exceptions has been Claude McKay, the Jamaican-born novelist whose portrayal of Black America in the twenties and thirties makes him one of the more significant precursors of the postwar West Indian novelists, particularly in his preoccupation with the experiences and values of Black self-identity. Indeed, in spite of the predominantly American materials of McKay's fiction, he can still be viewed, in a sense, as the archetype of the West Indian artist whose insights and techniques are shaped by cultural exile. Many other writers, since McKay, can be viewed in this way, such as V. S. Naipaul and Rosa Guy from Trinidad, Austin Clarke from Barbados, and Jamaica Kincaid from Antigua.

McKay provides an interesting parallel with Austin Clarke, the Barbadian novelist who has been living and writing in Canada for over three decades. In the 1920s and 1930s McKay contributed to the Harlem Renaissance, the dramatic awakening of Black consciousness in the arts and letters. In a real sense, the Harlem Renaissance represents the intellectual and artistic "fruits" of the movement begun by Marcus Garvey, the Black activist and crusader who was also a West Indian. Austin Clarke's relation to the Civil Rights movement in the United States was broadly similar. Unlike McKay, he has not abandoned the West Indian experiences as his primary topic, and his works are just as influenced by the emotional and intellectual issues of the 1960s ferment in Black America as his predecessors's were by the Harlem movement.

Clarke's major themes are similar to those of most Afro-World writers of the 1950s and 1960s—Black awareness, national identity, the hateful ambiguities of the West, and the heroic potential of the Black peasant. But the emphases and contexts through which he develops these topics are shaped by his experience with the African American consciousness that gained momentum during his stay in Canada and the United States. He, along with second-generation Barbadian American Paule Marshall, has, in effect, helped to contribute a North American dimension to the characteristic identity motif of the West Indian novel. As a major West Indian writer, he provides an invaluable perspective on an aspect of "British" Caribbean literature that has too often been minimized or ignored.

Clarke's first novel, *Amongst Thistles and Thorns,* is an invaluable contribution to the West Indian bildungsroman. His account of

Barbadian boyhood also showed Clarke's potential as a comic writer and as a vivid storyteller who can use the native island patois well. The identity theme that Clarke explores in all of his subsequent works appears in this novel, and its coherent structure and psychological complexity attest to the rapid development of Clarke's narrative techniques. He treats his racial and cultural subjects on a less exclusively external level than he does political misadventures; the moral and emotional conflicts become more coherent and psychologically interesting by being presented as the experiences of a single character whose introspection provides the work with a kind of subjective unity.

The novel portrays a weekend in the life of Milton Sobers, a nine-year-old boy in Barbados who runs away, temporarily, from both school and home. Milton's truancy is developed as a psychological quest, a search for identity that has racial as well as psychological overtones. The story's setting is Barbados in the 1950s, before independence from British rule. Milton runs away from a sterile educational system represented by a servile and sadistic Black teacher, an impersonal and detached White inspector, and the irrelevant offerings to a White "Motherland" during the colonial rites of Empire Day. This type of cruel teacher and White inspector was also seen in Lamming's *In the Castle of My Skin*. Strict colonial adherence to ceremony and obedience to the crown, flag and powerful figures are well known by every West Indian schoolchild prior to and even after Independence, "dressed in the white of colonial power."[11] At the same time, Milton is detached from the society of his village, for only Willy-Willy, who he does not yet know is his real father, shares his interest in the topic closest to his heart—Harlem, New York. Milton's Harlem assumes the dominant symbolic proportions it has in McKay's *Home to Harlem* (1928), and his daydreams of the famous Black community testify to the importance of American symbolism in Clarke's fiction. They also indicate the unifying subjectivity with which Clarke develops his themes of disconnectedness and desire to participate in a larger world. "I was looking at my mother holding the Book, but I was seeing the green pastures in our village stretching

11. Austin Clarke, *Amongst Thistles and Thorns*, 173. Further references to this work will be made parenthetically in the text.

far far out to sea all the way across the ocean to Harlem New York City America" (169). A daydreaming episode takes place after Milton's short-lived "ex- ile" and emphasizes the degree to which his weekend escapade has been a kind of catalyst for the rapid development of his insight and self-identification—both of which are symbolized by the racial and cultural "facts" of Harlem. He also dreams of Harlem during the escapade itself. While he hides beneath the village church one night, the service conducted by the Reverend Best becomes a part of Milton's vision of his village as a kind of Barbadian Harlem, and he seems to have been transported across the sea to what he has come to regard as "Willy-Willy" country.

The street was crowded with people. All the people were black people. And the street was paved; and was wide, wide as the sea. And there were large motor-cars such as I had never seen in Barbados. And in the middle of the street was something like a large long flowerbed with red flowers in it. . . . And there were policemen. The policemen were the only people who were not black like the people. They were white policemen. . . . They were walking and sauntering up and down the street looking at the black people congregated at the corner of the street which I thought was our Bath Corner. But it was not our Bath Corner. It had a funny name. Not like Bath Street or Bath Corner or Bath Place. It had a funny, foolish name, like 125th-Street-and-Seventh-Avenue, and it still looked like our Bath Corner. (90)

No other book or character in this study shows such poignant longing and depression. Milton's imaginings are a faithful re-creation of those held by foreigners hoping to emigrate. He hopes he will become an American and dreams of good things and a good place. The good place of his imagination is partly the "journey" theme in the novel. It transports the key character to another level of devel- opment. Milton's home situation is not ideal, but if he could talk to John Grimes, who lives in Harlem and wants to escape it, the stark reality of life there would also depress him. It seems that irrespective of place, a childhood mired in poverty and destitute circumstances has a universal sameness about it. The immediate effect of Milton's short-lived rebellion must therefore be found in the emotional and spiritual transformation embodied by his aspirations at the end of the novel, when he dreams of "discovering new worlds and countries and happiness like Columbus" (179).

From the onset of this terribly sad book, Milton is verbally and physically taught that he is worthless and will never amount to anything. He immediately becomes an isolated person, confined to a low and insignificant caste. Throughout the novel, all those who surround him and who are an integral part of his life repeatedly reinforce this theory. Most of the characters who know him have led desolate, desperate lives and vehemently dislike their situations, situations from which they cannot seem to escape. Subsequently, they take out their frustrations on him, through physical violence as well as verbal abuse. These actions can only cause him to wonder about his worth. It appears as though the society in which Milton lives is bent on stagnation, on an absence of mobility up the social ladder. This lack of mobility in the West Indies is maintained by the constant abuse that is endlessly fed to some children, as well as their elders, so a downtrodden and defeatist attitude resists any notions of advancement.

The reader is initiated into Milton's world with the jolting description by Milton of his own beating at the hands of the schoolmaster, Mr. Blackman (a name that becomes a metaphor for oppression). This prepares the reader for what is to happen repeatedly throughout the novel. At one point the schoolmaster wickedly beats Milton for his most unfortunate luck of having a coin fall at his feet—the crime he commits is to attempt to merely pick up the coin. The headmaster accuses him of being a thief and then tricks Milton into admitting a "crime" he did not commit. During the episode, Blackman uses words such as "beast," "pig," "demon," and "animul" to describe this innocent boy. Not only does he speak these insults to Milton's tearful face, but he says them so that the entire class hears. Humiliation among one's peers is as degrading an experience as one will find, especially at such a tender age. The scene is made more sadistic and a bit hypocritical as the headmaster has the boys repeat the Eighth Commandment, "Thou shalt not steal," as he whips Milton.

As the plot develops, Milton's own family also treats him in a confusing, demoralizing manner. Milton's mother, Ruby, is "married," but very "separated" from her man and the local society. This forces her into many different roles; one is that of a father, who has to levy punishment and who has to work, and another is as someone who is nurturing. Naturally, this pressure causes her to be nervous and tense—showing extreme emotions that eventually affect Milton severely. He is never quite sure whether he is loved or hated by either his supposed father, Nathan, or his mother. His world is confusing on many levels, from the conversations with his peers to everyday experiences. There is an attitude even within his society that blindly accepts the belief that Whites are better than Blacks. Milton discusses "who . . . is the wisest man in the world" (165) with his friend Lester. After Milton proposes someone named Haile Selassie, his nine-year-old friend's response is, "How could Selassie be the most wisest man in the world, when Selassie be only a black man? You expect a black man could be the most wisest man in the world when Selassie is *only* a black man?" (165). All around Milton are reminders for him to keep his rightful place. There is even the occasion on which he is attacked by a young White boy's dog and is then chastised for having hurt the dog. There is an invisible yet well-known barrier between the world of White people and that of the Black village, as is made clear to a young person through incidents such as this.

Milton and his Black, native culture have been degraded for his entire life. This necessarily must cause a large scar of insecurity and a very unstable perception of his own self-worth and the worth of others of his color. All of these factors influence his perception of himself and perpetuate the stationary and stagnant life that West Indian people appear to lead. If one is told incessantly in both blatant and unconscious ways that one has little worth except for service or despised menial labor, it seems impossible to avoid accepting it. This happens in the case of Ruby Sobers and her White employer and of Milton and everybody. His mother almost literally slaves for a White woman who continually criticizes her for her efforts in doing laundry. Although the abuse continues, his mother must still work in order to support them. Additionally, there is the White British inspector of schools who comes in to see if there has been educational progress, yet proceeds to thoroughly degrade the students. All around Milton there is ridicule.

The central events of the novel are bearable for the reader because they take the classic shape of tragedy. Milton's initiation starts at the beginning of the novel with the brutal beating by the school headmaster, as Milton learns the rules of the society in which he will have to survive. The beating is as formal a ritual as are learning the Ten Commandments and singing the British national anthem, "Rule Britannia." The narrative voice has a mature perspective, possibly adolescent, but not quite adult: "Rule Britannia, Britannia rules the waves; Britons, never-never-ne-verr shall be slaves! And singing, I saw the kings and the queens in the room with us, laughing in a funny way, and smiling and happy with us" (12). What Clarke does very well early in the novel, by way of that strong scene at school with the schoolmaster as slave master, is to set the historical basis for this story so that there is proper motivation for Milton's search for his identity and his father's identity. The headmaster had said that they were "little Black Britons" (13), but nothing in Milton's life at home or at school bore any resemblance to the "crowned heads" on the school's walls. Milton lives with his mother in what amounts to a shack, and she supports them on the five shillings per week she earns doing laundry. It is a job that takes her six days to complete, and for which she often has to purchase her own materials like soap and starch out of that five shillings, or from money borrowed from a neighbor, Girlie.

When Milton complains to Ruby about the severe beatings he has received at school from Blackman, she decides to speak with the teacher. But on meeting him, flattered by his compliments, she fades and "blushes" like a rose. On the way home she predictably beats Milton again, for making her look like a "damn fool." It is at this point that Milton runs away, disappearing into the night in search of Nathan, who has a reputation of being a bad man. Common-law marriages are not uncommon in the village, and Milton has already picked up this knowledge. He has heard the women at the stand pipe talk and seen them fight and compete for their men, and he has heard Willy-Willy's conversations and urgings that Milton is a "big enough man to start breeding the women of the village." But in terms of his own sexual orientation, the boy is confused because of a series of negative confrontations. Along the road, one day, he sees a black dog and a white dog connected, facing opposite directions. It is an ugly scene, and one could interpret it as an unsuccessful Black–White racial encounter, or as awakening the boy's awareness to unnatural sex. Girlie, who was rumored to like little boys, tugged at his testicles, which brought pain, fear, and degradation. Miss Brewster, who "looks like a man," seduced him, held him a "prisoner" in her house, and was going to suck his blood. As far as he knows, his mother is not sexual like Girlie; yet Ruby is the only close and positive "sexual" contact he has. After Nathan comes back to Ruby, "her footsteps are lighter now . . . love has placed a dancing-ness, a feeling of expectation. . . . But I cannot enjoy . . . her happiness" (115).

The novel is full of scenes in which the youthful Milton observes his mother toiling, sad, but always working. Her only "good times" are in conversations with Willy-Willy, who usually tells her of his American experiences, and in woman talk with Girlie. Those scenes are the most fun, earthy, and poignant in the book, and show a side of Ruby not often seen in the presence of her son.

> And once, out of girlish wickedness, my mother leaned over her paling, and called out next door for Girlie to come and see how many panties one woman could own and possess; . . . "Girlie! Girlie! . . . Come and see how people how decent people does live . . ." "Lord Jesus Jesus Jesus!" Her breath left her, when she saw my mother hold up twenty-four pairs of panties in her hands—all white! "Jesus God! Mistress Sobers, you mean to tell me that one woman . . . one person . . . Mistress Sobers, one human being does wear all them things? Lord have His mercy!" (31)

Ruby's laundry from the White woman across the "front road" and Willy's stories of America are her only contacts with the world outside her shack—her only "edication."

Milton is a very observant, sensitive, and realistic child. He understands his mother's predicament and struggles daily to help her get the wash done. He also understands that her often angry words and actions are the result of frustration. But she is also a wall, a hardened woman, he has to puzzle out. As Ruby says while addressing no one in particular: "This whole blasted world that I live in going backwards like them days during the war when a person was a lucky bitch if he had a grain o' rice to put inside his child' mouth, once a week. Christ, Christ, Christ! it taking everything outta me, just to live!" (47). Often Milton hears these soliloquies and ponders the complexity and hardness of his mother's existence. The moments of laughter for Girlie, Ruby, and Willy-Willy are simply those of comic relief because the possibility of a better life like that on the "front road" is as remote to Ruby, Girlie, Willy-Willy, and Milton as is the life represented by the singing of "Britannia." Like Lamming's collective story of four boys in *In the Castle of My Skin,* so does the world of the Sobers family exhibit a group spirit and consciousness that emerges in these scenes.

Yet Milton in the world of his mother suffers because of her need to be loved and wanted by a man. He is denied food, so that her men can eat. He is denied his mother's bed, and made to sleep where the rain leaks down on his makeshift bags on the floor, so that his mother can accommodate the "new love" in her life. He is banished from school. Nothing is friendly. The world aboveground is hostile. It is only from the dark place that "light" comes. When he runs away, he hears the word from under the cellar. His friends wonder "where Milton is." They want to give him a hero's praise because Nathan, "the bulldozer," had "beat up" the teacher. Despite the brutality of school and his life, Milton misses it all and longs to belong to that world again. He overhears the sexual act of his mother and Nathan from his cellar hideout and the plans they are carving out for his future. While under the cellar he also finds out who his real father is, from Nathan's and Ruby's conversation. He has gradually discovered that Willy-Willy, not Nathan, is his real father, and that Nathan had been duped into his paternal role as a substitute for the utterly destitute Willy-Willy. Hence, Nathan, initially presented as the strong father figure, is asked to avenge the savage punishments that his "son" receives at school. He is eventually dismissed by Milton as a contemptible and irrelevant boor.

Milton, like Ruby, is resigned to his fate. The two will continue to survive as best they can under conditions that seem possible for the time. Life has provided nothing wonderful, only faint compromises. Toward the end of the novel there is a telling scene between "son" and "father."

He sat there in that rocking-chair, not rocking, so quietly, and he continued to look at me as if I were a centipede, and he was deciding how best to
stamp out my life. . . . "You see this, you little bastard? . . ." I crept away
from him, although he had made no effort to grab me. He was so still, so
menacing! I sat on my mother's bed, yearning for the sun to come up, for
morning to come and release me from this prison. (179)

The meeting is by no means what one would imagine for a father
acknowledging a son for the first time. Milton Sobers is a tragic and
isolated figure because he is restricted by his age and status from
communicating his ideals to his Barbadian community.

To me, a father is like the coming of a rival in a love affair. My mother
has been my lover all these years. She had remained mine, alone with
me, mine all those nine miserable years of romance, of ups and downs,
but mostly downs. (115)

This last soliloquy is significant for the obvious sense of alienation
that accompanies Milton's newfound identity. His mother and
Nathan are apathetic figures, far removed from Milton's imaginative
world, limited to lovemaking and the daily drudgeries of eking out
a bare living—he as a rarely employed laborer and she as a White
prostitute's washerwoman. Milton's estrangement from both is dramatized in the evolution of his relationship with Nathan. Milton's
discovery of his real father is therefore linked with the Harlem symbolism of the novel, for in a real sense Willy-Willy, a former emigrant
to the United States, has also fathered Milton's transformation by
his stories of Black America. Both the parental and racial themes
thus cohere in the psychological experiences of Milton's rebirth.

Willy-Willy's own personality and experiences stress the tragic
irony that underlies the awakening of consciousness in *Thistles* as
well as in *Survivors of the Crossing* (1964), Clarke's second novel.
Transformation during his stay in the United States has alienated
Willy-Willy from the apathetic and self-hating society to which he
returns, a state illustrated by his role as the village drunk and local
eccentric. Willy-Willy's awareness, like Rufus's in *Survivors of the
Crossing,* is not translated into transforming action. It simply heightens a sense of futility, the frustration of being unable to communicate

the new consciousness to an insensitive environment. This failure is shown by his inability to acknowledge or support Milton as his child and by the eventual ignominy of drowning in a rainstorm, after being refused shelter by Ruby.

By the end of the novel Milton has inherited not only the triumph of his father's racial pride and awareness but also, by implication, its ironically painful consequences. Hence the aspirations expressed through his final vision of Harlem are undercut by the realities of the present; his overburdened mother has sacrificed her earlier ambition for Milton, in order to safeguard her own interests. She seeks to appease (and hold) Nathan by consenting to the latter's "plans" for Milton's real future—an abbreviated school education, followed by the lifelong futility of surviving as a semi-illiterate laborer like himself.

This attitude, ubiquitous on the island of Barbados and doubtless other places in the West Indies and United States, parallels society's treatment of Blacks and minorities universally. Most books, movies, television programs, newspaper articles, and magazines are geared toward the Caucasian, just as Milton's schoolbooks, stories, clothing, and even religion were all imported from England. This must have given him the feeling that he and his culture are of no importance, for they are never talked about, taught, utilized, or respected.

Milton lives in a society that mirrors the ghettos of America— crowded, poverty-stricken areas that are essentially "closed off" from the rest of the world. In these Black compounds, due to despondency and depression, it is extremely difficult to rise above such a demoralizing existence. This monotony and stagnation are the subject of the final line in Clarke's novel. When Milton's mother attempts to soothe her "husband," she ironically states, "Tomorrow going to be another, diff'rent new day, man. Patience . . ." (183). The irony comes from the fact that tomorrow, for her, Milton, and others in her village, will be, in effect, no different at all. In truth, the same depressing, degrading cycle will repeat itself.

Milton's dreams of Black pride have been inherited from his real father's views of Black America. But it is not enough that Milton, in his own way, has achieved a certain measure of self-awareness in ethnic and social terms, in learning that the full realization of self can be attained only in communicating these new insights with others, or with an unimaginative mother who blocks Milton's dream by removing him from school to work in a stone quarry. The horrors lie in the fact that almost all the people in the novel, including Milton, assume that things must be as they are, and they look with suspicion and some scorn on anyone who is outraged by the cruelty and unfairness of the world. The fact that Milton Sobers, a nine-year-old child, is victim and interpreter, hits us dead center.

■   ■

The novels *In the Castle of My Skin, The Year in San Fernando,* and *Amongst Thistles and Thorns* focus on particular aspects of a boy's growth into manhood in the West Indies. But the novels, regardless of plot, setting, and cultural circumstances, all have some basic elements in common—issues that are racial, cultural, familial, and sexual. The authors' narrative techniques also vary, but it seems as though they all follow the narrative strategy of most Black novelists of presenting a fractured reality.

In George Lamming's partly autobiographical *In the Castle of My Skin,* young G feels himself to be part of the communal village experience; he and his friends are close to the land and the "folk." But as G grows up he discovers himself to be more and more an individual, a stranger in his own society. His gradual alienation from friends, from the village, and finally from the island environment is more than a case of "growing up," of leaving the world of childhood behind—finally, it is a question not of class or even of education, but of sensibility. G has the questing, sensitive awareness of the creative artist, and as he develops the natural, undifferentiated world of the village and the world of literature and art inevitably draw apart. The gulf looms, even when there is no irresistible cultural pull. His overriding concern becomes the need to preserve this new identity, his integrity as a private individual, "the you that's hidden somewhere in the castle of your skin." It is a self-protective measure in a society that apparently can no longer contain or nourish the individual mind.

As Kenneth Ramchand says of *The Year in San Fernando,* it includes "us in the feel of a peculiarly open state of consciousness that is achieved by a scrupulous adherence to the boy's point of view, in a deceptively easy style that carries the necessary sensuous burden as well as sustaining the illusion of adolescent reportage."[12] Austin Clarke's *Amongst Thistles and Thorns* depicts the despair of those West Indians who find themselves locked into positions with little hope of getting out, with the protest likewise dramatized from the point of view of Milton Sobers, only nine years old. This novel tells of suffering, as an educational experience. Milton, in the "underworld," is like Ellison's Invisible Man whose initiation has no closure.

In all three novels, the boys exist in a woman's world. If one does not know who his father is, it is not a major disaster to outsiders and community. It does matter, though, for the protagonists. Black history and comparative diaspora studies have documented the pervasiveness of households headed by mothers or involving other types of family linkages that raise wonderful children. Milton's search is not only for a biological father but for the knowledge of who he himself is. The same is true of Fola in Lamming's *Season of Adventure* and countless other protagonists. They all seek the answer to those eternal questions of lineage, heritage, and kinship ties.

Clarke's *Amongst Thistles and Thorns* and Anthony's *The Year in San Fernando* offer the most truthful portraits of the passing of childhood of young boys in the West Indies, although Lamming's *Castle* has been the most acclaimed of the three, using the framework of childhood to show a group of boys and a place, Creighton's village, growing slowly into political, sexual, and racial awareness. Anthony's works have no political intentions beyond recording fully and faithfully that "season of youth," but the sociopolitical implications of Clarke's novels are important in the canon of Caribbean writing.

Baldwin's *Go Tell It on the Mountain* and Ellison's *Invisible Man,* although novels of initiation, also deal with blackness as a permanent part of one's being, coupled with the natural desire of an ethnic minority to blend, to assimilate, to become an integral part of the dominant White culture. There is, at the same time, the urge to blackness within the race, the need to feel a sense of identification. Hughes's Sandy in *Not Without Laughter* only begins to gain sight of this toward the end of that novel. The African American novels have a specific theme and statement to make about race, whereas the

12. Ramchand, *The West Indian Novel and Its Background,* 212.

West Indian novels stay closer to the basic tenets of the bildungsroman, using the protagonists' fidelity of consciousness to mirror their
initiations.

                ■   ■

Caribbean novels should be put into a social context because the
problems faced by mothers and sons in the West Indies are not the
same as those faced by Blacks in the United States, perhaps because
of locale and history. Nonetheless, the socioeconomic linkages are
very clear between Africa, the Caribbean, and the United States.

Recent evidence from census data and from surveys dealing with
the position of women in different societies has pointed to the growing
incidence of female-headed households, particularly in developing
countries. This increase appears to be closely correlated with the processes of modernization arising from specific strategies for economic
development.

One report provides striking evidence of the negative effects of such
strategies on women in general, and on those who head households
in particular. According to the report, the Caribbean data provide
"compelling evidence of the disadvantaged position for women who
are heads of households as compared to the female population in
general."[13] This had been a feature of the West Indian family from
the earliest days of the area's history, in addition to the slave history
that frowned on family units as threats to the institution of slavery.
Whether a family is headed by a male or a female, the needs for food,
clothing, and shelter have to be met. Factors that can lead to female-
headed households include women agreeing to live in a co-residential
union, or in an extended family situation without marriage. In addition, the emigration to the United States and Europe of men as
laborers especially during the 1940s and 1950s left women as head
of households. Since then women have been migrating equally, as
access to travel and work have become easier, and female independence has improved as socioeconomic conditions improved. One still
sees, however, nonresidential unions where the man comes and goes
in the household, thereby relieving him of any real responsibility

13. Joycelin Massiah, *Women as Heads of Households in the Caribbean: Family
Structure and Feminine Status,* 13. A good discussion/study in Edith Clarke's *My
Mother Who Fathered Me* supports this data also.

for women or children. This is Ruby Sobers's situation in *Amongst Thistles and Thorns*.

The literature suggests that female household headship has been a characteristic feature of lower-income family life, but little or no attention has been given to this form of household arrangement from the perspective of the woman. There are lots of West Indian women in "unionless marriages," but the novels *In the Castle of My Skin* and *Amongst Thistles and Thorns* show close "union marriages" of mothers with sons.[14]

Each West Indian mother makes three pledges to her child—to provide a clean bed, a "belly-full," and the best education money can buy. Lamming's *Castle* best illustrates all three points. G and his mother are introduced early, on G's ninth birthday. There is the intimacy of rain, warmth, and singing; the mood is one of a love scene. She is both mother and father to him. The novel does not deal with the absence of the father and the pressure it exerts on G's mother, but on the presence and closeness of the mother and what G takes away from that relationship.

It is through G's friends that we get additional summations of what a mother is. They state, for example, "there is nothing like a mother," "I love my mother," "mothers are stupid that's why men don't come around." These statements suggest also their close involvement with their mothers and the nature of their learned male and female roles. There is also the ritual repetition of the word *mother* by G throughout the book. "Miss Foster. My mother. Bob's mother. It seemed they were three pieces in a pattern which remained constant" (16–17). Interestingly, boys in the West Indies seldom become detached from their mothers, from birth into marriage and maturity. Even into middle age the maternal bond is one of nearly eternal Oedipal recognition and protectiveness.

In each case, boys seem to avoid contact with other women since their model for sexual attachments and the married state is their mothers. The boys are also "taken" by their mothers. The commitment is twofold. Like the other characters, G's experience is a blend of male and female—a rich, androgynous one. The most unloving

14. Geta LeSeur, "Mothers and Sons: Androgynous Relationships in African American and African–West Indian Novels of Youth," 23.

and violent people in the boys' lives seem to be men, who, despite their periodic absence, irresponsible attitude, and the presence of the mothers, want to exercise discipline and authority. How confusing this must be for a young boy, since it is obvious that it is his mother who is the dominant and rightful overseer of his daily life and growth. The blending of roles, emotions, and lifestyles is therefore "passed on" to each son, thus repeating the cycle of connectedness.

Whereas *Castle* and *Year* are quite autobiographical, *Amongst Thistles and Thorns,* according to Clarke, is a more fictionalized work, and should perhaps be read as a companion to *Growing Up Stupid under the Union Jack,* Clarke's autobiography. Although there are authentic experiences that the author might have had, *Amongst Thistles and Thorns* is generally acknowledged to be plotted to serve the purpose of expressing a mother–son relationship, and to show that Milton's life is a typical one for a poor West Indian youth, much like Clarke's early life.

Milton's adventures and dreams give insight into the West Indian culture, and his experiences illustrate the composition of a typical lower-class West Indian family. His immediate home life includes only him and his mother, Ruby, but they are interdependent. Because of the lack of a man in the house, Milton and Ruby assume roles other than the usual ones of mother and son. Milton is a son and a "little husband" to her and, for a nine-year-old boy, has a lot of responsibility. He does indoor and outdoor chores—makes beds, cleans the lamp, cleans the pigpen, fetches water, runs errands, helps keep track of money, and is his mother's confidant. Ruby also has several roles. She is mother and father to Milton—his support, his disciplinarian, his cook, and his provider. Their financial difficulties and their cramped quarters make them even closer.

The harsh reality of Ruby's life, however, is that she is utterly destitute, a poor washerwoman who works all week for five meager shillings that allow her and her son a minimum survival, with barely any savings to realize future dreams. Studies have shown that in the West Indies fathering a child out of wedlock does not require the man to assume responsibility for the child, financially or emotionally. It is only when the man assumes the role of husband and father that he is expected to be more responsible financially and act as a disciplinarian. Another character in *Thistles,* Girlie, has seven children, all of whom are born out of wedlock to different men. The village or yard community accepts this, and not much thought is given to who fathered whom. For a woman, surviving and providing for the child take priority over everything else.

Although there are two men in Milton's life, Willy-Willy and Nathan, both are on the outer fringes of his experience. It is his mother who is the center of his world. He completely understands and accepts her function in his life. Even though he did occasionally turn to Nathan for nonfinancial "support," it is his mother whom he turns to when he really needs someone for succor and comfort. In a nightmare Milton has about the Bath (public water stand) and getting in trouble with the Inspector, it is to his mother that he runs, not to Willy-Willy or Nathan.

This novel demonstrates a different perspective as mother and son are more distinctly linked than are Francis and his mother in *Year.* Ruby is in that category of West Indian women who seem to have gained a certain independence, and she tolerates a visiting situation with one man who is Milton's father and another who is a boyfriend. Ironically, both men depend on Ruby's small wages for "cigs," "rum," and "food." She willingly provides for them by often denying her own son a meal. Ruby seems to be the type of woman who must have a man in her life at all costs and who is forever hopeful for a father for her son. On one of her conjugal evenings with Nathan, she wishes to have for Milton "the best o' every-damn-thing possible" (104). They want to send him to Harrison College (like Clarke) to have a good education and find a job even more prestigious than a civil servant's, such as that of a schoolteacher or a sanitary inspector. She dreams of him singing with the choir in a cathedral, "more sweeter than if he was a blasted humming-bird" (105). She pictures him "riding 'pon a brand new-brand three-speed tick-tick bicycle, wearing his nice start-and-irn's khaki trousers and white shirt stiff stiff . . . whiter than the snows" (103). And her fantasies go on and on.

Milton, too, has dreams of other lives for himself, away from the hunger pangs and undeserved beatings and backbreaking labor he knows so well. He dreams of Harlem in "New York City, USA" far away from the little island of Barbados in the West Indies. But his dreams are more an escape from the reality he faces than a journey to a specific fantasy. His youthful visions and delusions are unfocused. But with all his "nine-years" innocence, he learns to accept his fate of hardship. And, since Nathan is determined to set him up with an iron drill in a rock quarry, and his mother has abandoned her plans for his education, Milton can only listen to the tragic irony of his mother's words and "see the sadness, the grief and the weakness" (177); so he continues to grope through the "thistles and thorns" of his impoverished world in search of his own happiness and contentment.

Milton has a more tragic life than the boys in *Castle* and *Year.* When the novel ends one wonders whether he will ever get the clean bed, the belly full of food, and the best education money can buy. Will he get Ruby back? The history of conjugal relationships in the West Indies suggests that Nathan will not stay with her. That situation is impermanent; Milton and Ruby's is permanent. Unlike the other boys—Francis, who returns to his quiet village; Christopher, who steps into a secure adolescence; G, who goes to Trinidad—Milton will, the next morning, go to the stone quarry to break stones. That "profession" is no different from the menial but necessary tasks he did for his mother all his life. He seems to have lost all around.

Mothers play a major role in the lives of all the male protagonists. The boys in the West Indies are conscious of the women's world and of women's work just as the writers are, and their growing experiences are outside the traditional American ones. In the West Indies, for example, there is a "rivalry" for the mother's love. This is not considered abnormal, however, but natural. In some circles such a boy might be considered a "sissy" or a "she-she man." Although the boys might lack father figures as role models, in the United States these relationships would be stigmatized, while in the West Indies they are perfectly natural because, as we have seen, lack of proper paternity is a fairly acceptable pattern in the culture.

In all aspects of home training, the mother is the principal actor. The child's most intimate relationship in the home is with her, even when the father is present and associates himself with the upbringing of the child. "The girl child identifies with the mother while the boy has already begun to build up a type of behavior which might be described as a husband substitute."[15] In other cases, boys take on the role of mother's helper, one that traditionally is associated with girls. The positive or negative influences on the male child's life have not been professionally assessed, but there seems to be little carryover in their treatment of women in general later as they mature. The dependence continues (as with Willy-Willy and Nathan), but the sharing and respect cease in some relationships. The consciousness of "a woman's world" thus must be presented by the mature male writer in some way other than through the immature male characters.

There is a natural rivalry for the mother between men and sons, so obvious in *Amongst Thistles and Thorns.* The boys know their responsibilities and they have a sense of mission and duty. The sexuality of the boys and their mothers is often ambivalent in all the novels. The merging of male and female in terms of work in the West Indies is very natural, as in the realism about women's work, even though some traditional duties are done by males. The reader never knows what Willy-Willy or Nathan does for a living. As they wander and "move around," it is Ruby who cares for them despite her destitute circumstances. In certain classes in the West Indies this practice is acceptable and customary. Even though some West Indian men depend on their women for "motherly care," not just sex, they do not feel castrated, unlike some African American males who blame Black women and society for their ills. One has only to contrast Austin Clarke's protagonists with James Baldwin's characters. The merging of maleness and femaleness in the West Indian bildungsroman puts the reader in touch with the truth and basic processes of that existence.

All the boys function in a world of women and their confidences; they watch women suffer pain and anguish. Ruby, for example, has no money to buy pads when her "ladies time" is upon her. She loses both her men but still has her little man, her son. Will these boys become caring husbands later? There is no data to substantiate this, but Edith Clarke's study, *My Mother Who Fathered Me,* further demonstrates that men in the West Indies continue a lifelong closeness with their mothers that is very different from the women's relationships

15. Massiah, *Women as Heads of Households,* 51.

with daughters.[16] The relationships of mothers with sons are not uncommon in other literatures, but they are striking in novels of the African diaspora because of the long history of Black women's experiences as heads of households, father substitutes, and "lovers" of their sons.

16. *My Mother Who Fathered Me,* 158.

III

"HIS GREAT STRUGGLE BEGINNING"
AFRICAN AMERICAN MALE INITIATION

The distance between this platform and the slave plantation, from which
I escaped, is considerable—and the difficulties to be overcome in getting
from the latter to the former are by no means slight.
                    Frederick Douglass, "Fourth of July Address"

The name and analytical concept of the initiation story are derived basically from anthropology, which has found that the most
important rites of traditional cultures center around the passage
from childhood or adolescence to maturity and full membership in
adult society. Certain "literary anthropologists" propose a concept
of initiation as a stage in all human life. For the most part, "initiation" in fiction has only a peripheral or tangential relationship
to the formal anthropological initiation. Only in some cases, as in
Faulkner's "The Bear" (1942), is the initiation of the fictional heroes
accompanied by ritual.[1] Some of the elements of the emergence into
manhood or the larger society of the protagonists in the works to be
examined here are separation or estrangement; growth and change;
isolation; the search for identity; racial and cultural violence with
its accompanying frustration; journeying or movement as a seeking
of knowledge; an examination of the relationship between mothers
and daughters, fathers and sons, mothers and sons; sexual awakening; and representative dominant images that are unique to each
initiation experience.

The various critical definitions of the initiation story fall into two
groups. The first group describes initiation as a passage of the young
from ignorance about the external world to the acquisition of some

1. Mordecai Marcus, "What Is an Initiation Story?" 220.

vital knowledge. The second describes initiation as the process of making an important self-discovery and a resulting adjustment to life or society. Thus, G in Lamming's *In the Castle of My Skin* belongs in the first group because of the well-delineated levels of learning that he grows from, seeks, and records. Francis in *The Year in San Fernando* and Milton in *Amongst Thistles and Thorns* belong to the second because of their unique family circumstances and settings and because their stories cover a briefer period of time—Francis's, one year; Milton's, one weekend—and do not take them into adolescence. Initiation for Black boys bears little resemblance to that of White boys. Huck and Jim, despite being thrown together, never do bond or share anything common in their individual backgrounds. Certainly, on one level Huck is oppressed and abused, but the historical and cultural contexts are vastly different.

Probably no other African American writer in the twentieth century made such a mark with both readers and critics with just one novel as Ralph Ellison. His *Invisible Man* has elements of the bildungsroman and carefully details the transition of a sensitive and artistic youth from innocence to perception and maturity, through a series of shocking and painful initiatory experiences. The author divides the book into three parts that move the narrator from purpose to passion to perception, and he calls it "a novel about innocence and human error, a struggle through illusion to reality."[2] There could hardly be a better statement of the process of initiation. The protagonist of *Invisible Man,* who is also the narrator, experiences a series of complications, which make his life's journey much clearer. This novel is very different from the other three books to be discussed here, Langston Hughes's *Not Without Laughter,* James Baldwin's *Go Tell It on the Mountain,* and Richard Wright's *Black Boy.*

All four works reveal a concern with defining an African American racial, historical, cultural, and political reality. In each of these very different texts, issues of self-identity merge with issues of African American consciousness and identity. The predicament of the writer as autobiographical subject, in the case of Wright, Baldwin, and Hughes, illuminates the collective predicament of the Black community. Their works emerge therefore as a means to an end rather than

2. Ralph Ellison, "The Art of Fiction: An Interview," 177.

as an end in itself. In Ellison's work, however, since he is not writing his life but a collective African American man's life, conventions of control and content do not dictate the story line. Ellison, therefore, does not experience a creative struggle, but deals directly with social and political issues. That his protagonist/narrator is also nameless affords more freedom for Ellison as artist. In fictive autobiographies like Wright's and Baldwin's books, the author's authority to omit portions of his life, change names and places, and intensify and highlight situations pushes the work into the bildungsroman mode. The voices in these novels tend to be in the first and third person, allowing the author to juxtapose self-revelation with the larger issues of the African American or West Indian context. Even though this is a good device to use, it creates tension in the works. Clearly in these novels, the "life" is in the service of something more than the story and the deeds done.

The protagonist of *Invisible Man* moves physically and emotionally through his series of separate experiences. We see him as a Black high school boy in a southern state, a college student at a southern Negro college, an employee in a paint factory, a leader of a Communist-type group called the Brotherhood, and self-exile in a brightly lighted basement. Even though some of these adventures may seem inconsequential and the movement of the protagonist aimless, still there is a thematic method to this structure. Because the picaresque novel is superbly suitable for the bildungsroman, individual episodes serve to express the theme of adolescent initiation and growth.

The first shock for the main character comes in early childhood from his grandfather, who, on his deathbed, advises him to continue the fight begun during Reconstruction, just after Blacks laid down their guns to conquer Whites by undermining them with grinning faces, by agreeing with all they think and say, and by overpowering them with accommodativeness. Neither he nor his father can accept this as his role in life. The boy envisions himself a potential Booker T. Washington and studies hard to fit himself for that role until the second shock, his obscene "rites de passage," introduces him to his real role in society and his journey into that society actually begins.

Invisible Man opens with the narrator's statements about the clarification of life he has experienced after his adolescence and young manhood. He realizes that he is an invisible man. In what really amounts to his notes from the underground he says: "I am invisible, understand, simply because people refuse to see me. . . . When they approach me they see only my surroundings, themselves, or figments of their imagination—indeed, everything and anything except me."[3]
What follows is a flashback to his experience of the past twenty years, beginning with his graduation from high school and his valedictory oration on the virtues of humility. Because of his brilliant performance he is invited to give the same address at a "smoker" for the leading White citizens of the community. His experience at the smoker turns out to be a nightmarish initiation rite. With nine other Black boys, he is made to watch a stark sexual act by a tipsy, sexually aroused White man who threatens to whip the boys if they don't look, while others threaten to do the same if they do. Thus begin the initiatory episodes. The narrator is shocked at the discovery of his own strong sexual drives. At the same time he is disgusted and frightened by the whole spectacle. Before he gives his speech he is made to take part blindfolded in a degrading fight with his Black companions. He takes a terrible beating from the boys before things come to an end. The frightening rite of initiation is not complete with that. He is then forced into another contest with his Black friends to pick his reward in gilt coins from an electrified mat and thus learns a valuable though painful lesson. He begins to understand what was so difficult to comprehend in his dying grandfather's injunction to him: "Live with your head in the lion's mouth. I want you to overcome 'em with yeses, undermine 'em with grins, agree 'em to death and destruction, let 'em swoller you till they vomit or bust wide open" (19–20). When he finally comes to make his speech he is appalled to find that his inebriated listeners regard his performance as an entertaining novelty. In a Freudian slip he substitutes "social equality" for "social responsibility." He is heckled into recanting and then awarded a scholarship to a Black college. He is also given a calfskin briefcase, which, he is told, will someday "be filled with important

3. *Invisible Man,* 3. Further references to this work will be made parenthetically in the text.

papers that will help shape the destiny of your people" (123), if he continues to develop along the right lines.

The next important initiatory episode occurs when he is expelled from the Black college where, for the first time in his life, he had begun to feel at home. After an incident, the president of the college, Dr. Bledsoe, reprimands him and sends him away with letters of recommendation to influential White patrons in the North. To make matters worse he dreams of his grandfather, who asks him to look into the briefcase for a message. He does, and the message reads: "To Whom It May Concern, Keep This Nigger-Boy Running" (136). It is only a dream, but it aptly foreshadows his future life.

The narrator's journey from the South to the North is an important stage of his initiation since it is a movement from the rural to the urban and, on a metaphorical level, from the darkness of ignorance to the light of knowledge. The movement of protagonists from the provincial setting to the urban is consistent in these novels, so much so that readers have come to expect it. Even in the case of Baldwin's protagonist John, who is already in the city, provinciality can be taken to mean the unenlightened and suffocating place where he lives, in that case, Harlem. The transition is also one from sightlessness to sight. Significantly the eyes on the statue of the founder of the Black school are empty, the eloquent preacher Homer Barbee is completely blind, and all the "Uncle Tom" figures the protagonist meets in the South are unable to see the true plight of Blacks. Ellison says that "the narrator's development is one through blackness to light; that is, from ignorance to enlightenment; invisibility. He leaves the South and goes North; this, as the road to freedom—the movement upward. The same thing happens again when he leaves his underground cave for the open."[4]

The painful initiation continues in Harlem. It helps him to understand his experience with Lucius Brockway, the half-crazy Uncle Tom character he works with at the Liberty Paints Factory. Brockway's strange truculent kind of Uncle Tomism drives the narrator to rebel for the first time, and they get into a fight during which the older man gets a sound beating followed by the young man blacking out. His blacking out is described in terms of a fall, the fall from ignorance into

4. Ellison, "The Art of Fiction," 174.

knowledge, and his coming to is described in terms of an initiatory second birth. When he is revived with the aid of an elaborate electrical apparatus, he can remember noting, "My mind was blank, as though I had just begun to live" (205). He doesn't even know who he is. He realizes that his freedom is tied up with the question of his identity, and he comes upon a very important initiatory insight: "I could no more escape than I could think of my identity. Perhaps, I thought, the two things are involved with each other. When I discover who I am, I'll be free" (237). Later he is taken care of by a surrogate mother, Mary Rambo, a well-known figure in Harlem, but the question of identity still bothers him: "And the obsession with my identity which I had developed in the factory hospital returned with a vengeance. Who was I, how had I come to be?" (253).

Pain and disillusionment have brought valuable insights, and along with them anger. He sees the Bledsoes, the Nortons, and the Emersons in a clearer light now. Although it conflicts with his grandfather's advice, he gives up the role of the docile Negro who was supposed to "yes 'em to death." He unashamedly accepts his Black identity and his southern origins. He is ashamed only because he was once ashamed of his ancestry, so he goes out and indulges his "southern Negro" taste for yams. When the old Black street vendor of hot yams expresses surprise at the quantity of yams he has eaten, he says, "They're my birthmark. I yam what I am" (231).

When he witnesses the eviction and dispossession of an old Black couple, his heart goes out to them. Using his powers of oration he passionately traces the history of Blacks since Emancipation and within a few moments has started a small demonstration that soon erupts into a full-scale riot. Ellison has called the book "the portrait of the artist as a rabble rouser,"[5] and a rabble-rouser is precisely what his protagonist becomes soon after this episode. The Brotherhood, a Marxist organization, employs him to rouse Harlem to a full realization of its plight and the necessity to do something about it.

The narrator thinks that at last he has found his true vocation in life, but he finds that he is again mistaken when he learns that the Brotherhood is just using him. They are interested more in the

5. Ibid., 179.

expediency of historical and dialectical materialism than in the problems of the Black people. His role once again changes from that of a
rabble-rouser to that of a pacifier and entertainer. The Brotherhood
removes him just as he seems most needed in Harlem. The women he
meets at the Brotherhood prove to be another disappointment. They
mouth the formulas of the party but don't seem to have any genuine
interest in it.

The narrator had thought that he had moved from blindness to
sight but now realizes that what he had achieved was only half-sight.
When he finally falls into a coal pit, his running and his incessant
changing of identities at last come to an end. His invisibility is now
a fait accompli. He has achieved the ultimate in invisibility—a black
man in a coal cellar. In a surrealistic dream he sees Brother Jack,
Emerson, Bledsoe, Norton, Ras, and others demanding that he return
to them. He tells them that he is through running. They hold him
and castrate him in a scene that recalls Joe Christmas's castration in
William Faulkner's *Light in August.* He decides to stay in the hole for
some time at least, and that is where his notes from the underground
emanate from. He illuminates the hole by tapping electricity from
Monopolated Light and Power Company. This illumination stands for
the enlightenment he has finally achieved. He comes to the view that
the world is one of infinite possibilities if a man first finds himself.
He says: "So why do I write, torturing myself to put it down? Because
in spite of myself I've learned some things. Without the possibility of
action all knowledge comes to one labeled 'file and forget,' and I can
neither file nor forget" (566).

At this stage his initiation is incomplete, but since his face is turned
toward society, there is hope that he will achieve decisive initiation
in the future. Unlike the protagonist of Dostoyevsky's *Notes from the
Underground,* he is not cutting himself away from society. Nor is he
plunging out of history. He has no doubt plunged into the cellar, but
it is in the cellar that he has sharpened his sense of perception; it
is there again that he has gained understanding. Furthermore, the
very act of narrating his experiences proves that the cellar is more
in the nature of a temporary purgatory than a permanent inferno.
The cellar as a place to gain knowledge recurs in literature, another
example being the cellar in which Milton is hiding in *Thistles* when

he learns for the first time the truth of his paternity. At the very beginning of *Invisible Man,* which is also the end, the narrator clearly defines his hibernation in the cellar as a "covert preparation for a more overt action."

Invisible Man was one of the more sophisticated examples of the bildungsroman at the time of its publication, but as an initiation story it has most of the traditional elements of the form. While the intention of most bildungsromane is not protest, Ellison has made his novel distinctly African American while staying close to the definition of initiation given earlier. The work's message of the peculiar conditioning imposed on its members by a society that denies the recognition of an individual is not unlike that of other novels such as Wright's *Black Boy* and *Native Son.*

While the journey is a physical one, it is, more importantly, an emotional and intellectual voyage. Ellison has explored, with intelligence and artistry, some of the more compelling issues of the meaning of American identity, the quality of Black–White relations, and the question of free will versus social pressure. *Huckleberry Finn* is universally accepted as one of the world's great books and one of the central documents of American culture; so, too, is *Invisible Man* a work that marked the height of Black achievement in this genre. More than that, it is a central document for an understanding of America's most crucial domestic dilemma. Although this dilemma contains deep complexities, and the paradoxes have been more fully recognized by such Black writers as Eldridge Cleaver, Malcolm X, James Baldwin, and Stokely Carmichael, *Invisible Man* still offers the classic delineation, in fiction, of what it means to be Black and male in America.

■   ■

Langston Hughes's only novel, *Not Without Laughter,* is different from Baldwin's *Go Tell It on the Mountain* and Ellison's *Invisible Man.* It is not written in the true protest tradition, but it does have much to say regarding racial politics, Black suffering, isolation, and what it means to be Black, male, poor, and "fatherless." What Hughes does well is to capture the folk tradition he knew so well and had used throughout his poetry, short fiction, and drama. Thus, although his only novel is not exactly idyllic, it is permeated with a feeling of innocence as suggested through three characters—Sandy, the boy who is the focal point of the story; his "absent" father, Jimboy; and his mother, Anjee, who is atypical of most Black heroines at the time of the novel's publication. The setting is a small rural town in Kansas in the early twentieth century, which again makes the family, lifestyle, and initiating experiences different from those in *Invisible Man*. Hughes, born in 1908, came of age during America's struggle with many changes and is best associated with the Harlem Renaissance era from the 1920s to the 1940s.

Not Without Laughter portrays a family that is very close to the Black folk culture and reveals styles of confronting the disorder and chaos that tend to hammer away at the precariously held sanctuary of Black family life. The novel portrays the tensions of a generation that came to adulthood not long after the hopes of Blacks for freedom had been dashed. The mainstay of this generation is the grandmother, Aunt Hagar, whose life is an epic of labor over the washtub. Getting ready to reach adulthood is her grandson, Sandy, a witness to the perilous hold on life managed by his grandmother, mother, father, and aunts. Although the events controlling the life of each member of the family absorb a good portion of the novel, the development and fate of the boy, and especially the extent to which he is exposed to the lives of his elders, provide him with opportunities from which to learn. What kind of man will Sandy grow up to be? What happens to boys reared primarily by women? Aunt Hagar is symbolic of the Black matriarch who rears not only her own children but also her grandchildren. She also represents an earlier generation of Black women who still carry the slave history and experience, and she has contempt for the "new ways" and the "new Black Woman" like her daughter Harriet. Sandy is with her constantly, and it is he whom she singles out to keep the old traditions alive. She is also the one who seems to wield the greatest influence on his upbringing. Perhaps Sandy is the alter ego of Hughes himself, who as an adult recorded the rich folk poetry, songs, and stories of his people. Sandy is privileged to the riches of Black life without knowing it. In this sense, then, this novel echoes the autobiographical components of Baldwin's *Go Tell It on the Mountain*, Lamming's *In the Castle of My*

Skin, and other works that show the indelible heritage some writers received from families. Aunt Hagar also represents the religious tradition begun in the secret "praise" meetings of slavery and further developed in the little whitewashed churches that once dotted the countryside and small towns.

Grandmother Hagar is represented as a "salt-of-the-earth" figure, and it is through her eyes that the action and flavor of life are communicated. Of her five children, Harriet, the youngest, is the most rebellious and liberated. Anjee's husband, Jimboy, has a reckless vagabond spirit. Actually he and Harriet have similar temperaments and tastes, but Jimboy is drawn to the road and ragtime music. He often disappears from home for months at a time without communicating with the family. Because of Jimboy's absence, he has no influence on his son's upbringing. Sandy is therefore reared in a world of women—namely Hagar, Anjee, and Harriet. As he listens and observes, his life is pretty isolated but also protected. He is not introduced to the world's realities until he goes to shine shoes and clean spittoons at a Black barbershop. The only other early experience he has of the outside, "better" world is in his Aunt Tempy's middle-class home, where he goes to live after his grandmother's death. The transition is difficult, and he would have preferred the "old home," which held such fond memories for him.

> Sandy had lived too long with three women not to have learned to hold his tongue about the private doings of each of them. When Anjee paid two dollars a week on a blue silk shirt for his father at Cohn's Cutrate Credit Store, and Sandy saw her make the payments, he knew without being told that the matter was never to be mentioned to Aunt Hagar. And if his grandmother sometimes threw Harriet's rouge in the alley, Sandy saw it with his eyes, but not his mouth. Because he loved all three of them. Harriet, Anjee and Hagar—he didn't carry tales on any one of them to the others. Nobody would know he had watched his Aunt Harriet dancing on the carnival lot today in front of a big fat white man.[6]

Sandy understands the little confidences between the three women. He is part of their inner circle. He respects the individuality of all

6. *Not Without Laughter,* 113–14. Further references to this work will be made parenthetically in the text.

three, and he is the only "man" in their lives. He is often referred to as an "apron string boy," which suggests femininity. This absence of a male as a model or giver of information is very common in some Black novels that focus on growing up.

> Neither Aunt Hagar nor Anjee had ever said anything to Sandy about love in its bodily sense; Jimboy had gone away too soon to talk with him, and Tempy and her husband were too proper to discuss such subjects, so the boy's sex knowledge consisted only in the distorted ideas that youngsters whisper; the dirty stories heard in the hotel lobby where he had worked; and the fact that they sold in drugstores articles that weren't mentioned in the company of nice people. (278–79)

Sandy tries hard to decipher those impressions and understand their meaning as well as that of the life around him. From his Aunt Harriet he learns that there is a potential for upward mobility and that his grandmother's generation has passed on.

Since he spends so much time with his grandmother he begins to accept what she presents as healthy and normal and feels contentment when he hears the "happy plantation songs." His father is disliked by his grandmother because of a traditional prejudice against mulattoes. She says:

> "First place, I don't like his name. . . . Who ever heard of a nigger named Jimboy anyhow? Next place, I ain't never seen a yaller dude yet that meant a dark woman no good and Anjee is dark." . . . But what she probably referred to in her mind was the question of his ancestry, for nobody knew who Jimboy's parents were. (18)

But Aunt Hagar does know the history of the white man's rape of Black women. Sandy was called "Sandy" because of his light brown color and sandy hair. In addition to Jimboy's questionable heritage, there is the problem of his representing, in the women's eyes, "the devil's musicianer . . . straight from hell" (32).

It is at his Aunt Tempy's house, however, after Aunt Hagar dies, that Sandy is exposed to literary works like those by Charles Chesnutt, Paul Laurence Dunbar, W. E. B. Du Bois, and Booker T.

Washington, and thereby to another aspect of blackness. By reading these books "he found, too, stirring and beautifully written editorials about the frustrated longings of the black race, and the hidden beauties of the negro soul" (259). All of this exposure makes Sandy think deeply about his rich heritage. As he lies in bed he says to himself:

> "But I want to learn!" I want to go to college. I want to go to Europe and study. "Work and make ready and maybe your chance will come," it said under the picture of Lincoln on the calendar given away by the First National Bank, where Earl, his white friend, already had a job promised him when he came out of school . . . it was not really so difficult for white boys. . . . No wonder Buster was going to pass for white when he left Stanton. (279)

Thus, in spite of his dislike for Aunt Tempy, Sandy realizes that a new phase of his growth or journey into understanding and knowledge has begun. At this level of initiation, "The Doors of Life" had opened for him. He succinctly ponders,

> The doors of life. . . . God damn that simple minded book that Tempy had given him! What did an old white minister know about the doors of life anywhere? And, least of all, the doors to a Negro's life? . . . Black youth. . . . Dark hands knocking, knocking! (280–81)

Just as Sandy learns about sex by listening and observing, he surmises that there is something hidden behind the information given him by his mother and grandmother. "Once when he asked his mother what his navel was for and she said, 'layover to catch meddlers.' What did that mean? . . . And how come ladies got sick and stayed in bed when they had babies? Where did babies come from anyhow?" (185). Sexual education is not made obvious in the novel, but Sandy knows about the girls at Maudel's from listening to the men at the local barbershop. He also finds out that his Aunt Harriet is a prostitute, and he does get propositioned by a homosexual on his arrival in Chicago later. In each case, common sense, instinct, and observation make him recognize precisely the sexual world and the realities of a world beyond Kansas.

What impresses Hughes and Sandy is the passionate spiritual power that sustains faith in life. Aunt Hagar would like for Sandy to be a Booker T. Washington or a Frederick Douglass: "I wants him to know all they is to know so's he can help with this Black race of our'n to come up and see de'light and take they places in de world. I wants him to be a Fred Douglass leadin' de people, that's what, and not followin' in de tracks of his good for nothin' pappy" (146). Hughes plays lovingly the notes of the tradition that involves a bouncing vitality and a defiant celebration of the sweet joys and pains of life, and Sandy finds himself drawn to the people who demand that life yield its more soulful fruits. However, Hughes has a very complex awareness, one that he cannot fully render within the novel. Because he is also an honest and realistic writer, he cannot make Jimboy's situation a very simple triumph and must report the costs of Jimboy's charm, joy, and exuberance in the increased deprivation experienced by his family as a result and in some rather painful childhood experiences for Sandy. Thus, despite Hughes's distancing of Jimboy's wide-ranging "amours," his explanations of the systematic oppression that tends to diminish Black men, the portrayal of him as a "rounder" who works and holds good intentions, and the dramatization of his ability to transform the atmosphere of his surroundings, Jimboy is never quite clear of the dubious stature that Aunt Hagar very early in the novel confers upon him. Jimboy is, after all, "boy."

Thus, the sensitive Sandy only gets to share "moments" of the tradition represented by his father. He can only feel that the swing and bounce that he represents ought to be a part of the richness of life. Because Aunt Tempy's choice to imitate White society represents an obvious surrender of the soul, her life embodies little that could promise richness to Sandy.

Sandy's consciousness does not develop dramatically, and there are contradictory statements about his degree of innocence. The novel ends logically, however, in the city where Sandy goes to join his mother after his grandmother dies. One wonders what the future holds for a young boy entering the "hostile" city after the secure rural setting and the "women's love" he had.

Especially significant is the spiritual that comes at the very end of the novel, "By an' By When the Mawin' Comes"—the spiritual ends

with the line, "An we'll understand it better by an' by" (303–4). It
tells of overcoming, suggests a determined struggle that cannot be
easily conceptualized or understood, as it is sung in the big, raw city
of Chicago. As Hughes has said, it is the music of a "people on the
go," who are somehow to break free from their cage. For those like
Sandy who "like to listen to the rambling talk of old colored folks . . . I
guess there won't be many like that in Chicago" (184–85). The vague
aspirations but settled determination of Sandy are appropriate for
someone entering the early stages of a second journey. This novel does
not allow the reader to assess Sandy's readiness for this. He appears
to be one of the most naive, at this stage, of the boys discussed.

■   ■

Generally regarded as one of the great American novels of the
twentieth century, James Baldwin's *Go Tell It on the Mountain* has
been called a psychological study of the clash between father and
son and a sociological examination of the role of the Black church in
the Black community; it is also a Black bildungsroman.[7] Baldwin's
themes, however, transcend the life of one Black youth and the lives,
past and present, of one family. He places his characters in a recognizable intellectual tradition and uses this tradition to express their individual destinies. The tradition from which Baldwin has benefited is
that of Du Bois, Booker T. Washington, Frederick Douglass, Langston
Hughes, Ida Wells Barnett, James Weldon Johnson, Richard Wright,
and others who had contributed to the Black autobiographical canon.
Mountain extends the strong tradition of African American autobiography and fictive versions of those autobiographies.

The autobiographical context of much of Baldwin's novel has been
noted by several critics.[8] The fictional protagonist, John Grimes, is,
like Baldwin, a first-generation Harlemite, a child of the great Black
migration to northern cities. John and the author are both sons of
proud, stiff-necked Pentecostal preachers who waste little affection
on their offspring. John's ecstatic religious "rebirth" on his fourteenth
birthday mirrors the author's personal conversion at the same age.
Like the youthful Baldwin, John learns early and acutely of "the

7. Charles Scruggs, "The Tale of Two Cities in James Baldwin's *Go Tell It on
the Mountain*," 1.
8. Robert Bone, *The Negro Novel in America,* 218–20.

weight of white people in the world," those people who live beyond the physical, economic, social, and psychological barriers that mark the boundaries of ghetto life. Indeed, "if this were in fact autobiography and not fiction, we might expect the writer's conventional exploration of his roots, . . . shaped and conditioned [by] emerging manhood."[9]

The novel examines three generations of a Black family whose history extends from slavery to the 1950s. It investigates, with warmth and perception, the Black man's possibility of achieving identity through the discipline of Christianity. Unfolding in a series of five major movements, the novel begins with the reach of fourteen-year-old John Grimes for recognition, a fearful, faltering reach, from a boy filled with guilt, hatred, fear, and love amid the stern religious frustrations of his elders and the rebelliousness of his brother, Roy. The second movement presents the tragedy of John's Aunt Florence, who is unable to overcome her internalization of the dominant cultural concept of blackness and is on insecure terms with herself and others. The third represents Gabriel Grimes, John's stepfather, who is blocked from complete fulfillment by his attempts to escape his worldly drives in a fierce, frustrated embrace of Christianity. The fourth portrays John's mother, Elizabeth, who, after a brief fulfillment from illicit love, retreats, frightened and awestricken, into the frustrated and frustrating arms of Gabriel. The final movement is John's questionable flight from his quest for identity into the supposed safety of religious ecstasy.

John's most serious problem is his inability to relate satisfactorily to Gabriel, who had married Elizabeth knowing that she had borne John out of wedlock but promising to love the boy as if he were his father. At the heart of Gabriel's generosity lies hidden guilt about his own sinful lusts of youth. Throughout their life together, he holds Elizabeth's sin over her, consciously hating her son and unconsciously seeking to destroy him emotionally. Gabriel's feelings, though unspoken, are transmitted to John. The guilt of both parents is also transmitted to John by the extreme emotionalism of their religious fervor and by the strictness of their public views on sex.

9. Richard A. Courage, "James Baldwin's *Go Tell It on the Mountain*: Voices of a People," 410.

They postulate a rigid either/or system in which a misdemeanor is as damning as a felony, demanding physical death and eternal hellfire. John's attitude toward Gabriel is a mixture of love and hate. To him, there are two Gabriels: the ideal Gabriel, whom he wants to love and from whom he wants to win love, and the man Gabriel, whom he hates. He sees Gabriel, the man, as an unworthy rival for the mother's affection, evidenced by the pregnancies that seem to take her further away from him. In John's mind Gabriel is unworthy of such advantage because he mentally and physically abuses Elizabeth.

The adolescent's most immediate and urgent problem, however, is his inability to handle adequately the sex drive that is building within him. After masturbating, on the eve of his fourteenth birthday, he feels dirty and disreputable. His anxiety about sex had started much earlier, when his father, while bathing, asked him to wash his back. As his eyes wandered inquisitively over the father's body, John felt that he was a true son of Ham and was terrified by his boldness.[10]

Complicating both problems is the boy's burning desire for more varied experiences than those provided in the house and church of his parents. He decides early that he will not imitate the life pattern of his parents, that he will raise himself above Gabriel and thereby finally win what he wants most, Gabriel's love. Up to this point, his is a portrait of any adolescent in whom individuality is emerging; but events impel him toward what seems a grotesque solution to his problem, suggesting a retreat from reality and a capitulation to cultural demands that are primarily racial. Not yet a "saint," in the sense of having undergone the highly emotional union with God required by his sect, John is nudged toward some outward manifestation of inner spiritual salvation by a young man named Elisha, three years older than he and already not only a saint but also a preacher in the church. From Elisha and from another saint, the mournful Sister Price, a spinster who is considered specially blessed by the members of the church because she has never engaged in sexual relations,

10. Ham in the Old Testament is said to be the head of a tribe of dark-skinned people who are eternally cursed because Ham viewed his father naked. Black people have been called the children of Ham who are doomed to suffer for their blackness and the low status given them by the dominant society.

John learns to see sublimation of sex in mystical experiences as the immediate solution to his more urgent problem. It is what Baldwin has called "the tyranny of the flesh," and John sees it as a way to win respect from Gabriel. Black religious ritual is permeated with color symbolism: "Wash me . . . And I shall be whiter than snow"; "For black is the color of evil . . . , only the robes of the white are saved"; "He that is filthy let him be filthy still"; "Fine linen, clean and white for the Righteous."[11] When John sweeps the church and his mother's carpet, they never get clean; they continue to be dirty—black. Dirt and grime are motifs that permeate the novel.

His ordeal of spiritual rebirth takes place, but the reader cannot be sure whether or not John believes in what is happening. At one point in the prolonged spiritual outburst, his rational mind urges him to stop writhing on the filthy floor, to get out of that place at once if he is not to be trapped in a life similar to that of "the other niggers." Turning to Gabriel, John smiles but receives no smile in return and knows that he has not won Gabriel's love. When John hears his mother calling to him he answers, "I'm on my way."[12] But which way he is going is the question the reader is left to ponder. This is also where the novel ends. This ending follows the tradition of a novel of development in that the protagonist begins his second quest.

James Baldwin does not deny that he was writing about his own experience in *Mountain*. During the summer of his fourteenth year, Baldwin fell to the spiritual seduction of a woman evangelist and found himself lying on a floor. The facts of this experience parallel his victimization by the White power structure. The world beyond the ghetto was remote and could scarcely be linked to his childhood experience. He felt a vague terror of what that world was all about, and its power was transmitted through his parents. But damnation was a clear and present danger to a young boy. Evidence of the "wages of sin" was everywhere—hallways, ambulance bells, scars on the faces of pimps and whores, knife and pistol fights.

11. Whiteness and blackness appear with frequency in spirituals, prayers, and folk sermons.
12. *Go Tell It on the Mountain,* 221. Further references to this work will be made parenthetically in the text.

Like Ishmael, son of the bond woman, John is the illegitimate and outcast son. The relationship between Gabriel and John is compared to that of Abraham and Ishmael, and the tableaux of guilty father and rejected son serve Baldwin as an emblem of race relations in America. He sees the Black man as the bastard child of American civilization. In John we have an archetypal image of the Black child, and using this extended metaphor, Baldwin approaches the meaning of the universality of the Black experience. Its essence is rejection, and its most destructive consequence is shame.

John's relationship with his mother, Elizabeth, is much better and clearer than one initially thinks, but it is subdued because of Gabriel's slavelike rule of the Grimes household. John sees his mother as a suffering person who needs help with the chores, so on his birthday he cleans house for his mother, even though there are girls in the family. His birthday appears to have no special meaning and is just another day. The other woman in his life is his Aunt Florence, a strong antagonist who helps to expose Gabriel's evil world. The balance in John's life comes from these two women. It is from them that he experiences goodness, honesty, humanity, and love similar to that Sandy experiences in Hughes's novel. John is the "man" to his mother that his stepfather cannot be, and Elizabeth is the "father" John could never have. Their bonding, though not verbally articulated, is felt strongly by both. As seen in the West Indian novels, "the absence of the father . . . and ever-present proximity of the mother [causes] a binding relationship between mother and son . . . [so] the child is always aware of the mother's changing moods and emotions."[13]

The Black child, rejected by Whites for reasons he cannot understand, is afflicted with shame; he thinks, therefore, that something must be wrong with him for him to be so cruelly ostracized. In time these feelings are associated with color—the basis for rejection. He feels dirty, unclean; life seems an unending struggle with the blackness symbolized by the family name, *Grimes*. Gabriel's sermons also begin with his obsession with original sin.

Class, sexual awakening, and what it means to be a Black boy growing up in America are the major themes of *Go Tell It on the Mountain*. As the twin pressures of sex and race mount in John, he

13. Lawrence, "Mother-Child Relationships," 11.

strikes a desperate bargain with God. In exchange for sanctuary as a member of the church, he surrenders his sexuality and abandons any aspirations that will bring him into conflict with White society. It is through the adults that we perceive the boy's conversion. This is his initiation into conscious reality of the choices made. But as John Grimes moves out of the "Temple of the Fire Baptized" into the New York morning, there is no doubt that he is on his way into manhood, and a world much more debilitating than that of the Grimes household.

In a brief early scene in *Go Tell It on the Mountain*, John takes a headlong run down a hill of melting snow and ends by extending the distance he is beginning to recognize between the White and Black worlds.

> At the bottom of the hill, where the ground abruptly leveled off onto a gravel path, he nearly knocked down an old man with a white beard, who was walking very slowly and leaning on his cane. They both stopped astonished, and looked at one another. John struggled to catch his breath and apologize, but the old man smiled. John smiled back. It was as though he and the old man had between them a great secret. (34–35)

We can speculate that part of their secret is that even though they both live in the same country, they had never been in such close contact before. Or it could be that both reactions were spontaneous. The passage also suggests a simplistic answer to race relations— deny invisibility and acknowledge a shared history and destiny— while illustrating that despite their shared smile and secret, the Black boy and the White man do not speak or meet again. It is a ritual that is repeated in America daily. It also establishes early for John that a meeting with the White world could be pleasurable, but he later learns that a friendly coexistence is impossible no matter what one's age.

The novel seems at times to be more Gabriel's story than John's and, if examined from that perspective, has elements in common with *Invisible Man*. There are many scenes in Black American novels where a child is going along happily until someone (often at school) points out the "difference" in his life, which is also the difference in his future. At that revelation the child flees in panic to a mirror in order to stare at himself, to see himself for the first time as the White world sees him, as something "other." From that point on, life becomes a series of oppositions.

Baldwin has consciously used a number of narrative voices to tell John's story. At times there are flashbacks and ambiguity in the shifting viewpoints. We can visualize the narrator moving through the story with numerous masks: a young John, an implicitly older John whose persona appears suspiciously like that of the author, a young and wild Gabriel, an old and bitter Gabriel, and so on. The voices also embrace male and female, rough and refined, secular and religious, but find a common matrix in the Black experience. The novel's shifting viewpoint creates a composite picture of a Black family whose experience over generations comes to represent the experience of all Black people, "a racial, cultural bond forged in slavery and tempered by continued racial oppression."[14]

Baldwin's bildungsroman is fascinating, sad, and glorious at the same time. It instructs us about what it means to be a kid trapped in the ghetto; the son of a man who believed he was a "nigger," yet was self-righteous and cruel; a child born out of wedlock on Park Avenue in uptown Harlem; a boy told he is a worthless human being; a part of a church that used itself to get back at the White man; the ugliest child anyone had ever seen; a person abhorred by the White world; one who cannot live in the White world or Harlem; the son of a woman who suffered emotionally and physically because of her gender, color, class, and history. How could a boy from these circumstances survive to dream the American dream of becoming what he wishes—a writer?

At age fourteen, Baldwin discovered, like John, three important things: that books are connections to the world, that nobody actually cares what a writer looks like, and that writing is an act of love and the greatest consolation anyone could have. This novel, like Black gospel music and the blues, is what Robert Bone calls "a poetry of suffering . . . a ritual enactment of daily pain." Baldwin also states in *The Fire Next Time,* "I became during my 14th year, for the first time afraid of the evil within me and afraid of the evil without."[15]

14. Courage, "Baldwin's *Mountain,*" 425.
15. Bone, *Negro Novel,* 224.

Yet we must be careful in thinking of *Go Tell It on the Mountain* as autobiographical, because the autofictive voice of the narrator incorporates the use of imagination and creation. If we consider Dickens's David Copperfield or Richard Wright's Richard in the context of authors who also wrote of their own painful initiations and journeys, then Baldwin's voice is certainly unique and extends the body of the "male" bildungsroman. Just as girls have wretched and tense relationships with their mothers, so do boys with their fathers. The body of Baldwin's work illustrates the repetition of poor father–son relationships and the continued search for answers from "the father"—answers that he also sought from America so as not to give that world power over him.

■   ■

Whereas *Invisible Man* and *Not Without Laughter* are read as works of fiction, Richard Wright's *Black Boy,* like Baldwin's *Go Tell It on the Mountain,* is often studied as a childhood autobiography. In the case of Baldwin, his title essay in *Notes of a Native Son* and the long autobiographical essay in *The Fire Next Time* are usually read as companion pieces or at least referred to when discussing *Go Tell It on the Mountain.* Many scholars of autobiography find the comparisons helpful to justify their arguments about the purpose and function of a text. *Black Boy* has been acknowledged to be the original suggested title for the autobiographical *American Hunger,* but for Wright it ended up as "not only a title but also a kind of heading to the whole general theme."[16]

Michel Fabre in his book *The Unfinished Quest of Richard Wright* treats all of the biographical components of Wright's life and discusses their inclusion and exclusion in *Black Boy,* especially the omission or creation of specific personages.[17] A reader of both pieces, *Black Boy* and *American Hunger,* is prepared to say to a reader of *Black Boy,* "The function, the psychology, of artistic selectivity is to eliminate from all those elements of experience which contain no compelling significance. Life is as the sea, art a ship in which

16. Michael Fabre, "Afterword" to *American Hunger,* 144.
17. *The Unfinished Quest of Richard Wright,* 533.

man conquers life's crushing formlessness."[18] The devices used to construct such pieces will of course be those of fiction as the work enters the level of art. Charles T. Davis in his provocative essay "From Experience to Eloquence: Richard Wright's *Black Boy* as Art" argues for *Black Boy* as an autobiography in the strictest sense:

> Some critics, carried off by the impact of *Black Boy,* tend to treat *the autobiography* as if it were fiction. They are influenced by the fact that much great fiction, Joyce's *Portrait of the Artist as a Young Man,* for example, is very close to life. Another tendency here is reinforced by the fact that the author himself, Wright, is a creator of fictions. Yielding so is a mistake because many of the incidents in *Black Boy* retain the sharp angularity of life, rather than fitting into the dramatic or symbolic patterns of fiction.

Davis continues his argument for autobiography by pointing to descriptive details as only a way for the author to highlight the themes of "mundane tedium," "profound distress," and the "confusion" of a small Black boy in the South. He continues that *Black Boy* "does not display the perfect design of serious fiction."[19]

Stephen Hero, Joyce's autobiographical piece, preceded *Portrait of the Artist as a Young Man,* and *Portrait* is read almost exclusively as fiction. The question should be asked as to how much should be left in or out of these autobiographical works to make them qualify as novels. Gwendolyn Brooks's *Maud Martha,* "partially based on Brooks's own experience as a young black girl growing up in Chicago in the 1930s and 1940s[,] contributes to the authenticity one feels while reading this work . . . [and] distinguishes a memoir from an autobiographical novel by calling the former 'a factual account' while the latter is nuanceful, allowing."[20] I imagine that similar comments could be made about Maya Angelou's *I Know Why the Caged Bird Sings* and Lamming's *In the Castle of My Skin,* both based on their authors' lives and experiences.

18. Charles T. Davis, "From Experience to Eloquence: Richard Wright's *Black Boy* as Art."
19. Ibid., 141.
20. Barbara Christian, *Black Feminist Criticism: Perspectives on Black Women Writers,* 13.

It also seems obvious that these works fall into a gray area between fiction and autobiography and pose problems for objective
discussions. It is possible to look at Wright's *Black Boy* as a modern
bildungsroman, because it has enough of the criteria noted in this
study to be one, and at the same time to see it as an initiation story,
that is, as leading the main character toward the adult world. If only
in its style of presentation, descriptive language, colorful details,
imagination, nuances, and the poetic qualities of Wright's prose,
Black Boy is more novelistic in form and content than the standard
autobiography. The use of the Black sermon tradition of the anaphora
in various passages, for example, demonstrates a conscious use of art.

The protagonist of this novel, then, experiences the many cruel
circumstances of a Black boy growing up in the American South.
Richard's household, like Baldwin's, is chaotic and restrictive to his
imagination, so he sets the fluffy curtains on fire "to see how [they]
would look when they burned."[21] Richard's father, who reigns over
the household, is described as antagonistic to him, a poor provider,
a "fat," "alien," and "remote stranger," indicating the noneffectual
presence he will have in Richard's life. This is borne out as the story
develops. Only short remembrances and glimpses are given of the
father. When Richard meets him again, twenty-five years later, he
is still "a strange Black sharecropper in ragged overalls holding a
muddy hoe."[22]

Richard's mother, like all the mothers in these novels, is not a
"strong" woman in the sense of the ironlike Black matriarchal figures, but her presence and closeness to him are expressed throughout
his life. There are two reasons for this. One is that in the household
there is another matriarchal figure—the grandmother, who looks
almost White, "as nearly white as a Negro can get without being
white" (48). It is she who keeps everyone in check including his
mother, grandfather, and brother. Second, his mother becomes chron-
ically ill early in his life, so there is always this "helpless" dependent
woman who recoils under pressure as well as from the grandmother's
commands and demands. It is a household of displaced persons,

---

21. *Black Boy*, 11. Further references to this work will be made parenthetically
in the text.
22. Davis, "From Experience to Eloquence," 143.

and the fact that they move from Arkansas to Mississippi and back to Memphis, Tennessee, drives home the theme of the despair and hunger that the Depression years created. Those years were hard on everyone, but seemingly more so on the poor, Black American. Richard's placement in an orphanage early in his life validates the desperation of this family.

As in other novels, especially *Native Son,* Wright establishes the themes and messages to be explored, via the narrative voice, quite early. For example, the grandmother's whiteness makes implicit the slave experience of Black women being raped by White masters. The dilemmas of what it means to be a Black man in America are symbolized by Richard's father, who "from the white landowners above him had not been handed a chance to learn the meaning of loyalty . . . sentiment . . . or tradition. . . . A creature of the earth with no regrets and no hope" (43). Richard also talks about the ongoing abuse of Black bodies from slavery to the present, where Blacks do not get "whipped" but are "beaten," and about the senseless murder of Uncle Hoskins, his Aunt Maggie's husband, because he dared to want to be more than a boy all his life. Uncle Hoskins's thriving liquor store business, it seems, was the envy of Whites. Richard then goes on to say, "A dread of white people now came to live permanently in my feelings and imagination. . . . I had already grown to feel that there existed men against whom I was powerless, men who could violate my life at will" (83). Other themes such as violence (killing the cat), rebelliousness (drinking and cursing), hunger, and the Black woman as domestic (his mother) are also inherent in this work.

Having laid out these protest-like themes so common to African American novels of development, Wright then begins the initiatory journey of the protagonist, the first step of which is his "leaving home" to enter the larger metropolis. In Richard's case the larger world is school. There a new language is learned—the language of beginning adolescence. The word *nigger,* for example, is used freely among his peers. They "play the dozens," "signify," and use sexually suggestive language; "we spoke boastfully in bass voices; we used the word nigger to prove the tough fiber of our feelings; we spouted excessive profanity as a sign of our coming manhood" (88). Richard's yearnings, ambition, and imagination are displayed when he begins to write.

When this is discovered by his peers, it makes him a kind of oddity; whoever heard of a Black boy writing? When he declares "I want to be a writer" (162) to a White teacher, she says, "Who on earth put such ideas in your nigger head?" (162). Earlier in the text, Richard tells us he got a similar reaction from a girl to whom he had read his story about an Indian maiden: "I never forgot the look of astonishment and bewilderment on the young woman's face. . . . Her inability to grasp what I had done or was trying to do somehow gratified me" (134). Davis in his essay says that Wright omits a lot of information about his schooling both for thematic purposes and to make his work effective for intelligent readers of the protest tradition. There were, Davis says, sympathetic teachers at the Jim Hill school in Jackson who recognized and nurtured Richard's ambition.[23]

Once the hero of the bildungsroman has made certain commitments to his future, a number of setbacks always follow, and the overruling context of Richard's life is the poverty and hunger that permeate the novel. Only in Austin Clarke's *Amongst Thistles and Thorns* has it been so vividly portrayed—to the extent of provoking distress, shock, and disbelief—that one could be so outside a system that mouths equality, under the law, and be so poorly treated by it.

The circumstances under which he suffers, however, make Richard seek outside work to help the family. Interestingly, it is through his selling of a Chicago newspaper with a friend that he learns more about prejudice, racism, and the Ku Klux Klan. His other jobs as a "handyboy" for a White woman and an errand boy in a store pale by comparison to one of his most wretched experiences, that of working in a lens factory but not being allowed to learn the trade for fear he would "move up." These racist situations placed before the reader by Wright are timeless and recognizable.

Learning about life in all its forms takes Richard from the "old world" and places him in a new one and into a new role, even though he will also have to continue struggling with the old world because it is still a reality. His confrontation with Uncle Tom, one of a series of uncles who come and go in his life, is a reminder of the old ways and synonymous with the process of breaking in a mule or breaking in a slave. Tom wants to beat him for not complying and for showing

23. Ibid.

arrogance; in Tom's eyes he is being disrespectful. Although Richard realizes that Tom is a broken man, having lost his job and status as a teacher, he does not bow to this forgotten figure of authority. The confrontation was precipitated by Richard's refusal to read the valedictory speech written for him by the Black principal of his high school and by various other incidents. At this point in the novel, the reader knows that the protagonist is "poised for flight." Besides, he tells us, "in me was shaping a yearning for a kind of consciousness, a mode of being that the way of life about me had said could not be, must not be" (187). Wright takes the time to give us a historical marker for the first time; it is 1925. What relevance this has for the novel is unclear, although it does posit the idea of an autobiography. The reader already knows that Richard Wright was born in 1908 and now at the age of seventeen was finishing high school.

In the larger metropolitan setting, Richard notices how Blacks follow the roles of expected behavior put down by White men, leading the "Jim Crow life," being street smart and cheating the system, trafficking in sex, drinking, and prostituting themselves for easy money. Despite his shock at seeing these things, it is certain that he knows that this education is important if not critical for his survival. At lunch, he and his Black coworkers discuss "the way of white folks towards negroes. . . . Each of us hated and feared whites, yet had a white man put in a sudden appearance, we would have assumed silent, obedient smiles" (251). These scenes are complements to earlier ones showing Richard's school friends speaking in bragging tones about Whites. They have become, in their mature years, those men who still can only act out their hostilities against the White world in private. Also, in a scene reminiscent of the opening of Ellison's *Invisible Man,* the custom of pitting Blacks against Blacks is played out again with the planned boxing match between Richard and Harrison. All of this is done for the White man's enjoyment, providing the two young Black men only five dollars for food.

Richard's other journey is that which takes him to the world of books and authorship; his sponsor is a sort of "everyman" one meets in most Black novels in this genre. This is the good White person, a "patron" of sorts who gives him a "forged" note to the public library. This entrée into the White world allows him to get books by H. L.

Mencken, Sinclair Lewis, Conrad, Poe, Twain, and others. None were Blacks or African American. He says, "I knew of no Negroes who read the books I liked, and I wondered if any Negroes ever thought of them" (275).

He does know, though, that an intellectual Black educated elite exists—the Harlem Renaissance writers, his contemporaries—although he has never "seen" one, so of course he ponders his differentness. Two educated figures in the book, the schoolteacher Uncle Tom and his high school principal, had both sold out and cowered under a White power structure. Another, Ella, a schoolteacher/boarder, would not have been considered a role model because she was female, Black, and, even then, working in an unappreciated profession.

The end of *Go Tell It on the Mountain* finds a younger John Grimes groping his way into the sunlight, and we think of another journey, another chance to prove himself worthy of recognition as a young man saved from destruction by the forces of evil. Ellison's narrator is also moving into a new awareness as he surfaces from his "underground" into the light and says: "No indeed, the world is just as concrete, ornery, vile, and sublimely wonderful as before, only now I better understand my relation to it and it to me. I've come a long way from those days when, full of illusion, I lived a public life and attempted to function under the assumption that the world was solid and all the relationships therein" (*Invisible Man,* 563). In the conclusion of *Not Without Laughter,* in keeping with Hughes's folk wisdom, it is not Sandy who speaks of the direction his life will take, it is his elders. Sandy is the most innocent of the four young men discussed here, and it is his mother who states, "that boy's gotta get ahead—all us niggers are too far back in this white man's country to let any brains go to waste. . . . Hagar want him to be able to help the black race, . . . You hear me? Help the whole race!" (*Laughter,* 303).

Unlike the other three novels, however, *Black Boy* ends by forecasting the things that Richard Wright would be most concerned about later, "the southern swamp of despair," "fear," "hate," "cowardice," a "heritage of guilt and blood," "burden," "anxiety," and "compulsive cruelty" (284–85). The South had become for him a metaphor for evil, a world that seemed to have no relationship to anyone or anything except itself. That Wright left it and wrote books like *Native Son* and short stories like "Almos' a Man" using the metaphors of anger—guns, blood, fright, all modern versions of slavery—is not surprising. The wonderful and yet controversial thing about a bildungsroman like *Black Boy* is that we know the ending before we pick up the book. We know what Richard will become. This is precisely what happens when art, imagination, and autobiography meet. Black forms of the bildungsroman reconstruct the race's history, culture, place, and dilemmas through personal narratives to present old information in new ways, to instruct and bring those realities to an understandable level.

All four novels, *Invisible Man, Not Without Laughter, Go Tell It on the Mountain,* and *Black Boy,* though very different in their plots and settings, deal with the common experience of growing up Black and male in America. The variety of the novels' content is evidence of the varied upbringings and initiation experiences of Black children, and the varied circumstances of Black families. All of them touch on the racial issue and the "castaway image" found in other diasporan literatures. None of the boys have close relationships to their birth parents. Evident in all of them are the many themes and customs of Black life—Baldwin's church rituals; Ellison's questing journey, isolation, and suffering; Hughes's use of the folk tradition and the transference of Black oral history; Wright's exploration of Black poverty, racism, and America's unjust institutions. These authors have explored numerous facets of African American life in unique ways to project the Black experience of male initiation; their protagonists all grow from innocence into knowledge and the realities of the American perception of its slave descendants and communities of color.

In these novels, the male protagonists, on reaching adolescence, leave the sanctuary and relative safety of "home" to face a White and hopefully multicultural cosmopolitan world. A Black boy smiles at a White man who smiles back. The moment is construed as accidental. It is not. It is their essential relationship, only made to appear accidental by a cruel history and unnatural fears. The boy who smiles at the man recognizes him, and recognizes the man recognizing the boy. They may choose to treat that act as a mere acknowledgment and a separate-and-equal nod, or to elaborate on it by communicating at a humane level.

These examples of the African American male bildungsroman are therefore basically sociopolitical since, regardless of their plots, the theme is inevitably the confrontation with one's race. Ellison, Baldwin, Hughes, and Wright all suggest that young Black boys must confront Black history painfully and realistically in the early stages of their lives. The African American's increased awareness of self has heightened his perception of indifference and antipathy to his blackness. The Black boy who discovers himself discovers that he is isolated in an alien society, where the journey to manhood is painful and will continue to be so, as long as he resides in a racially charged society.

IV

WOMANISH GIRLS
AFRICAN AMERICAN FEMALE INITIATION

i usta wonder who i'd be
when i was a little girl in indianapolis
sitting on doctors porches with post-dawn pre-debs
(wondering would my aunt drag me to church sunday)
I was meaningless
and i wondered if life
would give me a chance to mean
                    Nikki Giovanni, "Adulthood"

Black woman writers as well as others who exhibit a feminist/
womanist consciousness have had to recast the old European and
male forms of the bildungsroman to accommodate stories of the lives
of women who have been excluded from the normal processes of development for centuries. The early slave narratives and autobiographies
like *Our Nig* and *Incidents in the Life of a Slave Girl* give us one
version of a well-documented history of African American women's
lives, while historical novels like Margaret Walker's *Jubilee* extend
that existence from slavery to beyond Reconstruction. Several others
over the past decades have documented in various genres the Black
woman's multifaceted experience.

Black women writers do not concentrate only on youthful recognition by the dominant society; rather, they collectively depict the Black
woman's internal struggle to unravel the immense complexities of
racial identity, gender definition, and the awakening of their sexual
being. In short, they seek to discover, direct, and re-create the self
in the midst of hostile racial, sexual, and other forms of societal
repression, producing a literature not confined to the "usual" *Bildung* model. Because of Black women's different racial and cultural

history, the Anglo form does not work for them, especially when one looks at the younger ages of the typical protagonist in the White novels of this genre. One example of this is Betty Smith's *A Tree Grows in Brooklyn*. Overall, as Sondra O'Neale has pointed out in her interesting essay on various aspects of the bildungsroman, Black female protagonists tend to be older, such as Janie Starks in Zora Neale Hurston's *Their Eyes Were Watching God*, Maud in Gwendolyn Brooks's *Maud Martha*, Sula Peace in Toni Morrison's *Sula*, Meridian in Alice Walker's *Meridian*, and the three young women Sassafras, Cypress, and Indigo in Ntozake Shange's novel of the same name. Even when they have not passed adolescence, they are still generally older than their White peers.[1]

Many Black female characters share some of the same situations faced by their White sisters and are often seen as victims, sex objects, mother haters, little mammies, and rebellious outsiders. Often they are seeking a new, viable existence distinct from their historically and culturally predetermined roles, and thus seek transformations that are often unachievable or disrupted.

The five bildungsromane to be discussed in this chapter are Gwendolyn Brooks's *Maud Martha*, Paule Marshall's *Brown Girl, Brownstones*, Toni Morrison's *The Bluest Eye*, and Ntozake Shange's *Sassafrass, Cypress, and Indigo* and *Betsey Brown*. Although all show a variety of protagonists and a variety of outcomes, they share the issues of race, color, gender, class, and age as critical elements of their initiations and development.

Gwendolyn Brooks's only novel, *Maud Martha*, has traditionally been given secondary status to other novels of Black female development. It has been described as being not as rich, complex, or well developed as Toni Morrison's works, for example. Barbara Christian says of Brooks's work, "Her understated rendition of a Black American girl's development into womanhood [did not] . . . arouse in the reading public the intense reaction that Baldwin's dramatic portrayal of the black male did." The novel, according to Christian, became the forerunner of Marshall's *Brown Girl* and was also the first African American novel not to deal with the stereotypical portrayals

1. "Race, Sex and Self: Aspects of *Bildung* in Selected Novels by Black American Women Novelists," 25.

of Black women as "mammy, mulatto, wench, or downtrodden heroine." Christian's discussion of *Maud Martha* and its place in the
African American canon explains the many qualities of Gwendolyn
Brooks's novel, most notably its poetic tone, its lack of the heavy-
handed protest mode, and its presentation of a new Black heroine with realistic recognizable traits "like many of us . . . ordinary."[2]
Brooks's work, therefore, represents a new approach, another version
of the Black novel of development. *Maud Martha* deals with the
themes of beauty, love, and what it means to be accepted fully or
initiated properly, as a Black woman, into society as a whole.

Brooks's work has no real plot but consists of a sequence of vi-
gnettes that suggest a chronological progression from childhood to
courtship to marriage, and from marriage to motherhood. The novel
is a thinly disguised autobiographical account that depicts a young
Black woman in a ghetto, similar to the one in which Brooks grew
up. Brooks says of this genre, "An autobiographical novel . . . is a
better testament, a better thermometer, than a memoir can be. Who,
in presenting a 'factual' account, is going to tell the absolute, the
inclusive, the horrifying or exquisite, the incredible truth? . . . An
'autobiographical novel' is nunceful, allowing. There's fact-meat in
the soup, among the chunks of fancy."[3] That Brooks has to give the
audience this explanation seems to anticipate readers' reactions to
her work. It is common with the bildungsroman for content to be
questioned, for parallels with the author's life to be looked for; art,
fact, and form are often at odds with each other. This distrust of
text has authors always defending and clarifying their works. *Maud
Martha*'s poetic qualities, like those in Lamming's *In the Castle of
My Skin,* are one of its major contributions to story and genre. As
Ntozake Shange has said on several occasions, "Can't [we] have an
imagination?"

The novel considers how Maud Martha looks at the world and how
she thinks the world looks at her. Maud has doubts about herself
and where and how she fits into her world. Her concern is not so
much that she is "inferior" but that she is perceived as ugly and
the wrong color. This attention to the importance of physical beauty

2. *Black Feminist Criticism,* 127, 128, 129.
3. Gwendolyn Brooks, *Report from Part One,* 190–91.

will be echoed by Pecola Breedlove in *The Bluest Eye.* Even Maud's husband, who is light skinned, makes her conscious of it.

> But it's my color that makes him mad. . . . What I am inside, what is really me, he likes okay. But he keeps looking at my color, which is like a wall. He has to jump over it in order to meet and touch what I've got for him. He has to jump away up high in order to see it. He gets awful tired of all that jumping.[4]

Sibling rivalry or, more specifically, female rivalry between Maud and her sister is also evident in this novel. Maud's sister, Helen, was still the one they wanted in the wagon, still "the pretty one," "the dainty one," "the lovely one." Whereas, Maud tells us, "My hair is longer and thicker . . . I'm much smarter. I read books and newspapers and old folks like to talk to me" (34–35). The rejection of Maud in favor of Helen by young Emmanuel suggests the advantages enjoyed by the lighter skinned Helen. Maud in turn idolizes the White world, does not like life, and feels isolated. Like Pecola, she believes that if she were attractive, then life would be beautiful and good for those around her. Like Maureen Peal in *The Bluest Eye,* Helen is a representative of the favored, idolized, and blessed female. The very name *Helen* echoes back to Helen of Troy, a symbol of all that's acceptable in White womanhood. Thus, Maud feels that the main reason for her deprived circumstances is her appearance.

Maud is very aware of everything around her. She has an acute sense of male–female relationships and character and feels inadequate because of her early insecurities at home. She refuses, however, to compromise in adjusting herself to jobs, ideas, and functions. When she does have a sexual encounter, it is with a boy from a different background. Maud's favorite flower is the dandelion because of its "everydayness," and in it "she saw a picture of herself, and it was comforting to find that what was common could also be a flower" (2); this image also occurs in *The Bluest Eye.* Maud sees herself as being nothing special, unpretentious and simple. Beauty for her is only in the eye of the beholder. She tries, therefore, to cultivate those traits

4. *Maud Martha,* 229–30. Further references to this work will be made parenthetically in the text.

that are more fundamental to one's basic relationship with others. She goes inside herself in a healthy fashion, and her imaginative spirit suggests that "what she wanted was to donate to the world a good Maud Martha. That was the offering, the bit of art, that could not come from any other" (22).

Her initiation is one of despair because it seems that she will never be those things valued by Black culture, White society, and her family. Brooks depicts a sensitive young woman grappling with the difficult problem of reconciling her human need to be cherished with society's preferences and insensitivity, which exclude her from its ranks.

Brooks's novel represents a major contribution to the Black novel of initiation and education as well as the broader form of the auto-biographical novel. "*Maud Martha* is a fusing of . . . two qualities, the sensitive and the ordinary, not only in its characterization of the protagonist, but also in the moments the writer chooses to include in her compressed rendition of an urban Black woman's life. Yet these moments, as they form a whole, both look back at the novels of the 1940s and toward Black women's novels of the 1960s and 1970s."[5] Its true importance for this study is in its recognition of race, color, gender, and class as barriers to feeling complete in American society. It is a lesson that Maud learns early. If Maud has a negative view of herself because of looks, color, and class, then Pecola Breedlove takes her self-hatred to the extreme of paranoia. We feel that Maud Martha will recover herself and move on, but such an end is not foreshadowed in Morrison's novel of despair, *The Bluest Eye*.

■   ■

Toni Morrison did not publish her first work until eleven years after novelist Paule Marshall published her first novel, *Brown Girl, Brownstones*. The latter was and still is a wonderful work, one of the finest in the Black female tradition. In fact, it launched the Black women's literary renaissance that came to fruition in the 1970s and 1980s. Perhaps because Marshall's work was seen as deceptively "easy" and "different," it did not attract the attention of the major critics, who were still focusing primarily on the male writers' work or

5. Christian, *Black Feminist Criticism*, 132–33.

were ill equipped to discuss or engage Marshall's novel. Another facet of the lack of attention paid this novel might have been that Marshall was writing from several perspectives and platforms: West Indian, American, urban, bicultural, cross-cultural, bilingual (West Indian creole), matrifocal, with androgynous characterizations, negation of stereotypes, protest, and many other elements. That Marshall was a second-generation Barbadian American did not help to place her on the traditional track to American recognition. She has, however, taken a special place in the canon of Black women writers, and *Brown Girl* continues to be one of the most read, discussed, or written-about texts in the body of her work because it can be looked at on so many levels. Like Gwendolyn Brooks, Paule Marshall has decidedly provided a voice, a model, and a form from which her younger literary sisters have benefited.

Because Marshall's parents are Barbadian immigrants, she, like Claude McKay, provides a bridge between the African American and the West Indian literary traditions. Although the West Indies and the United States both claim her as one of their own, she has managed to weave her themes and stories from both perspectives. *Brown Girl* addresses therefore the problem of dual cultures, American and West Indian. Marshall's Selina Boyce has a concern for roots regardless of the fact that she lives in Brooklyn and has never been to her parents' homeland of Barbados. Like Ralph Ellison, Marshall believes that the "Negro American writer is also an heir of the human experience which is literature."[6] From Eliot and Joyce, Marshall learned the value of tradition; but she did not forget the value of Black folk materials. Her succeeding works of fiction—*Soul, Clap Hands and Sing* (1961), *The Chosen Place, the Timeless People* (1969), *Reena and Other Stories, Praisesong for the Widow* (1983), and *Daughters* (1991)—all reveal a distinct balance between content, culture, and art. For this and other reasons her "first novel seemed to bear little relationship to Black literature that preceded or followed it . . . and [pays] close attention to the portrayal of the Black female and male characters within the context of their own culture."[7]

6. Catherine Ward, "Self-Realization in the Fiction of Paule Marshall."
7. Christian, *Black Feminist Criticism,* 104.

Marshall learned the first lessons of the narrative art from listening to her mother and her friends, "the talking women" who,
after their hard day of scrubbing floors, talked out their hurts and
humiliations. They taught her that "in the African tradition, art was
an integral part of life and that form and content were one."[8] She,
too, like other West Indian writers in exile, stresses the need for identity and the understanding of one's past—individual and historical.
Marshall endorses the revival of the African cultural heritage that
gives supremacy to man over "the machine." When Marshall writes
of Blacks, often West Indians, she does so because writers write best
when they make use of what they know best. *Brown Girl* is modeled
from countless émigré experiences, and it raises familiar issues like
those in Maxine Hong Kingston's *The Woman Warrior.* Marshall's
novel is a unique contribution to the bildungsroman because of its
subject, growing up as a first-generation West Indian American girl.

Marshall's fiction presents an invaluable portrait of the psychological struggles of immigrants who came from a colonized people and
who, because of racial prejudice, continue to suffer some of the effects
of colonization despite their new country of residence. Although her
protagonists and locations vary, the body of her work has a central
subject matter and theme: the struggle of West Indians to achieve
wholeness and self-realization. Ultimately, Marshall rejects assimilation into the new culture as desirable or even possible. Instead she
proposes that West Indian Americans live in two worlds and that
their real "home" must not be any one place or one culture but should
rest within themselves—selves that are constantly renewing and
redefining their identities through interaction with their ancestral
heritage as it is redefined in the present.

Brown Girl, according to Barbara Christian, "ushered in a new period of female characters in Afro-American literature . . . and merged
together qualities of earlier Black women's novels . . . like Zora Neale
Hurston's lyrical novel *Their Eyes Were Watching God* . . . and Gwendolyn Brooks exquisite novella *Maud Martha.*"[9] Its place in this
study therefore is critical because its theme transcends class, race,

8. Ward, "Self-Realization," 2.
9. *Black Feminist Criticism,* 103.

gender, and place and forecasts the womanist themes of writers like Walker and Shange in the 1980s and 1990s.

Brown Girl, until the early 1980s, was unusual among West Indian or African American novels of childhood. Part of its fame rests on the fact that it is the story of West Indians struggling not in the colonial homes of the Caribbean, but in the United States, sharing that experience with their Black American brothers and sisters. Marshall's use of a protagonist's dual cultures is not the first in African American literature, but it clearly develops the theme more deeply and in a broader scope than did the works of her predecessors such as Harlem Renaissance writers Rudolph Fisher, Nella Larsen, Claude McKay, and Eric Walrond.

As soon as they arrived in the United States in the early 1920s, new West Indian immigrants encountered racism in various forms, including ostracism by American Blacks who had not long before come from a Southern plantation system. "Monkey chaser" was and still is a derogatory term used for West Indians. For the first time, many West Indians were finding that race and color were more critical to their existence and success than class. These migrants, therefore, clung to each other, not unlike immigrants from other countries who were also coming to America for the same purpose about the same time. Stories from "back home" were told over and over again by women who were mostly mothers and domestics, as well as by men. It was these stories with their solidly Black West Indian base that laid the foundation for the sense of celebration evident in Marshall's stories. Marshall says: "I do not know that their need to establish a sense of themselves each afternoon by recalling their past life nurtured in me a desire to understand that combined heritage which was at once Afro-American, Afro-Caribbean and to a lesser degree American, that was mine."[10] All of her fiction presents an invaluable portrait of the psychological struggles of immigrants who come from a colonized people and who, because of racial prejudice, continue to suffer some of the effects of colonization in their new country.

Brown Girl, set in the 1930s and 1940s, details the growth and reaching out of Selina Boyce amid a community of Barbadian immigrants in New York City, a community powerful in its cohesion and

10. Marshall, "Shaping the World of My Art," 106–11.

demanding in its criteria for acceptance, a community pitted against a world that has prejudiciously shaped its strategy for survival and improvement. This depiction of the Barbadian community, of essential significance in the context of the protagonist's search for self, is symbolically unveiled in Marshall's vivid description of the Brooklyn brownstones where Selina lives. Marshall stresses that, although the buildings were short, "they gave the impression of formidable height," and although they appeared as a unified whole, each of the brownstones was distinct in its complicated design, sharing "the same brown monotony. All seemed doomed by the confusion in their design."[11] Thus, in its solidarity, its sharing of heritage and color, the community exudes wholeness, and in that wholeness, strength. The confusion in design, the double consciousness, the fact that part of their identity is defined by glazed-over White eyes, is that which Marshall refers to as their "doom." Such is the setting for the physical and mental growth of a young girl, American by birth, Barbadian by parentage.

Selina is caught between her divided loyalties to her father and to her mother. Her parents' marriage gradually disintegrates because the father, Deighton, a romantic dreamer, yearns to return to Barbados and build a house on two acres of land he has inherited from a sister. The mother, Silla, who has no romantic illusions about her native island where she had labored as a child in the cane fields for meager wages, will do whatever it takes not simply to survive in America but to insure economic and social success for her two daughters. To achieve her ends, she first scrubs floors, then sells her husband's land behind his back, works in a factory, and finally buys a brownstone where she takes in boarders whom she exploits and tyrannizes.

Marshall introduces Selina by emphasizing her eyes and foreshadowing her ripeness or "womanishness," as well as the complex development Selina is to experience and the fact that Selina's starting point is not that of complete unawareness. She says that Selina's eyes "were not the eyes of a child. Something too old lurked in their centers. They were weighted, it seemed, with scenes of a long life. . . .

11. *Brown Girl, Brownstones,* 3. Further references to this work will be made parenthetically in the text.

She seemed to know the world down there in the dark hall and beyond for what it was" (4). Aware of what waited in the external world, beyond the cozy respite of the familial represented by the brownstones, ten-year-old Selina longs to transcend the security of the familiar for the challenge of the larger outside world. Thus, even at an early age, Selina is conscious of a need for fulfillment and confrontation with a reality that she must use to overstep the threshold of the community.

The first intimation of Selina's perception of her mother is given in reference to the silence of the house, in which Selina rejoices. Marshall states, "Above all, it was a silence which came when the mother was at work" (5). Inferentially then, the presence of the mother incorporates an intrusion on the welcomed silence and has a negative connotation. Of equal significance is Selina's concept of whiteness and the perception of herself in relation to it. Selina, imagining herself the center of attention of the White family who had formerly lived in the house, envisions herself "no longer a dark girl alone and dreaming . . . but one of them, invested with their beauty and gentility" (5).

Selina's feeling of beauty, importance, pride, and elegance in embodying White standards is exemplified as she "threw her head back until it trembled proudly on the stalk of her neck and, holding up her imaginary gown, she swept downstairs to the parlor floor" (5). Thus, the protagonist, at the outset of the novel, judges her physical self through a White lens. Her own blackness is unacceptable to her; it falls short of White people's aesthetic criteria and thus of her own. When Selina catches sight of herself in the mirror, her illusion of White-defined beauty is shattered and she returns to being "only herself." When the reality of her blackness confronts her, she feels estranged—a sad misfit unworthy of the White elegance and refinement of the house. After taking notice of a family photograph in which she is not present, Selina is overcome by a desire to make her presence known and experiences an urge to yell, to break the silence of the house, and to awaken her sister. This spontaneous impulse is a symptom of her awareness of her existence as a unique individual, distinct from the dead baby brother whom she replaced. She is angered when her mother refers to her as if she were the dead brother, shouting, "I keep telling you, I'm not him. I'm me. Selina"

(47). She attempts to affirm her own identity as separately and distinctly hers, not his—with a vehemence that wants to establish the validity of her own existence. She wants to "bring someone running" in order to confirm her "self," and to make her existence known and important to the external world.

The foundations of Selina's oncoming search for self are firmly established in the first few pages of the novel, and Marshall invests Selina with natural qualities for survival. In contrast to the meek, defeatist, complacent, quiescent Ina, Selina, although younger than her sister, takes a passionately active role in her relationship with life, in terms of the intensity of her feelings and desires, her self-assertiveness, her iron will, her defiance, and her pride. Unlike Ina's smooth journey into and through adolescence, for Selina a tumultuous passage lies in store, a passage that will arm her for the harshness of life outside the family. Unlike Ina, she will never be "defenseless . . . as though . . . never really fit for the roughness of life" (7).

However, at this point in her existence, Selina's need for affirmation expresses itself negatively. Characteristic of ten-year-olds, her only strategy for easing the frustration of her inner discord is to lash out blindly at those around her. Aware of her sister's vulnerable nature, she awakens Ina to tell her that she was an ugly baby. But she fails to wreck Ina's emotional composure and, forbidden to strike her sister, feels an impotence symbolic of the broader impotence she feels accruing to her unimportant existence. Furthermore, Selina is physically immature (having a "flat body" and long legs) and ignorant of menstruation, childbirth, and sex (she knows only that Ina is "sick," believes that babies must be cut out of a mother's stomach, and refuses to accept the truth as she hears it from her friend Beryl, because it threatens her own firmly rooted convictions)—all of which compounds her isolation from the familial unit that surrounds her.

Marshall provides a significant intimation of some of the feelings Selina must confront in her developmental passage. Selina's feelings of insecurity and her need to formally establish her existence as an individual stem (at least partly) from the fact that her own birth had barely waited for the last bit of dirt to cover her baby brother's coffin, and that her parents (in their grief) had not taken pictures of her. Her

brother's inability to hold on to life seemed to choke her out of existence in the mind of her mother. Her parents' sadness over the death
of her brother made their acceptance of her—a healthy child—more
difficult. Of equal importance to her later struggle, Selina cannot
conceive of her mother as the young woman with "a shy beauty" and
a smile of "girlish expectancy" who appears in the family photograph.

Pitted against the overwhelming personality of Silla, "the mother"
(she is never addressed or described without the *the,* which emphasizes coldness, formality, and distance), is her husband, Deighton,
an impractical but lovable character who is nostalgically attached to
Barbados and refuses to don the straitjacket of his wife's fierce zeal
for "buying house" in Brooklyn. Silla flays him with her wrathful
tongue, dividing her attack equally between his lack of ambition and
his attachment to his "keepmiss" (mistress).

The seeds of tragedy are sown when a sister of Deighton's dies
in Barbados leaving him two acres of land. Silla sees this as an act
of Providence and urges her husband to sell the land so they can
make a deposit on the Brooklyn house. This he refuses to do, for
his dream is to return home eventually and build on the land. His
intransigence acts as a goad to her house-owning ambitions, and she
contrives to sell the land behind his back. Feigning acquiescence,
he maneuvers her into allowing him to cash the bank draft and, in
a burst of revengeful generosity, at once squanders the entire nine
hundred dollars during a single shopping spree.

At the factory where he works, Deighton is involved in an accident
that disables an arm. He finds God in a peace movement, and his relationship with his family becomes detached and ethereal. He leaves
home to take charge of a Peace Restaurant for "Father."[12] Silla, after
passing through the emotions of anger, frustration, remorse, and self-
righteousness, informs the immigration authorities that Deighton
has entered the country illegally, and he is subsequently deported.
But, before the ship docks in Barbados, he jumps overboard and

12. The "Father" referred to here is probably the popular Father Divine, a
Black minister and religious "guru" who, besides preaching, had a series of homes
where hundreds of "unfortunate" followers, including entire families, lived,
worked, and donated money to his church. His enterprises included restaurants
like the one in which Deighton works.

drowns. Silla, impelled by the memories of her poverty in her native Barbados, is fixed in her resolve to carve a more secure place for herself and for her family in the brave new world to which she has emigrated. It is as a first means to this end that she is determined to acquire on the installment system the old brownstone house, part of which she occupies, then to let it as a roominghouse and move into the more fashionable residential area of Crown Heights. She pursues this objective with an implacable determination that is at times frightening.

In the descriptions of the efforts of Barbadian women to acquire a home of their own, the novel at times takes on the qualities of a saga. One can see beyond Selina and the desperate efforts of her possessed countrywomen the epic struggle of Black America to establish for itself a precarious foothold in an alien world. There is something primeval and overpowering about the intensity with which these women claw a path for themselves and their kin through the jungle that is Brooklyn. For as long as Selina can remember, this intensity has intruded upon her consciousness.

Silla, like most West Indian mothers, goes beyond the traditional role. She is a merging of the traditional male and female. Also, because as I've suggested earlier paternity, by tradition, is often viewed differently by West Indian women than by African Americans, her position in the household is not a subservient one. Selina rebels against the materialistic values of her mother, and the story therefore expresses this antagonistic relationship at critical times in Selina's existence.

Though she begins to understand her, Selina still questions her mother's acquisitive, materialistic nature when she visits the factory where her mother works. Not only is Selina deeply shaken by the massive technological power that the machines personify, but the sight of her mother, who seems perfectly at home there, is frightening. She is almost like one of the machines, coldly functional, impersonal, and powerful.

Her movements were attuned to the mechanical rhythms of the machine-mass. She fitted the lump of metal over the lathe center and, with a deft motion, secured it into the headstock and moved the tailstock into position. The whine of her lathe lifted thinly above the roar as the metal whirled into shape. Then she released the tailstock and held the shell up for a swift scrutinizing glance before placing it with the other finished shells. Quickly she moved into the first phase of the cycle again. (99–100)

The repugnance Selina feels for all this eventually causes her to break with her mother, and she leaves home determined to order her life in a way that will permit her to love and feel. Silla, despite her Barbadian accent and West Indian loyalties, has seemingly taken on Americanness for survival purposes.

Selina's attempt to become an initiate into the Barbadian Association does not work. She attends a meeting to discover what her parents' heritage is about. There she feels the clash of cultures despite the motto on the banner, "IT IS NOT THE DEPTHS FROM WHICH WE COME BUT THE HEIGHTS TO WHICH WE ASCEND" (220). As the speaker proposes that West Indians and Americans unite under the word *Negro,* the audience shouts "Hear, Hear," a common Briticism. But another voice says, "Look how that man want us to let in the Sammy-cow and Duppy for them to take over" (223). In summarizing her sentiments about the association for her boyfriend, Clive, she says: "I think it stinks. . . . It's a band of small frightened people. Clannish. Narrow-minded. Selfish. . . . Prejudiced. Pitiful. . . . That's your Association" (227). Her attempted initiation into the larger community of West Indians fails.

Through Clive, Selina maintains an unconscious tie to her father. Clive is a dreamer, an artist, and is not involved in the Barbadian Association. Like Deighton, he seems to lack ambition or motivation and simply lies on the sofa reading. Selina can gain true initiation into the culture and regain her lost identity only by joining her father in attempting to return to the island of his origin. She will do what her father wouldn't or couldn't—go back to the Caribbean roots, seeking the truth and answers to life.

As a girl, Selina's natural sympathies are with her father, whose charm and gaiety appeal to her independent, willful spirit. She withdraws from her "watchful," "wrathful" mother, whose tongue lashes "the world in unrelenting disgust" (11). Selina thinks her mother carries "a theme of winter" (16), while the father is a creature of sunlight. Yet Selina is ambivalent; part of her "always wanted the mother to win" (133). Although Selina gradually grows to admire her mother and eventually to understand her, her father is the pillar of reality and stability in her early life. He is the source of comfort, understanding, and reassurance. He affirms her existence by sharing an intimate, confidential relationship with her and by nurturing her individuality. This is evident as an anxious Selina runs upstairs to the sun parlor to bond with her father in "their circle" (9). The sun having penetrated her closed lids, Selina opens her eyes to see a luminous halo about Deighton's head, symbolic of her idolatry of him. This extreme closeness to and blind infatuation with her father impedes Selina from communion with her mother and from the realization and acceptance of the positive significance of their ties to her, a view expressed through Sondra O'Neale's conviction that in Black women writers' bildungsromane, "Where fathers are present, strained relationships with mothers exist."[13] Selina scorns her mother as the embodiment of a negative womanhood exemplified in "those watchful, wrathful women whose eyes seared and searched and laid bare, whose tongues lashed the world in unremitting distrust" (10–11). *Brown Girl* is also important as the first work of literature to show a close warm relationship between a Black father and daughter.

Unlike Deighton, Silla sees where the power is and sullies herself to grab some of that power. Later, at a Barbadian wedding, Selina imagines her mother as she had been as a girl, young and passionately in love with Deighton. At other times Selina abhors her mother's values and actions. When Silla reports her husband to immigration authorities as an illegal alien and causes him to be deported, Selina hates her mother and screams that she is a "Hitler." Yet afterward, Selina spends the night cradled in her mother's arms. She is "Deighton's Selina" as well as Silla's Selina, although she seems to totally reject her mother's values after she attends a meeting of the Barbadian Homeowners' and Businessmen's Association with her mother. There Silla spells out her credo and argues against a proposal to allow American Blacks into the association, saying, "power is a thing that don really have nothing to do with color. . . . [It] don make you nice. . . . People got a right to claw their way to the

13. "Race, Sex and Self," 27.

top and those on the top got a right to scuffle to stay there" (224–25). This statement shows Silla's ambivalence about acculturation and the American Dream as she has come to understand it.

Throughout most of the novel Selina is lost. She cannot identify with either parent. She is repulsed by her mother's rash pursuit of power and "abandoned" by her father. Neither can Selina find anything in the Barbadian community to admire. Her girlfriends, even Ina, seem lost in their pursuit of crass materialism and have been coerced into accepting roles of submissive domesticity.

When the novel opens, the ten-year-old Selina is repulsed by her cultural identity. She daydreams about the house's former occupants and yearns to be one of them, "invested with their beauty and gentility" (5). She feels "vulgar in a holy place" (6). But neither can Selina identify with other Barbadian girls, who seem to her "prim, pious, and pretentious" (226). Later, in order to get enough money to escape from her people, Selina lies and schemes, just as her mother had done when she sold Deighton's land. Selina pretends to be a dedicated member of the Barbadian Association in order to win a scholarship the group is sponsoring. She actually intends to take the money and run away with her young lover to a place where she can be free to be herself, unencumbered by her cultural heritage. However, by the time she wins the scholarship, she has been forced to realize that Whites will always consider her culturally inferior.

The moment of realization comes when Selina is celebrating her brilliant solo performance as part of an otherwise all-White dance troupe. At a party after the dance recital, the mother of one of the other dancers puts Selina in her place by reminding her that she is still Black and inferior, like one of the family's ex-servants. For the first time Selina learns "the full meaning of her black skin" (289) and realizes that she has almost "robbed" herself of her identity by her longtime hatred of "her blackness." Selina sees that to the White community she is both feared and hated because she embodies "all their own dark instincts" (290). For the first time Selina sees her own capacity for evil as she reflects on her planned duplicity of the scholarship committee. In the end she rejects the White idea of the potential evil in blackness and embraces her racial identity. Then as a young Black woman of Barbadian extraction she accepts her basic humanity and aligns herself with all the good she has observed in the people of all races and cultures. She now admires her mother, whom she had always referred to in a generic, impersonal fashion as "the mother." Yet Selina is not ready to follow totally in her mother's footsteps. After winning the scholarship, she confesses her scheme to the Barbadian Association and rejects the money. She then decides to get a job on a cruise ship to pay her fare to return to Barbados. She does not intend to remain on the island but instead hopes to discover there the culture that she and her fellow Barbadians have lost. Once enriched by her true cultural heritage, Selina plans to return to America and work out an assimilation of the best in the two cultures.

A further characteristic of Selina's preenlightened state is her lack of recognition of racism. Unlike the traditional adolescent recognitions within the Western tradition of the bildungsroman, works by African American women do not concentrate on youthful perceptions of racial rejection.[14] Thus, Selina is unconscious of the racist implications when she learns of how her father, as a boy, dove for coins thrown into the water by White American tourists. Rather than questioning this exploitation, Selina "closed her eyes again and in the orange void tried to see him diving after the coins" (100).

At one level, *Brown Girl* is the story of Selina's growing up, but on another level, it is the story of "any people undergoing fundamental change and disruption, . . . it was a story of two opposing forces in life: the poetic as suggested by the father in the story and the practical and materialistic as symbolized by the mother and the necessity to reconcile, to balance these two forces is pointed up in the character of the daughter."[15] Marshall forecasts the coming of a more experienced Selina whose journey does show her tired maturity.

In the initial process of her physical and mental development, Selina rejects the traditional Black Barbadian womanhood and all that it signifies. Her emerging womanhood threatens to tie her to the qualities, in her mother and her mother's friends, that she finds repugnant. Thus, when Florrie Trotman casually and benignly brushes Selina's small breasts, she cries in outrage and reacts violently to the

14. Ibid., 25.
15. Marshall, "Shaping the World of My Art," 108.

"rite which made her one with Florrie's weighty bosom and Virgie Farnum's perennially burgeoning stomach" (78).

In contrast to John S. Mbiti's findings that "in the African psyche, there are not mentors, sympathetic or polemic, ready to aid in the passage ritual," Marshall gives Selina two mentors and surrogates through the characters of Suggie and Miss Thompson.[16] Suggie introduces Selina to the concept of sex as pleasurable, desirable, and fulfilling and offers a model in herself of an unconventional alternative to Barbadian mores of marriage, motherhood, and monogamy. In contrast, premarital sex is depicted by Silla as evil and unacceptable, as grounds for being labeled a whore. Furthermore, Suggie teaches Selina to embrace life rather than dwell self-destructively on death. She persuades her finally to replace her black mourning attire with more colorful clothes, symbolic of life, after the death of Selina's father. Miss Thompson teaches Selina that she must first acquire an understanding of her people and their political objectives before she can self-righteously reject them and persuades Selina to attend the meeting of the Barbadian Association at which Selina's inner conflicts are emphasized.

Selina's own convictions concerning the possibility of a different world devoid of classist, materialist aspirations toward mobility are threatened by the purposefulness of the Barbadian community's struggle toward economic betterment through imitating the strategy of the oppressors. "Selina again felt that certainty within her threaten to topple and break on the floor of her mind. It was her own small truth that dimly envisioned a different world and a different way" (225). Although Selina was envious of the purposefulness of the association's members, she felt alienated from their convictions. But Selina's entrée into womanhood is carefully advancing. Miss Thompson gives her her first set of curls and recognizes Selina's imperative need and determination to confront her mother at work in order to tell her not to sell Deighton's land. Selina's first awareness of the meaning of racism is stimulated by Miss Thompson when she describes for Selina how her foot had been gouged out by a White southern racist's rusty shovel. In her realization that the ulcerous sore that resulted is what has given Miss Thompson a tragic look,

16. O'Neale, "Race, Sex and Self," 27.

Selina "ached for violence. . . . It came to her like a thirst. In a wild pulse beating at the pit of her body . . . to grab the cane and rush into some store on Fulton Street and avenge that wrong by bringing it smashing across the white face behind the counter" (216). Thus, Selina gains an adult understanding of what the sore signifies, and her urge to avenge a brutal racist act is an adult response.

Selina's growing sexual awareness is evident in her envy of the sexual awakening experienced by her schoolmate. She sees this awakening as a freedom—the same type of freedom that the lovers in Prospect Park had—and as a type of transcendence into a higher realm apart from and beyond the turmoil she feels. She also admires it as a bold act that rebels against family and society. That day, for the first time in her life, she wishes for a boy. Selina's sexual awakening culminates in her relationship with Clive, through which she expresses her sexuality and feels the strength of her womanhood. She senses that she is stronger than Clive and "possess[es] a hard center that he would never have" (246).

More subtle changes attest to Selina's progressing maturity. For example, she no longer wants to hurt Ina's feelings. In contrast to her former behavior, Selina apologizes to her sister after yelling at her and "wish[es] that she could summon more eloquent words to ask forgiveness for all her abuse" (252). Selina comes to the realization at the wedding that she must understand her mother in order to understand herself, whereas previously she simply resented Silla and had no desire to understand her. Furthermore, at her friend Beryl's party, Selina seems to have transcended the mentality of those her age; she has been pushed ahead and out of their circle by the long year of grief that has weighed her down like winter. Thus, Selina, at a young age, confronts death and a reality that her friends have not experienced, as is evidenced by their awkwardness upon her arrival at the party. While these new, important qualities develop, other qualities eminent in Selina at the outset are retained: her determination, her pride, and her defiance of tradition are positive and represent her individuality. For instance, at the wedding, Selina, unconcerned with public opinion, insists on dancing with Beryl, even though a male-female couple is the acceptable American norm. Since dancing with another girl in the West Indian culture is normal and acceptable,

Selina's act of dancing with Beryl demonstrates the transformation and cultural merging taking place within her.

In her relationship with Clive, her pursuit of academic education, and her joining of the dance club, Selina's life becomes very full and fulfilling. "She was happy that for the first time she was living at a pitch and for a purpose. . . . She visualized her mind as a faceted crystal. . . . Each facet was a simple aspect of herself, each one suited to a different role" (30). Through dancing, Selina finds a satisfying outlet for her creativity and a means for self-expression. At the recital, she performs the dance motions of the life cycle, symbolic of her own passage into adolescence and maturity.

One of the most important awakenings Selina experiences is her harsh, forced confrontation with White racism. Having been fairly sheltered from racist attitudes, she recognizes herself in humanistic terms and believes in an untested truth that makes her struggle for recognition and fulfillment no different from or more difficult than that of anyone else. Margaret's mother's racist insinuations and inquiries force Selina to realize that regardless of her personal accomplishments and individuality, White eyes will always define her solely as Black, and stereotypically so, as if the color of her skin in itself speaks for her complete identity. At this point, she understands that part of her has hated her blackness and has evaded her racial identity. Selina is "seeing, clearly for the first time, the image which the woman—and the ones like the woman—saw when they looked at her. . . . Her dark face must be confused in their minds with what they feared most: with the night . . . which seethed with sin and harbored violence. . . . Like the night, she was to be feared, spurned, purified—and always reminded of her darkness" (291).

When Selina sees the full racist meaning of her Black skin reflected in the woman's eyes, she realizes in horror and outrage that in addition to her own struggles she must also battle racism—the White illusion of her blackness, which she must prevent from "destroying her inside" while finding "a way for her real face to emerge" (291). Selina has been jolted into consciousness of the shared bond between herself and her people, necessitated by the imperative of conquering racism in order to enable full development of human potential. In this sense, Selina begins to comprehend what lies behind her mother's harsh outbursts and actions and her people's need for coalition.

Selina also realizes, when Clive deserts her for his mother, that she must face her problems alone, relying on the inner resilience and formidable strength that she has inherited from her mother and that make her her mother's child, and on the "mysterious endurance" of her people, for whom she now feels admiration and love. "They no longer puzzled or offended her. Instead their purposefulness—charging the air like a strong current—suddenly charged her strength . . . and her heart calmed" (303). In her speech to the association, Selina explains her deception, that her perceptions had been based on simple, unrealistic extremes of good and evil. She rejects the scholarship money because it signifies a norm she does not desire. O'Neale affirms that while Black heroines "are not at odds with any 'collective ethos' in the Black community, they certainly do insist upon separate collective feminine strategies within that ethos." Consistent with O'Neale's assertion that the protagonists of Black women writers' bildungsromane "discover, direct, and recreate the self in the midst of hostile racial, sexual and other societal repression, Marshall's protagonist discovers and confronts truth and directs herself toward rectifying her past mistakes, determining her own future and reconstructing her conceptions and values in light of her newfound consciousness amidst the racial illusions of whites and false aspirations of her own people."[17] Thus, Selina no longer embraces White standards of beauty and is able to value the Barbadian community and herself. Eugenia Collier's important assessment is that "for Selina . . . to dream of being white is essentially to reject the community of the oppressed and to long—futilely—to be part of the oppressor . . . this dynamic . . . has been a vital factor in the perpetuation of oppression."[18] Selina, rather than internalize the ideology of the oppressor, actively refutes it through knowledge of her identity, through her rejection of White acceptance, and by coming to terms with her mother and her people, both of whom are incorporated in herself. She decides to continue her quest for answers in Barbados.

17. Ibid., 27, 25.
18. Collier, "The Closing of the Circle: Movement from Division to Wholeness in Paule Marshall's Fiction," 299.

Selina's search for her place in the world forces her to learn about people and their weaknesses. In order to overcome those weaknesses, one must rely on oneself and make an effort to get away from that which is oppressive. In Selina's case, her family, community, and society put her into a special category where she does not want to belong. She needs, therefore, to free herself from all, including her heritage. As a way of separating herself from the past, she removes one of the silver bangles she has worn since birth and throws it into the air, marking her detachment from all that she once knew. It is time for her to live for herself. Selina believes in what the wise Suggie once told her, "They'll down hand on you, mahn, and when you hear the shout you wun be able to call your soul your own" (207).

Through Selina's physical journey, Marshall asserts the need for Blacks to make the spiritual and psychological journey back into their past. John McCluskey Jr. states:

> The refrain of the woman who with love and compassion must be willing to define herself and the responsibility such an act demands rings throughout her [Marshall's] work. The refrain is not flattened by resignation, but sharpened by affirmation, by an insistent "I am?" All the while, however, . . . the awareness of sociocultural history adds a new dimension to personal identity, defines quest and mission.[19]

Selina positively affirms her desire for individuality and an independence that parallels her mother's. She asks Silla: "Remember how you used to talk about how you left home and came here alone as a girl of eighteen and was your own woman? I used to love hearing that. And that's what I want. I want it!" (307). Selina has come to a deep realization of her personal and collective self, which she will incorporate in shaping her quest for meaning and fulfillment. Thus this protagonist of *Brown Girl* has progressed from a fragmented self through a turbulent awakening to a realigned whole.

■   ■

Toni Morrison's contribution to the women's literary canon and American literature is invaluable, and her first novel, *The Bluest*

---

19. "And Called Every Generation Blessed: Theme, Setting and Ritual in the Works of Paule Marshall," 333.

Eye, gives a depressing view of growing up Black and female in an environment that is not only closed but stagnant. Morrison typically does not conform to the usual fictional modes, but rather takes what readers consider the real and brings it to another level of believability to get the messages home. Pecola Breedlove was new to 1970s scholars of Black American literature, as was Maud Martha to those in the 1950s. She is still new to some audiences because her journey into experience leaves the reader reeling with the realization that such a life could have been lived. Even Maya Angelou's *I Know Why the Caged Bird Sings,* despite its scenes of confusion and suffering, has some joyful moments. Pecola's story reminds us of Milton Sobers's in Clarke's work because of the socioeconomic, cultural, and racial contexts used to highlight stark realities. Also, presenting girls as victims in the "new literature" since the 1970s allows the novelist to express an awareness of female vulnerability.

Morrison's striking creations of dual characters are central to her style of making the reader understand the story through the qualities of the people she portrays. In *The Bluest Eye,* Morrison shows the impact of racism and society's definition of physical beauty on the self-worth of the main character, Pecola Breedlove, and the narrator, Claudia MacTeer. In *Sula,* she constructs complementary opposite personalities in Sula Peace and Nel Wright to illustrate individual differences in female friendship and the understanding of good and evil. Milkman Dead, the protagonist in *Song of Solomon* (1977), and his best friend, Guitar Bains, serve as contrasting characters to help develop the theme of different routes in the search for identity. In *Beloved,* Morrison presents the theme of love by showing the different types of love exhibited by daughters Beloved and Denver toward their mother, Sethe.

In *The Bluest Eye,* the contrasts between the positive feelings of self-worth of the narrator, Claudia, and the low self-esteem and loneliness of the main character, Pecola, serve to emphasize the effect of both internal and external forces on the emotional development of the two girls. The impact of those forces influences the direction and destination of their lives. Morrison says that the central theme of all her work is: "Beauty, love. . . . Actually, I think, all the time that I write, I'm writing about love or its absence. Although I don't start out that way.... But I think that I still write about the same thing, which is how people relate to one another and miss it or hang on to it."[20] Certainly, this theme is evident in *The Bluest Eye* and *Sula*, whose female characters search for love, valid sexual encounters, and, above all, a sense that they are worthy of acknowledgment in their society and community.

Traditionally, the initiation rite is painful but enlightening and forms a part of the chief theme of novels of adolescence, a theme that has been identified as "the individual's search for genuine values."[21] Morrison's early works explore the dilemma of Black women whose values are real and powerful but designed primarily for middle-class Whites. From the outset, these values are known by some of Morrison's female characters to be useless, even damaging. Claudia, the narrator of *The Bluest Eye*, recognizes her position as "a minority in both caste and class [being poor, Black, female] we moved about anyway on the hem of life, struggling to consolidate our weaknesses and hang on, or to creep singly up into the major folds of the garment."[22] For Pecola Breedlove, Sula Peace, and Nel Wright Green, as for many other female characters, "female aspiration is a joke. Female rebellion may be perfectly justified, but there is no good universe next door, no way out. Young potential revolutionaries can't find their revolution. So they marry in defeat or go mad in a complicated form of triumph, their meaning the inevitability of failure."[23] Toni Morrison joins her basic theme with the initiation motif, and the initiation experiences, trying and painful as they are, fail. Sula rebels and is rejected; Nel marries; Pecola attempts to transform herself and goes mad. All live lives of profound isolation in a society that does not want them, or wants them for various reasons. The Black community of Medallion seems no different from the larger White American society in its treatment of individuals like Sula or Pecola.

The Bluest Eye is the story of eleven-year-old Pecola, seen, for the most part, through the eyes of her classmates and friends, Claudia

20. Jane S. Bakerman, "The Seams Can't Show: An Interview with Toni Morrison," 60.
21. Fredric I. Carpenter, "The Adolescent in American Fiction," 315.
22. *The Bluest Eye*, 11. Further references to this work will be made parenthetically in the text.
23. Patricia Meyer Spacks, *The Female Imagination*, 158.

and Frieda. As the child of a drunken father and an aesthetically impoverished mother, Pecola is universally considered ugly, despised,
and ignored. She rarely smiles; she looks "whipped" and her eyes are
haunted. Any act of violence, such as a dog's death or her parents'
quarrels, makes her ill. She is keenly aware of the world around
her; her sensitivity and feelings are very near the surface. The indifference of the White storekeeper, the harassment of the boys in the
schoolyard, the bullying by a sadistic little rich boy are real tortures
for her. She is accepted by the three friendly prostitutes, China,
Poland, and Miss Marie, who live in the upstairs apartment, and
by her sister, who also has problems communicating with grownups
and understanding the values of the adult world. For the most part,
however, her interaction with other human beings serves only to
reinforce her self-image of worthlessness.

Morrison constructs this novel in two ways. The first demonstrates
the elementary school primer's standards for family behavior and
beauty. The second is the family life of the MacTeers. The text announces this early, visually, as the reader sees the simple childlike
storybook epigraphs to each of the early sections in Autumn. As
the story progresses, we see/hear more abbreviated versions of the
elementary school reader's repetitive depictions of lives:

> Here is the house. It is green and white. It has a red door. It is very pretty.
> Here is the family. Mother, Father, Dick and Jane live in the green-and-
> white house. They are very happy. See Jane. She has a red dress. She
> wants to play. Who will play with Jane? (7)

This is a deliberate and loaded paragraph as Morrison places before
us a White model of an American household; quite obviously this is
the stuff of storybooks, and most certainly a life alien to many Black
children.

Morrison then proceeds to tell us in sum what the story is:

> There were no marigolds in the fall of 1941. We thought at the time, that
> it was because Pecola was having her father's baby. . . . We had dropped
> our seeds in our little plot of black dirt just as Pecola's father had dropped
> his seeds in his own plot of black dirt. (9)

What remains for the reader now is to ask the how, why, where of this tragic event.

When Claudia tells us the story of her friend Pecola, she also describes her own stable family as a point of comparison and contrast. Subsequently the reader witnesses a simultaneous development of more than one Black girl in the same household. Narrator and subject thus meet in an interesting fashion. Their unique experiences emit from their reactions and individual responses to events around them. Early in the story, Claudia makes it clear that she does not accept the injustices and inequities of life. Her dislike for White baby dolls and White girls marks her defiance against White society. It is the rejection of the standards set down by society and the naive belief that beauty is in the eye of the beholder that encourage Claudia's security with herself. Pecola, conversely, is drawn to White objects.

Claudia has a strong, supportive home life that builds security, even though her parents do not always seem to express love openly to her. She remembers "love, thick and dark as Alaga syrup" (14). Because Claudia is able to integrate events into her psyche and associate them with warmth and security, the reader comes to understand that she is making this type of association when she relates her memories of the time she is sick and remembers that she can "think of somebody with hands who does not want me to die" (14).

Claudia does not bend under the arrogance she sees in the White people she comes in contact with; instead she wants to lash out against it. Morrison is able to present a clear vision from the perspective of the child Claudia of what prejudice looks, sounds, and feels like. Although Claudia's relationship with her family seems to be positive, she feels rejected by society in general because of her blackness. Claudia sees how people act, but she does not "accept without question what everyone else seems to assume: that little black girls are somehow lesser beings because of their blackness." Pecola does not have any similar or happy memories to strengthen her. Her mother thinks she is ugly from the time she is born and through her actions sends this message to the child. Mrs. Breedlove, for example, shows affection to the daughter of her employer but shuns Pecola, reinforcing the message that little White girls deserve love because they are beautiful or better. It is no wonder then that "Pecola really believes that the world would be better if viewed through the blue eyes so highly valued according to the white standard of beauty."[24] The world of injustice and oppression outside her family affects Pecola negatively as well. When Maureen Peal insults Pecola, Claudia, and Frieda, the girls react in different ways. The two MacTeer girls hurl their best insults back, but Claudia tells us that Pecola "seemed to fold into herself, like a pleated wing" (61). The constant strikes against Pecola's self-worth drive her inward in her yearning for escape. Unfortunately, there is no internal salvation for Pecola because she does not have the strength to reject the standards by which society and her own family measure her. Pecola's reaction to Maureen's insults upsets Claudia. She thinks that her friend should stand up against the insults and not wilt. Thus, the difference in character between Claudia and Pecola is illustrated in Claudia's frustration with her friend's passivity.

Pecola's aching search for kindness is revealed to the reader through a hauntingly simple question: "how do you get somebody to love you?" (29). This young girl starts to crave an unattainable symbol of beauty to fill her need for love. The ideas of romantic love and physical beauty, which Morrison calls "the most destructive in the history of human thought" (97), become an obsession. She begins to believe that the only way to attain love is by being something that she is not.

While Claudia rejects the blond-haired, blue-eyed dolls and girls, Pecola is fascinated with drinking milk from the Shirley Temple cup at the MacTeer house. We can see the different paths that the two girls take toward security. Claudia has no envy of White features; in fact, she abhors them. Eventually, Claudia loses her naive outlook and contempt for Shirley Temple, but, because she has a firm foundation from which to deal with her metamorphosis, she sees the change in her outlook on life only as "adjustment without improvement" (22).

Pecola's envy and preoccupation with appearance take over her life because that life is empty and frightening. She does not have the strength to fight for herself partly because her own parents do not seem able to find their own self-worth and thus cannot give that ability to her. Her mother, Pauline, has low self-esteem mostly

24. Donna B. Haisty, *"The Bluest Eye,"* 193.

because she has accepted the standard of beauty that she assimilated from movies. She believes that she cannot live up to those standards herself and certainly holds no hope for her daughter. Furthermore, Barbara Christian says, "the Breedloves despise themselves because they believe in their own unworthiness, which is translated into ugliness for the women of that family."[25]

Morrison helps the reader see the differences between the lives of the MacTeer girls and that of Pecola. When Pecola is raped by her father, her mother beats her and the whole town talks about the incident as if it were, at least partly, Pecola's fault. In a scene that parallels the rape of Pecola, Mr. MacTeer throws out the roomer who has fondled Frieda and then throws the children's tricycle at his head. Pecola's role as victim of White society stands out against Claudia's success at dealing with the world. The story can be seen as Claudia's because the events that affect Pecola leave a lasting impression on Claudia, too. In a way the novel consists of two bildungsromane, just as George Lamming's novel tells multileveled stories of G and of his friends.

By the end of the novel, Claudia realizes that she and Frieda are just as guilty of seeking beauty at another's expense as the people she despises. "We were so beautiful when we stood astride her ugliness. . . . We honed our egos on her, padded our character with her frailty, and yawned in the fantasy of our strength" (159). Although she still believes society's image of beauty to be wrong, Claudia has come to define it against the devastated Black child who does not have the resources to deal with life. "The mother's own internalization of the desirable woman as beautiful, well-taken-care-of, cuddled, results in her rejection of her own daughter, who by virtue of her blackness and her poverty cannot possibly obtain such a standard."[26]

Pauline Breedlove undoubtedly embodies Black women's slave history; her class and status are those of the Black working poor. She is an uneducated product of the great migration North. Like so many of her Black brothers and sisters she is a victim of urbanization. Her household is not exactly matriarchal in that she does what she

25. *Black Feminist Criticism*, 73–74.
26. Ibid., 74.

has to do to make ends meet by working as a domestic for a White middle-class family. She is not a "Sapphire" or a "Mammy." Yet it is very difficult to figure out just what makes Pauline Breedlove a memorable character. What one gets is her suffering, quiet strength, and acceptance about her circumstances and her family. She seems to have, like Silla, no time for anything except work. Even when we learn of how Cholly swept her off her feet and brought her North, we are not really sure if this is what she wanted. Pauline's feminine world is an extension of her work. What, therefore, can this brooding, distanced woman give her daughter? Love? Tradition? Practical sense? Pauline watches her daughter grow but does not raise her. She is raised by the prostitutes, China, Poland, and Miss Marie, the MacTeers, and the community. The three real and unpretentious prostitutes become her surrogate parent, each offering the girl a part of herself. The freedom Pecola shares in conversations with them never happens with her mother, who is formally addressed as Mrs. Breedlove, never mother, or mom, or mama. Again we see the formal distancing of the relationship between mother and daughter. At the end of the novel, she is completely alienated from her mother.

Pecola seems to sense that the Breedloves are damaged people, undervalued by both Whites and Blacks. She wishes to emerge not only from the isolation of childhood, but also from the isolation of this family. They are poor and they are "ugly."

> You looked at them and wondered why they were so ugly; you looked closely and could not find the source. Then you realized that it came from conviction, their conviction. It was as though some mysterious all-knowing master had given each one a cloak of ugliness to wear, and they had accepted it without question. (34)

Because White children appear to be beloved by both White and Black adults, Pecola is determined to achieve beauty and acceptance by acquiring blue eyes. "Each night, without fail, she prayed for blue eyes. Fervently, for a year she had prayed. Although somewhat discouraged, she was not without hope. To have something as wonderful as that happen would take a long, long time" (40). Morrison's point is clear:

When the strength of a race depends on its beauty, when the focus is turned to how one looks as opposed to what one is, we are in trouble. . . . The concept of physical beauty as a virtue is one of the dumbest, most pernicious and destructive ideas of the Western world, and we should have nothing to do with it. Physical beauty has nothing to do with our past, present or future. Its absence or presence was only important to them, the white people who used it for anything they wanted.[27]

But there is no one to explain this point to Pecola. Her parents, Cholly and Pauline, have accepted the idea that they are ugly and in doing so have come to hate one another. Of equal importance, they do not know how to love; they cannot give their children a sense of self, for they have none of their own. Pauline's isolation is exacerbated by the couple's removal to the North, where she is different from other Blacks and unaccepted by them. Eventually, Pauline's loneliness and Cholly's futile struggle to support the family decently destroy every possibility for love, and they learn to use their children as weapons against one another.

Morrison incorporates the motifs of race and ugliness so that at every turn the reader is made to understand that Pecola's state is hopeless. Even the most casual exchanges teach her that she is unworthy. At school, the boys taunt her; she is the scapegoat for their own humiliation and pain: "Black e mo. Black e mo. Yadaddsleepnekked. Black e mo black e mo yadaddsleepsnekked. Black e mo. . . . That they themselves were black, or that their own father had similarly relaxed habits was irrelevant. It was their contempt for their own blackness that gave the first insult its teeth" (55). Buying the Mary Jane candies that she likes to eat because of the blond, blue-eyed child on the wrapper, Pecola is made aware that for many people, she doesn't really exist. At the local grocer's she realizes that "he does not see her, because for him there is nothing to see. How can a fifty-year-old white immigrant storekeeper . . . his sensibilities blunted by a permanent awareness of loss, see a little black girl?" (42).

Seemingly befriended by a pretty little "yellow" girl, Maureen Peal, the darling of the teachers and the demon of the other children, Pecola begins to relax, only to discover that she's being tricked into

27. Toni Morrison, "Behind the Making of the Black Book."

revealing "humiliating" facts about her family in exchange for pretty Maureen's specious information about sex.

> "Did you ever see a naked man?" Pecola blinked, then looked away. "No. Where would I see a naked man? . . ." "I wouldn't even look at him, even if I did see him. That's dirty. Who wants to see a naked man?" Pecola was agitated. "Nobody's father would be naked in front of his own daughter. Not unless he was dirty too." (59)

Nakedness is "disgusting" or shameful for most girls of Pecola's age, whether it's theirs or someone else's. A father's nakedness before a daughter is admittedly humiliating to Pecola, and Maureen shows her own superiority in class and knowledge by suggesting that children, being basically honest and unassuming, often reveal truths needlessly.

The most terrible of her rejections occurs when a young boy makes her the scapegoat for his own pain, which stems directly from the fact that his mother, embracing White, middle-class standards, forces him to reject his own blackness and invests her affection in their cat. The lifestyle to which the mother, Geraldine, exposes her son and her own attitudes about blackness isolate the boy from the realities of Black life. Her negative attitudes toward Blacks are instilled in the boy, who exhibits them cruelly toward others, rather than toward his mother, whom he silently hates. "She was deep in admiration of the flowers when Junior said, 'Here!' Pecola turned. 'Here is your kitten!' he screeched. And he threw a big black cat right in her face" (73). Pecola is unable to save the cat from further torture, and she is unable to save herself, for Junior's mother, interrupting, cannot allow herself to see the moment for what it really is; to do so would be to acknowledge kinship with Pecola, poor, ugly, and Black. She exclaims instead, "You nasty little black bitch. Get out of my house" (75).

Thus, Pecola is carefully taught that there is no one to love her—that Whites do not see her and that Blacks scorn her. For her, a healthy sexual encounter symbolizing initiation into the adult world is forbidden, for when someone does see her as lovable, it is her father in the act of sexually attacking her. The resulting baby dies, but Pecola lives, and makes one more attempt to come to terms with the world. Because her prayers for blue eyes have come to no account, she seeks the aid of a magician. If he can give her blue eyes, all will be reversed. The result is bitter and ironic; she finds the only refuge available to her—madness. Through her false belief that she has, indeed, acquired blue eyes, she escapes to the deepest isolation of all. "The damage done was total. She spent her days, her tendril, sap-green days, walking up and down, up and down, her head jerking to the beat of a drummer so distant only she could hear" (162). For the community, Pecola's madness, coupled with her family history, brings scorn rather than sympathy. She becomes the scapegoat not merely for frustrated children, but for all of society.

The ultimate images are very different for Claudia and Pecola because the experiences that lead to the points of intersection in their lives are quite different. Claudia is able at the end to look back and analyze the tragic effects of race prejudice and the absence of love on a human being. She becomes strong and mature because of the lessons she learns. Pecola, Claudia reveals, "stepped over into madness, a madness which protected her from us simply because it bored us in the end" (159). So Pecola, who wanted whiteness and blue eyes, and Pauline, who dressed up like Jean Harlow, are no better off at the novel's end. They simply live together in "separate" worlds on the *edge* of town.

The novel is effective because of the importance of its theme and the skill with which the inevitability of a failed initiation and brief unhappy childhood is developed. It is inevitable, but unfortunate, that the voice of the economically deprived and socially depressed woman is little heard except through the mouthpiece of her literary sisters; Frieda and Claudia by telling Pecola's story become Morrison's literary mouthpieces. They are her singers. This underscores the lesson that oppressed voices seldom speak and, when they do, are seldom heard.

■   ■

Since the 1970s there has been an amazing and spectacular renaissance in Black women's writing. They have extended their boldness, experimentation, activism, and energy into new works of fiction, poetry, drama, and essay, adding variations of all of these to the American literary tradition. For their energies and talent some have received prizes, applause, visibility, and monetary rewards. Toni Morrison and Alice Walker have received the Nobel and Pulitzer, respectively. Gloria Naylor and Alice Walker have had their works adapted to film, and Walker's *The Color Purple* was nominated for eleven Academy Awards in 1985. Maya Angelou and Rita Dove have been named Poets Laureate. Paule Marshall received the prestigious MacArthur Prize.

Among their most exciting contributions are the new angles through which Black women have looked at such issues as single motherhood, spousal and child abuse, aging, lesbianism, incest, rape, womanism—and their creation of a new Black female bildungsroman clearly different from the form used by their earlier literary sisters and brothers. Some of the greatest excitement about literature of the last thirty years has been that created by Black women within the African diaspora. It is fitting therefore, that the last discussion in this chapter focus on Ntozake Shange, who has revolutionized form and language in African American literature like no other writer of the last twenty-five years.

Shange holds a unique place in the African American woman's contemporary literary canon. With her dramatic choreopoem *For Colored Girls Who Have Considered Suicide When the Rainbow Is ENUF,* and novels such as *Sassafrass, Cypress, and Indigo* and *Betsey Brown,* she joined the ranks of prominent Black women writers whose messages are clear, provocative, and womanist. Her works expose issues facing Black women as they develop into adulthood. She explores the issues of racism, sexism, classism, and ageism as they impact on their lives. Although each of her characters finds a definition of herself as a Black woman, the path taken by each is unique. In *Sassafrass, Cypress, and Indigo,* for example, each woman fulfills herself with a particular interest from which she derives power, be that interest music, dancing, or weaving cloth. These women also learn to relate to and separate themselves from the men in their lives. With strength of character, Shange's women imprint themselves permanently in our memories. Shange dedicated *Sassafrass, Cypress, and Indigo* to "all women in struggle." Within that statement lies the power of her writing. Her works are about Black women, but they are indeed for all women. She uses Black English in a manner that does not exclude any gender, class, or culture but invites all readers to enjoy, to understand as well as confront the many issues facing them. Shange said in a 1987 interview that "unless black women are writing the pieces, we're being left out in the same way we used to be left out of literature. We don't appear in things unless we write them ourselves."[28] The oppressions of Black women are addressed by and through the many characters in her writings.

Black women are often deprived of their sense of childhood because they must immediately begin striving for recognition in the home and community. In *For Colored Girls* one of the dancers, the lady in brown, sings solemnly of "dark phrases of womanhood / of never havin been a girl" and continues with the realization that the invisibility of Black women is like death:

> somebody/anybody
> sing a black girl's song
> bring her out
> to know herself
> but sing her rhythms
> carin/struggle/hard times
> sing her song of life
> she's been dead so long
> closed in silence so long
> she doesn't know the sound
> of her own voice
> her infinite beauty.[29]

Through the choreopoem, Shange plays out the many concerns of Black women. Betsey, Sassafrass, Cypress, and Indigo tackle the invisibility of Black women who carve out their own places in society, along with the nameless women dressed in the varied rainbow colors of *For Colored Girls*. This wonderful, groundbreaking piece also explores the never-ending experiences of women—rape, abortion,

28. Barbara Lyons, "Interview with Ntozake Shange," 690.
29. *For Colored Girls Who Have Considered Suicide When the Rainbow Is ENUF,* 3, 4. Further references to this work will be made parenthetically in the text.

abuse, love/hate relationships, mothering, death, philosophies of life, Third World concerns, what it means to be an Egyptian goddess, and "being sorry and colored at the same time" (*For Colored Girls,* 46). *Sassafrass* presents a good example of how a homeostatic relationship can be achieved. Shange is so creative and original that her book presents this formulation on three complimentary levels— culture, education, and the development of four women, Hilda Effania and her three daughters, Sassafrass, Cypress, and Indigo. By examining the importance of rivals in the novel, Shange's style, and the characters she uses to tell her story, the reader can grasp a new alliance in writing—in essence the creation of a new subgenre of the female bildungsroman. Shange weaves together the stories of the three "girls" so well that they become a triad growing in unison, yet at different stages of their development.

By including poetry, recipes, letters, songs, and instruction, Shange creates a different kind of book—not a cookbook, not a book of poems, not a crafts book, and most likely not entirely a work of fiction. She has created a new medium for expression, one that is magical in quality and distinctly feminine. By doing so, she has balanced various elements of the common female culture and Black culture to show that complete expression requires an acknowledgment of one's heritage while breaking new creative ground.

Sassafrass, Cypress, and Indigo relies heavily upon the shared heritage from which each of the women grows. First, the importance of cooking, a traditionally feminine activity, is emphasized. Recipes are shared, descriptions of meals and the corresponding preparations are given, and locations are determined by the various aromas from different kitchens. For example, "Mrs. Yancey's house smelled like collard greens and corn bread, even when she fried oysters and made red sauce" and "mother's apron always smelled like cinnamon and garlic no matter how many times it was washed."[30]

Second, sewing or weaving is a skill taught to all three daughters by their mother. Even though sewing is often thought of as a traditional task for women, Shange turns it into an exquisite art form, which it is. From Indigo's dolls, to Sassafrass's weavings, to

30. *Sassafrass, Cypress, and Indigo,* 9, 21. Further references to this work will be made parenthetically in the text.

Hilda Effania's weavings for Mrs. Fitzhugh, each piece is described as an expression from the soul; a potentially mundane task becomes beautiful self-expression. Women's culture (manifest in sewing and handicrafts) reinforces feminine roles; yet it is a mode of breaking away from oppression through expression.

Third, Shange makes a point of describing the neighborhood in Charleston as all Black. She makes the racial and cultural connection even stronger by noting that all of Indigo's dolls are dark-skinned, and that she and her dolls will converse only with Black folks. To further emphasize the cultural aspect, she uses folklore to add richness and depth to the story. For instance, in the beginning, while focusing upon Indigo, Shange tells us about moon journeys, determining suitors with the moon's blessing, and what to do "If Your Beloved Has Eyes for Another":

> If Your Beloved Has Eyes for Another
> Sleep on your left side with 6 white roses by your head. Fill your pillow with 2 handfuls of damiana leaves. . . . (Use blue if you merely desire fidelity). With the damiana-cubeb berry-filled pouch anywhere on your person in the presence of your beloved, your way shall be had. (15)

The folklore Shange uses to highlight cultural markers in the novel also works on another level. These devices allow her own education and cultural experience to shine through. While the book is sociologically informative, it also is consistent with the theme of all her writing, which is to convey "what it means to be of color and female in the twentieth century."[31]

Sassafrass, Shange's first novel, thus details the developmental patterns of three sisters simultaneously. Indigo, the youngest, is the child who possesses the most obvious power. She establishes herself with magic. "Where there is woman there is magic. If there is a moon falling from her mouth, she is a woman who knows her magic, who can share or not share her powers" (3). She surrounds herself with dolls that are more than just toys—they are her companions. The

31. Lecture given by Shange at the University of Missouri–Columbia, March 1990.

dolls have their own thoughts and questions that push Indigo to seek answers.

Shange blurs the line between reality and a child's imagination to illustrate that Indigo's wisdom goes far beyond her years. Indigo also plays the fiddle and uses it to speak her own language. She creates spells and converses with spirits. "There wasn't enough for Indigo in the world she'd been born to, so she made up what she needed. What she thought the black people needed" (4). Indigo is fiercely independent and draws on her magic and fecund imagination for strength. No one told her she could work this magic; she does it on her own. Because of this inner power, she is able to grow on her own as well. She backs off Spats and Crunch with the power of her fiddle and becomes a Junior Geechee Captain, thus gaining access into the behind-the-scenes world of adults in The Caverns. However, she recognizes the time to resign that position and move toward womanhood. She also decides in her own time when to give up her beloved dolls, despite all the previous hounding by her mother. When she finally sends them to the attic, it is with the knowledge that she is saving them from growing up. She has recognized her fate, but she wants to spare her friends the pain involved in the passage to adulthood. She explains this poignantly to her mother: "Bein' a grown colored woman is hard, ain't it? Just like you tol' me. Just cause I haveta grow up, my dolls don't haveta. I can save them" (52). Indigo has a remarkable grasp of life for one so young, and she shares this knowledge with those around her. She is able to gain maturity without developing the hard edges of Cypress or the vulnerability of Sassafrass.

Indigo's escape from the troubles that befall her sisters may largely be attributed to her focus on magic rather than on men. When she announces that she enjoyed the Schuylers' party but liked her fiddle better than the boys she met, her mother is pleased. "There'd be not one more boy-crazy, obsessed-with-romance child in her house. This last one made more sense out of the world than either of the other two. Alfred would have liked that. He liked independence" (64). Alfred is the girls' deceased father. Cypress and Sassafrass each have special talents on which to focus, but both of them allow men to play large roles in their development as women. Indigo is perhaps the strongest of the three sisters, and her story could make its own fascinating novel.

It takes Sassafrass a long time to declare independence from her love interest. She lives with Mitch, a chauvinistic musician who dominates her life, and with whom she has a cacophonous relationship. He wants her to pursue her interests but at the same time wants her to wait on him and cook his meals. This is an interesting characterization of the renewed male of the 1970s, and of the conflict faced by women of that era. These interactions among male and female characters expose degrees of sexism, but as Shange says, "It's like creating a world of women that's women-centered, so aberrant male forms really look aberrant."[32] Sassafrass doesn't muster the strength to leave, until Mitch's sexist behavior reaches gigantic proportions. He, with the companionship of two friends, directs a sexually explicit song at her. She, finally, explodes:

> I am not about to sit heah and listen to a bunch of no account niggahs talk about black women; me and my sisters; like we was the same bought and sold at slave auction . . . breeding heifers the white man created 'cause y'all was fascinated by some god damn beads he brought you on the continent. (89)

Her long overdue self-defense is followed by a beating from Mitch, so she moves in with Cypress. Yet, even after all of the abuse and humiliation she has endured because of Mitch, she believes that she loves and needs him. "She needed Mitch because Mitch was all she loved in herself" (98). With this knowledge, she returns to him as soon as he asks her to come back. Sassafrass has her weaving and her writing, but her man is her way of defining herself, so she endures his negative attitudes. It is not until she and Mitch go to The New World Found Collective that she finds a focus that can save her from her destructive relationship. Once she finds completeness within herself, she no longer needs him. She realizes that she can live in her looms and that that is enough; her self-awareness is complete.

Cypress's road to self-discovery is also a rocky one. She wants most of all to be a dancer. "She knew dancing was in her blood . . . every

32. Lyons, "Interview with Shange," 687.

step" (135). Yet she allows herself to lose sight of her goal by dabbling in alcohol, drugs, and many sexual relationships. She is living the empty life the lady in red describes in *For Colored Girls:*

> you'll have to go now/i've
> a lot of work to do/& i cant
> with a man around/here are yr pants/
> there's coffee on the stove/its been
> very nice/but i cant see you again/
> you got what you came for/didnt you. (36)

Cypress is determined to be a dancer. She studies dance in New York and travels with an African American troupe to San Francisco. When she returns to New York, she dances herself into two whirlwind relationships that force her to accept herself as a woman and an artist.

Although Cypress enjoys the company of many men, it is her first love relationship with a woman, Idrina, that derails her sense of self. She allows herself to fall in love, even though she knows from the beginning that Idrina has a steady lover. "Idrina knew some things that Cypress didn't know: loving is not always the same as having. And Idrina loved Cypress, but not to have . . . and Cypress didn't know that" (149). When Idrina's lover returns from Holland, Cypress suffers a devastating blow. After much alcohol consumption, she runs into her old friend Leroy and finds her focus on dance again. As she fulfills herself with her dancing she is able to fulfill her need for love with Leroy and accepts him as part of her life. By the novel's denouement, she has agreed to marry Leroy. Cypress has not defined herself in terms of her man, but has developed her own individual sense of self, through her dancing, and is now able to have a good relationship with a man.

Hilda Effania, the mother of Indigo, Sassafrass, and Cypress, is an interesting woman and differs substantially from Jane Brown, the mother in *Betsey Brown* who disappears almost completely from her daughter's life. Shange uses Hilda as a catalyst, a context and frame for the story, but she definitely has her own story, one that raises many questions: Why are all three daughters so creative?

Why are they so steeped in the South and southern culture? Why do they, and she, seem to function outside the ordinary mundane things with which we associate poor Black women's lives? What qualifies her to mother such extraordinary young women? Hilda had prayed for a husband and got one. She made all ordinary occasions like Christmas and the onset of menstruation and meals major and creative events for celebration. She essentially got on with life despite single motherhood. Hilda thinks, "she looked good for a widow with three most grown girls" (66). She writes nurturing and supportive rather than destructive letters to her daughters no matter where they are, such as this one:

> My two big girls, Sassafrass and Cypress,
>   Well, looks like you are having a veritable family reunion. I wish I could be there, not just to see you both (which I really would like), but so I could finally be at one of Cypress' parties! Cypress, you be sure to introduce Sassafrass to some nice young men . . . watch that your sister doesn't spend up all her money entertaining folks. (116–17)

This mother, although a bit unrealistic, is what many of us wish mothers would be more like—that is, compassionate, creative, patient. She, like Jane in *Betsey Brown,* touches her daughters and molds them without seeming to take a proactive part in their lives. Important, though, is that whatever Indigo, Sassafrass, and Cypress become, they become because of what Hilda gave and exposed them to as children. Indigo, the last child, benefits from all who preceded her—sisters, mother, "the geechees, long gone," the South, and, additionally, Africa and the Ibos. Hilda can be any kind of woman she wants to be because she has been the mother her heritage intrinsically deemed her to be. It was not effortless, but easy. We also see Hilda and Indigo in a special mother–daughter bonding, and we suspect that the two older daughters have received the same experience and teaching about life and Black woman's history from her. Ultimately, Sassafrass, Cypress, and Indigo are wise women. Like their mother, they find out how to live and how to express themselves in a nice/mean world, or what Paule Marshall calls the "beautiful/ugly."

Each child thinks that good fortune will follow her; Indigo thinks, for example, that only boys who are "pure of mind and strong of body" will come to her (22). When her mother slaps reality into her, a feeling of pain and confusion can be felt. The reality of slavery and discrimination is brought to life with one sentence: "White men roam these parts with evil in their blood, and every single thought they have about a colored girl is dangerous" (22). The idea of evil and hatred planted into the mind of innocent Indigo reminds all of us of our slow growth into reality. Prejudice comes alive in Indigo's mind; she has to fear White men. The passage also shows the fierce attachment between Indigo and her mother when Hilda adds, "I would just kill anybody who hurt you" (22).

Some readers will say that they do not know Hilda at all and that she refuses to let her daughters go by writing those probing, advising letters. In fact, what Shange does in those letters is to let the reader see a slow evolution from the worry, anxiety, and concern for the girls' choice of lifestyles expressed in Hilda's early letters:

> My Littlest Angel, Indigo,
>   Wouldn't I look simple, keeping a house full of grown women, aching to be part of the world, from being part of the world, just so I wouldn't be quite so lonely. That's enough of that. You all have your 'mends to make with the world & so do I. . . . I keep looking for Cypress' face to be on the news, when they talk about those youngsters who've lost their minds in California. I swear, I feel in my soul that she's wandering around San Francisco all painted up with stars & peace symbols. I pray the TV cameras never find her. She might do a dance, then what would I say to all my neighbors. I got a painted dancing daughter in Haight-Asbury? (74–75)

The letters show Hilda's slow evolution to wholeness, acceptance, and truth; a process similar to that of her daughters.

Each woman takes her own route to complete womanhood, yet all achieve that end. For Indigo, growing into a complete person means giving up her dolls (not entirely, one suspects) and turning toward her brand of music for self-expression, wherein she finds power. At times she abuses that power by using it to entertain White folks or to frighten her Geechee Captain friends. After a time, she realizes that the power in her music is from her self-expression. The fiddle does not have the power, she does. Her renaissance, this time as a whole woman, occurs as she returns to the Black woman's community and aids in bringing life into it, as a midwife.

For Cypress, growing to completeness takes a much rockier road. She must deal with various opposing emotions—fear, jealousy, depression, and guilt. She never tells her mother of her female lover. She knows her mother would be appalled. Still, in her letters, she wants to share so much with her. The guilt and pain accrue. Her lesbianism does, however, teach her about womanness and not being completely male-identified like her sister Sassafrass. Finally, she becomes whole in herself as she decides to dance for the Civil Rights Movement.

For Sassafrass, most of her development occurs when she is with Cypress and away from Mitch. But her deep love for Mitch prevails. Becoming pregnant, preparing to bring life into the world, makes her feel fulfilled.

Hilda, as an older woman whose children have grown into affirmed womanhood on their own, does not grow much herself until her daughters begin their respective journeys. Afraid of the unknown, she keeps trying to reel them back into her nest. Still, she is proud of their accomplishments; hence, she grows with them and through them—by proxy. "Hilda Effania couldn't think enough to cook. . . . She looked at Alfred's portrait over the parlor fireplace, a little embarrassed. 'You know, Al, I did the best I could, but I don't think they want what we wanted'" (225).

Sassafrass, Cypress, and Indigo try to make it on their own, but they are forever linked to mama. Through her letters, recipes, and weaving, she has a loving hold on the girls no matter how far away they are. In this novel, Shange's poetic sensibilities provide an energetic yet calming lyricism. Her characters have an inherent dignity and are in rhythm with life.

The book closes at the point when the three sisters have achieved self-awareness. They are at various stages in their lives: Cypress is about to be married, Sassafrass is about to have a baby, and Indigo continues to move at her own pace. But they are all strong, magical, talented women who have selected a path for life and will follow it.

Shange has shown us what life is all about for these young women and created a piece that will endure for the next generations. She says that she does not want children brought into this world without a past to hold on to; she wants them to have heard about themselves. "I want to recreate and save what our being alive has been so their being will stay alive, won't be such a surprise."[33]

Teasing out the different layers of analysis in this book is like an adventure, because Shange masterfully weaves a multitude of elements—characters, genres, poetry, recipes, drama, letters, and cultural trademark—into a beautifully feminine tapestry. As indicated by her personal work history, Shange herself dances, writes theater pieces and poetry, weaves, and sews. Furthermore, she is obviously a bit of a dreamer, like Indigo, with a powerful voice of her own. Like Shange, these characters have all become complete women by balancing their education, culture, and art. Perhaps this wonderful novel is part of Shange's *Kunstlerroman,* but it also contains many elements of the Black female bildungsroman, primarily in Indigo's story of development and the age differences and range of all four women. *Sassafrass, Cypress, and Indigo* is a paradox, because somehow this shaman of a writer manages to integrate tradition with rebellion, chaos with peace, reality with fantasy, and poetry with life. Meanwhile music, art, and food become literature and the result is a lively/tranquil story that is painful/joyous and magical.

■   ■

Shange's second novel, *Betsey Brown,* portrays a black family in St. Louis in the late 1950s, focusing primarily on the struggles of the oldest daughter, Betsey. A concern of many Americans at that time was integration, open schools, and civil rights for the disenfranchised; it was a time of Black pride, Black Power, and the gravitation to African and African American arts, heroes, and ethnic self-expression. The novel gives us the family members' varying perceptions of life and depicts the choices available to Black women in modern society. By virtue of their ages, comparisons between Indigo and Betsey seem natural. They are also the only two children that Shange has devoted extensive attention to in her fiction works to date. Both girls have

33. Ibid., 690.

an incredible ability to perceive situations and an uncanny grasp of life for their young age. Indigo, however, is much more secure in her growth than Betsey, who must deal with constant family turmoil. Shange says: "Indigo has a knowing sense of what's possible and who she can be. We discover with Betsey what her possibilities are, which is different, I think, from Indigo giving us permission to share what she already knows."[34]

Betsey is a dynamic, imaginative thirteen-year-old beginning to learn about her Black heritage. Her mother, Jane, is a light-skinned woman absorbed by fashion. Her father, Greer, is a dark-skinned man who tries to instill Black pride in his four children, much to his mother-in-law's dismay. She says of her daughter, "She was most white. Slaves and all that had nothing to do with her family, until Jane insisted on bringing this Greer into the family and he kept making family."[35] Jane herself clashes with her husband's desire to keep the family in touch with its African and African American roots. This creates great turmoil in Betsey, who is experiencing the trials and tribulations of her passage into womanhood, amid this household in conflict. She is also experiencing the effects of integration in the St. Louis school she attends. Because Betsey's parents are affluent, she has never understood completely the Black culture her father relishes nor the prejudices against Blacks. "Betsey didn't know yet that white folks could get away with things a Negro'd be killed for. That's what was wrong with this integration talk" (30).

Betsey learns quickly though. She has White girlfriends and knows that something is wrong when she is not allowed to visit their homes while their parents are there; her friend Susan Linda says that "niggahs" aren't supposed to be in their house. This is Betsey's first real experience with the prejudices of Whites. She must fight with her conscience over her friendship and the unjust treatment she receives. Even more violent clashes with prejudice occur within the integrated school system. Betsey is left with a helpless sense of frustration when a White teacher tries to rob her beloved writer, Paul Lawrence Dunbar, of his merits: "this teacher tried to make me think that being

34. Ibid., 689.
35. *Betsey Brown,* 19. Further references to this work will be made parenthetically in the text.

colored meant you couldn't write poems or books or anything . . . she doesn't believe that we're American. . . . I tried to tell them but nobody listens to me cause it's just another nigger talking out the sides of her mouth" (183). Already, at thirteen, Betsey senses something wrong with the dominant culture's view of Blacks, especially since in her household, her father delights in the beauty and greatness of Black history and culture.

These conflicts often send Betsey to her private hiding places either on the stairs or in a tree in order to reflect on life. These secret places are stopping points on her journey to her own self-discovery. She has reached the age when she must start to think about her future role as a Black woman in a White-dominated society. Her power to acquire knowledge hinges on these stolen moments of solitude. Because of this, she guards the privacy that is an integral part of her life. When the new housekeeper, Bernice, gives away her secret spot in the tree, Betsey goes to war. The loss of her secret place also signals her loss of innocence and separateness.

It is only after Betsey has successfully driven away Bernice that her friend Veejay forces her to confront her privileged living conditions. Veejay says, "That coulda been my mama and you don't care" (67). When Betsey realizes from that conversation that many Black people do domestic work and other less-than-desirable labor in order to support their families, she vows then never to hurt another Black person.

Mixed with the difficult questions that racism raises in her life are her feelings for Eugene, her first love interest. She watches the maid, Regina, moon over her boyfriend, Roscoe, and ponders the meaning of love. She begins to think of marriage and a family, but at the same time is torn because her grandmother treats the Regina-Roscoe romance as something that can lead only to trouble. All of this confusion in her young life pushes Betsey to her decision to run away from home. She decides to go to Mrs. Maureen, the hairdresser, to learn a trade and remove herself from the frustrations of love and from White people so that she can finally immerse herself in Black culture. She sees herself as different from everyone else in her family, and the only way for her to discover her identity is to start a new life.

Once again she finds that things are not always the way they appear. There are no ideal worlds. Mrs. Maureen wants to send her home, telling her that her household is not suitable for a young girl. In fact, Mrs. Maureen runs a brothel, and Regina (sans Roscoe) is a part of it. Betsey learns that there are different kinds of colored people—not an easy concept to grasp at the age of thirteen. While she is able to see the good in all colored people, she finds that others are much more judgmental.

> She bet money some of these negroes wouldn't give a stone's throw if something happened to Roscoe, they didn't care what was gonna happen to Regina's baby. "Niggahs" they'd say and leave it to the will of God that people, especially colored people, suffered. Yet, they couldn't go anywhere else to get their hands done but a bordello. (138)

Betsey's return home marks a passage for her into true understanding of her situation. She learns through her experiences not only that she *is* different, but also that it is all right for her to be different. As she begins to realize that, Betsey becomes her own person. Her love of Black writers and Black music does not have to be a setback, but can instead lead to a broader appreciation of her race.

Betsey's mother, Jane, gets a later start on the road to her self-awareness, but she, too, "runs away." This is an interesting development in this bildungsroman, since it is the child who should "run away." Shange is also, therefore, charting Jane's earlier suspended development. After defining herself as Greer's wife, her mother's daughter, and the mother of four children, she takes off, by herself, to define herself on her own terms. Having given up control of her household to Greer and the housekeeper, she chooses to reflect and learn about the larger world. When she returns, she also has grown. She is no longer defined by her man, but her identity is enhanced by him; "this man . . . this particular colored man was hers forever and ever . . . those thoughts so provoked her, made her see anew who she was and who they were. Jane wanted Greer to feel how she'd grown. To actually grasp her new understanding of him, what he stood for, for their people, for the children" (190). She is less disturbed by Greer's interest in everything Black because she is coming to an understanding that being Black is part of her life. In her depiction of Jane, Shange created a new image of the African American mother; she incorporates none of the stereotypes seen in early Black writing. Shange also draws readers' attention to the new concept of an ongoing female bildungsroman, which has no specific age demarcation and is influenced by feminism and the new women's movement of the 1970s.

From "colored girls," to Betsey, Jane, Sassafrass, Cypress, and Indigo, Ntozake Shange has created journeys of self-discovery. She has woven tales that reach out to the "searching and yearning" of her own adolescence.[36] These are extended stories that touch the lives of women of all colors. She has suggested that women's novels are like breathing for her. The development of women as they struggle to find themselves seems to be the essence of her works. It is impossible to simply read her works and walk away; they linger in the mind. Shange is "for colored girls who have considered suicide / but are movin to the ends of their own rainbows" (*For Colored Girls* 64). Shange writes for anyone interested in a greater sense of self-awareness, yet she touches us all.

> i found god in myself
> & i loved her
> i loved her fiercely
> (*For Colored Girls,* 67)

Shange is also her own universe from which she embraces the mythical and mystical. Consistently and successfully she creates myriad representations of blackness that celebrate and weave history, heritage, culture, and language. The core of her work is the contemporary experiences of Blacks, especially women, but crafted so uniquely that what we have are revolutionary ways of expression, form, and content. She writes of Black women's experiences in ways that have not been done before. Like Toni Morrison, Alice Walker, and others, she forces language and experience to blend, in order to force the reader to experience old events in new ways. Girls experience the

36. Lyons, "Interview with Shange," 690.

pain and confusion of growing up every day, but never have those feelings been handled and presented with such technical agility and joy as in Ntozake Shange's works.

■   ■

The portrayals of African American protagonists by Brooks, Marshall, Morrison, and Shange are very real, believable, and unromantic. The self-hatred Maud and Pecola feel is primarily because they are individuals who lack the power to shape their lives. Because of the White American standard of color and class, the African American girl's self-concept becomes a crippling factor in her development. Pecola and Maud Martha dislike themselves because they are "ugly," but Brooks's Maude, Marshall's Selina, and Shange's "womanish" girls somehow manage to carve out a life for themselves despite their environments and the pervasive attitudes of the dominant society. It seems that the major difference between these girls is their family circumstances. Selina, Sassafrass, Cypress, Indigo, and Betsey Brown have a well-defined family "culture" and structure, despite the conflicts within them. Their environments are not so overwhelming that they have to relinquish control over them, consequently they derive, from them, positive self-concepts.

V

JOURNEYS TO SELFHOOD
AFRICAN WEST INDIAN FEMALE INITIATION

You are lucky, Beka. You are being given advantages most [young] people
in this country far smarter than you are not going to get. Therefore, you
have an obligation to serve, a responsibility to produce under the most
adverse circumstances. You must go as far as the limitations of your life
will allow. Find a way to do what you can, even though things seem to
be crashing all around you. Sometimes they are not breaking down at all,
sometimes things are taking a different shape. Try to recognize the pattern
even if it is one you don't like, then maybe you can do something about it.
    Zee Edgell, *Beka Lamb*

A study of West Indian culture and literature reveals that women
play a dominant role in that society, and perhaps for that reason
West Indian literature abounds with unforgettable female characters, even though very few of the early novels were about young girls
or about girls growing up. Claude McKay is credited with creating
the first recognizable West Indian heroine in Bita Plant. Women in
the literature of the West Indies are multifaceted, and their stories
make for fascinating reading. Often they are portrayed as strong, in-
domitable, verbose, and fiercely loyal to their children and their men.
Sometimes they are the butt of sexual ribaldry, as evidenced in the
oral literature of the calypso.[1] The physical appearance and lifestyle
of the young West Indian woman have always been of primary interest to the calypsonian, although since few females are calypsonians
themselves the story line again is always male engendered. Hence, as
with early African American writing, it is mainly through the eyes

---

1. In the folk tradition of the Caribbean, a calypso is a song based on a local
event or person. Calypsos are often satiric or bawdy and can involve very sensitive
and personal subjects.

of the male creative artist that the West Indian woman has been portrayed. Some of these creations are stereotypes, and some are romantic versions, but few describe bona fide recognizable women. This has only happened with the writers since the late 1950s and 1960s. The West Indies has also had its equivalent of "mammies," Sapphires, and "madonnas." There are a few notable women's slave narratives, and they show us another face of the West Indian woman. The best known is *The History of Mary Prince: A West Indian Slave, Related by Herself*.[2]

Caribbean writers of fiction wrote primarily "novels of manners" during the first half of the twentieth century.[3] However, by the 1950s, having firmly established a milieu for their prose fiction, Caribbean writers were ready to devote whole novels to the celebration of childhood. As West Indian literary scholar Michael Gilkes notes, "It is the world of childhood that returns to the freshest images of the most deeply imprinted experience of a native landscape of sensibility." While Louis James has heralded the movement as "a sad initiation," the West Indian bildungsroman carries on the canon established in the nineteenth and early twentieth centuries by British, American, and African American writers.[4]

The West Indian novelists' nostalgia for childhood takes on an extra dimension when we note that they are often displaced from their places of birth in order to pursue a writing career. A good number of writers have explored the varieties of education open to

2. Moira Ferguson, ed. *The History of Mary Prince: A West Indian Slave, Related by Herself*. First published in 1831, this is the oldest known female slave narrative, predating *Incidents in the Life of a Slave Girl* (1859). Prince was the first Black British woman to escape from slavery and publish a record of her experience. The narrative recalls her life as a slave in Bermuda, Antigua, and the Turks and Caicos Islands. She escaped in London in 1828. Also interesting is Mary Seacole's *The Wonderful Adventures of Mrs. Seacole in Many Lands* (1858), which utilizes diary, memoir, travelogue, and other journalistic styles to create an "autobiography." Mrs. Seacole, a very unusual creole woman, seems to have been conscious of "voice," reader, her time, and the immortality of texts. Her work is also one of the first important histories written by a Caribbean-born woman.

3. The phrase *novel of manners* is being used here to suggest a prescribed model used by eighteenth- and nineteenth-century British authors. Most students were British-educated in the English-speaking Caribbean system and had become accustomed to its labels. Almost all school materials were sent from England in the form of readers, as well as fiction, poetry, essays, drama, and annual exams.

4. Gilkes, *The West Indian Novel*, 116.

the West Indian in traditional forms of the bildungsroman. Outside the British sphere of influence, Joseph Zobel's *La Rue cases nègres* (1950), a novel set in Martinique, depicts the struggle of a village boy to succeed once he wins a scholarship to attend high school in the city, is, technically, the first West Indian bildungsroman. However, since it was first published in French, Zobel's novel has been unavailable to most English-speaking West Indians until its translation into English as *Black Shack Alley* in 1980. *A Brighter Sun* (1952), written by Samuel Selvon of Trinidad, deserves citation as the first West Indian bildungsroman in English, with full-scale treatment of the growing-up process in the West Indies.

The most significant type of bildungsroman written between 1950 and 1980 is the one in which the young protagonist is poised on the verge of departure from the native soil; George Lamming's *In the Castle of My Skin* stands out as a prime example of the form. Other important bildungsromane of that period, in addition to those previously noted, are Jan Carew's *Black Midas,* Peter Kempadoo's *Guyana Boy,* and Ian McDonald's *The Hummingbird Tree,* all by male authors.

Dominica's Jean Rhys wrote a now well known novel, *Wide Sargasso Sea* (1966), which explores the neurosis of identity and creole status of its antagonist, Annette Bertha Cosway. Despite the Caribbean setting and the writer's nativity, neither she nor the book has been grouped under the West Indian canon, either because Rhys is White or because of the subject matter. The book has been acknowledged to be about the "prelife" of the wife of Mr. Rochester in Emily Brontë's *Jane Eyre,* who goes mad during the course of that novel. In her novel, Rhys suggests how Annette got to England, what kind of life she led, and the nature of the victimization she suffered. Besides Rhys's White heritage, her landscapes are almost always European, which helps to explain her designation as a non–West Indian writer. Unlike Paule Marshall, who is accepted by most West Indians, Rhys is recognized in the West Indies primarily for a few short stories, a novel, and her unfinished autobiography, *Smile Please.*

Some female characters were created by White male writers in the early part of the twentieth century, but often they were paper heroines and quite unrealistic. Examples occur in Herbert De Lisser's *Jane's Career* and *Susan Proudleigh* and Tom Redcam's *One*

Brown Girl and . . . A Jamaican Story. Their young female protagonists seem to be modeled after the British romantic tradition of the
displaced swooning woman at the mercy of the city or a cruel situation, or the tragic mullata created by African American male writers
in the late nineteenth and early twentieth centuries—William Wells
Brown's *Clothel* (1853) comes to mind. C. L. R. James, a Black West
Indian scholar and writer from Trinidad, noted, "The most appropriate definition and assessment for me and [one] which obviously
serves my interest is writing about childhood."[5] He does this very
well in *Minty Alley,* in which he began the unfolding of the positive
mother images that came later in works such as *In the Castle of My
Skin* and Jamaica Kincaid's *Annie John.*

Although Claude McKay's *Banana Bottom* was published in 1933,
it bears consideration because of McKay's interest in exploring personal roots in order to declare identity, as well as the effect of a
colonial culture on a character's growth. When Merle Hodge's 1970
novel, *Crick Crack, Monkey,* is seen in the context of McKay's work,
it becomes richer and more substantive because of the many issues
McKay does not raise. Trinidadian writer George Lamming's fourth
novel, *Season of Adventure,* focuses on Fola, an intelligent and privileged girl who witnesses a ceremony of souls at the "tonelle" and
begins a backward glance into her origins. That event actually marks
her initiation. Like *In the Castle of My Skin, Season of Adventure* has
many of the elements of a bildungsroman and also contains a wealth
of African Caribbean political messages and implications, something
not seen in novels by White West Indian writers. Fola and Bita, the
protagonist in *Banana Bottom,* are strong heroines and provide an
interesting contrast with other protagonists created by West Indian
women. Their actions and initiations also differ from those of their
African American sisters.

■   ■

Bita in *Banana Bottom* and Tee in *Crick Crack, Monkey* are from
two different West Indian environments. Born into culturally and
materially impoverished worlds, they are given the opportunity ei-

5. From a lecture given by C. L. R. James at Indiana University, Bloomington,
fall 1978.

ther to leave the stultifying confines of their society or to seek a viable means of escape from unacceptable personal situations.

Claude McKay's novel was published more than two decades after the author had left his native Jamaica for the United States. This fact perhaps accounts for the somewhat romantic treatment of the female characters who people this work, although Bita is not the first Black West Indian woman in a West Indian novel. She is the daughter of a fairly wealthy farmer, Jordan Plant, of the mountain village of Banana Bottom. The place name here is also ironic. Bita's mother dies in childbirth, and she is brought up by her aunt Naomi, who marries Jordan. When Bita is twelve years old, she has her first sexual experience. She is raped by the village musician, a supposed "harmless" idiot, who often played with Bita by the riverside. The setting is idyllic, and Bita is drawn like a natural creature "creeping upon her hands and feet up the slope to him" (35); he is involuntarily possessed and seduced by her. This notion of both being enchanted— she by him and his music, he by her female sensuality—is a bit unrealistic. This incident establishes, however, Bita's natural connection with the Banana Bottom world, and it also precipitates a change in Bita's life. Because of the setting and era of this story, the idea of rape is not developed. Although this is the first time that this issue is addressed in a West Indian novel, what its treatment indicates about the culture and about the place of women in that culture is bothersome for contemporary readers. Other, later women writers have more openly treated the subjects of abuse and the powerlessness of women.

A villager, Phibby Patroll, reveals Bita's experience to the Reverend and Mrs. Craig, the English minister and his wife who are her benefactors. Acting on their missionary impulses, they adopt Bita and send her to a boarding school in England for seven years. At the end of her studies she returns to her small village in Jamaica. The reader is not told much about the educative process in Europe but is made to feel that it was in the long run a "good thing" for her. It is with Bita's return home that her second journey begins. "Bita's homecoming was an eventful week for folk of the tiny country town of Jubilee and the mountain village of Banana Bottom. For she was the only native girl they had ever known or heard of who had been brought up abroad. Perhaps the only one in the island."[6] Prior to the 1950s, not many West Indian girls got the opportunity to be educated abroad; those who did were usually the mulatto descendants of former slave masters. After emancipation, some mulattoes who had succeeded to the estates of their parents sent their children abroad to be educated.

In colloquial language, Bita is called a "been to"; she has traveled to England, to the cosmopolitan city, but, much to the consternation of Mrs. Craig, Bita's seven years abroad seem to have aroused her curiosity in the rich folk culture of her childhood. This curiosity is further reinforced by Squire Gensir, a White creole anthropologist, who also finds the island's rich culture unique and satisfying. He has decided never to return to England, which cannot provide the joy and celebration of life he finds in Banana Bottom. Bita has many conversations with him, gaining further motivation to pursue her background and its history and culture. She now wishes to become immersed in all the local experiences. Although as a young girl she had frequented the local market with the Craigs' maid, Rosyanna, for the first time Bita is conscious of the spirit of this unique place with its rich dialect patterns, musical speech cadences, coarse humor, the odor of tropical fruit, and the jostling of buyers and sellers. She is aware of a kinship with the people and with the sounds and scents of the marketplace. With the realization of these feelings, she acknowledges that this new awareness of the environment is a result of her having resided for seven years in an alien land whose culture never really touched her soul. She grew up, after all, in Banana Bottom and not in England, yet the expatriate experience has given her the distance she needed to understand and appreciate as well as experience the local life: "Bita mingled in the crowd, responsive to the feelings, the color, the smell, the swell and press of it. It gave her the sensation of a reservoir of familiar kindred humanity into which she had descended for Baptism. She had never had that big moving feeling as a girl" (40).

But this is only the beginning of the baptismal experience, which is to further include the joy and excitement of eating "pure native cooking" (53), of surreptitiously attending a tea meeting, of swimming

6. *Banana Bottom,* 1. Further references to this work will be made parenthetically in the text.

in the nude in her favorite childhood swimming hole, and finally of allowing herself to be drawn into the communal spirit of an erotic dance:

> The scene was terrible but attracting and moving like a realistic creation of some of the most wonderful of the Anancy tales with which her father delighted and frightened her when she was a child. Magnetized by the spell of it, Bita was drawn nearer and nearer into the inner circle until with a shriek she fell down. (250)

This passage suggests a comparison to the declaration in the closing sentences of Neville Dawes's *The Last Enchantment:* "I was a god again, drunk on the mead of the land, and massive with the sun chanting in my veins. And so, flooded with the bright clarity of my acceptance, I held this lovely wayward island, starkly, in my arms."[7]

Throughout McKay's novel, Bita Plant is linked with nature, not only in the developing consciousness of her own sexuality but also in her love for Banana Bottom, the land, and its people who live close to nature. Bita's return to the folk is confirmed when she witnesses a religious ceremony held by a drumming cult during a period of drought: "A mighty shout went up and the leading woman shot out prancing around Bita with uplifted twirling supple-jack, but a man rushed in and snatched her away before she could strike" (250).

Bita's increasing sense of her rootedness in the Banana Bottom community is reflected in her deliberate flouting of Mrs. Craig's good wishes and plans for her. A climax of a kind is reached when the two women clash over an ordinary villager, Hopping Dick, who comes to the mission to escort Bita to a dance. Mrs. Craig wants to know if Bita loves Dick. Bita says that she could love him, much to the dismay of Mrs. Craig.

> "A low peacock," said Mrs. Craig, "who murders his h's and altogether speaks in such a vile manner—and you an educated girl—highly educated."
> "My parents also speak broken English," said Bita. (210)

7. Dawes, *The Last Enchantment,* 288.

Moving from this show of antagonism between the two women, and with the weight of similar demonstrations in earlier episodes behind him, McKay enters the consciousness of Bita:

> Bita was certain that the time had arrived for her to face the fact of leaving Jubilee. It would be impossible for her to stay when she felt not only resentment . . . because it was to Mrs. Craig, a woman whose attitude to life was alien to her, and not to her parents, she owed the entire shaping of her career. . . . Mrs. Craig had never referred to it directly before that unhappy day. There had always been something about the woman proclaiming: you are my pet experiment! (211)

Even before her complete break with the Craigs, Bita begins to come to terms with her own sexuality. At the childhood swimming hole she consciously enjoys her naked swim in the pond and is not angry afterward when she discovers that her clothes have been taken by someone. She is, however, justifiably angry when she finds that it is Tack Tally who has taken her clothes and is peering at her. Yet what is memorable about this scene is Bita's awareness and ease with her body, which is so closely associated with nature—as the ferns and the mangrove bushes surround her. Of much more significance is Bita's reaction after being called "nuttin' more'n a nigger gal" (262) by a mulatto aristocrat as he threatens to rape her. She hollers back at him, "but this is a different black girl, you disgusting polecat" (262). The silence and acceptance she exhibited in earlier years have been replaced by femaleness, spiritedness, defiance, and a sense of what is right or wrong for her.

Every point of Bita's awareness and acceptance of her blackness and her sexuality is expressed in nature imagery. Finally, Bita's acceptance of Jubban as lover and husband is simple, natural, and appropriate since Jubban as a Black peasant is intimately associated with natural things. In her gravitation to an earthy man she anticipates Zora Neale Hurston's Janie Crawford in *Their Eyes Were Watching God*. Both break the stereotype of the Black heroine as "mammy" and "mule." Bita, like Janie, is coming to terms with who she is and what she wants. Both are symbols of "self-affirmation and independence, combining richness of metaphor, the humanizing of nature's elements, the celebration of Black culture . . . the depiction of a positive heroine."[8] Their second initiations to their indigenous roots seem to be the natural and real.

Although Bita Plant is older than some of the other protagonists of the bildungsromane in this study, her initiation is important within the framework of her total development. It can be seen in three phases. The first phase, which takes place in the West Indies, is the negative and painful sexual encounter of rape and the loss of her parents. The second is the initiation into the new and foreign culture of England, synonymous with exile or isolation. The third is her return and integration back into her native culture. Some Blacks, like Bita, are forced to function and form images of themselves under the influence of a White society, consequently they often must incorporate what is of value to them in White Western culture into their Black consciousness. For Bita, it is a question of integrating her origins, female and gender concerns, and Black pride with her White education.

■   ■

Whereas McKay depicts a quasi-perceivable heroine in her cultural initiatory process, Barbadian George Lamming gives us a new type of woman never before seen in West Indian literature. Like Bita Plant, Fola in *Season of Adventure* is older than some of the female protagonists of the African American writers, and she strides through the pages taking on all kinds of institutions—political, cultural, familial, parental, and, most important, her relationship to the colonial system and the Motherland, Africa.

The African presence in Lamming's fiction must be seen in the context of the distinctive relation of his ideas between personal and political, and more specifically in the context of the problematic role of the creative imagination in West Indian society as it is first visualized in *In the Castle of My Skin* but most fully treated in *Season of Adventure*. That this novel was published at the beginning of the movements for Black consciousness and Caribbean independence is significant.

8. Russell, *Render Me My Song*, 41.

It should already be clear that Lamming's purpose goes beyond a mere satirizing of the middle-class West Indian condition. He neither sentimentalizes the peasants nor invokes Africa as a convenient fetish, explicit both in the details of his presentation of a voodoo ceremony and in the use to which he puts this ceremony in *Season of Adventure*.[9] But before focusing on this key element it is necessary to give the frame of *Season of Adventure*.

If the previous novels in this study provided us with unusual characterizations, style, and structure, then Lamming's novel provides new content. *Season of Adventure* is unique in the genre of the bildungsroman because of its focus on Fola as a political activist. An examination of both its content and its form will help in understanding the re-created role that the female bildungsroman seeks to fulfill.

The central character is Fola Piggott, an educated West Indian girl who visits a voodoo ceremony in the slum section of her island and finds herself participating in the rites. "Part product of that world, living still under the shadow of its past disfigurement, all her emotions had sprung from a nervous caution to accept it as her root, her natural gift of legacies. Fear was the honest and ignorant instinct she had felt in the tonelle."[10] The visit to the tonelle arouses Fola to a consciousness of the incompleteness in her life and sets

9. A ceremony described in George Lamming's *The Pleasures of Exile* would appear to be the basis of the ceremony in the novel: "in the republic of Haiti . . . a native religion sometimes forces the official law to negotiate with peasants who have retained a racial and historic desire to worship their original gods. We do not have to share their faith in order to see the universal significance of certain themes implicit in the particular ceremony of the Souls. The celebrants are mainly relatives of the deceased who, ever since their death, have been locked in water. It is the duty of the Dead to return and offer on this momentous night, a full and honest report on their past relations with the living. . . . It is the duty of the Dead to speak, since their release from that purgatory of Water cannot be realized until they have fulfilled the contract which this ceremony symbolizes. The Dead need to speak if they are going to enter that eternity which will be their last and permanent future. The living demand to hear whether there is any need for forgiveness, for redemption, different as they may be in their present state of existence, those alive and those now Dead—their ambitions point to a similar end. They are interested in their Future" (9–10).

10. *Season of Adventure*, 221. Further references to this work will be made parenthetically in the text.

her off on a single-minded and, at times, cruel search into her origins, both personal (she has known only her stepfather, Piggott) and racial (her mother, Agnes, is uncertain whether Fola's father is European or Black). Lamming explores Fola's crisis through several sets of relationships in the novel: with Agnes, whose secrecy Fola interprets as guilt and whose sexual attractiveness Fola harshly condemns as vulgarity and cheapness; with Piggott, whose physical sterility tightens the affection he feels for his stepdaughter and who becomes a destructive beast when she begins to slip away from him and the privileged world in which he has sought to capture her; and with Charlot, the European teacher who instructs her in history, and who in a strange mood of self-contempt and unconscious superiority takes his pupil/mistress to witness the voodoo ceremony. Lamming also presents the development of Fola's relationship with the peasant world in a way similar to McKay's presentation of Bita's development in *Banana Bottom*. He does this through Fola's involvements with Chiki, an artist full of compassion, but troubled in his own right by an apparent drying up of inspiration, and with Powell, the political fanatic who finally makes an uncompromising and murderous assault upon her because he thinks it impossible and too late for people of her "type" to break with their traditional attitudes to the Black masses.

Each of these relationships is presented with such realistic particularity as to become absorbing in itself rather than as a segment of Fola's complex problem of adjustment. Furthermore, each relationship carries a symbolic burden that Lamming wants us to respond to as intensely as we do to the literal situation. Agnes is not only a secretive mother unable to communicate with an impatient rebellious daughter, she is, like the islands, both "the willing prostitute of the ages" and the passive victim of a rapacious history, waiting, like the islands, to be made respectable to those she has nourished. And Powell is as much an embittered individual as the extreme, somehow subtle spirit of Black Power repudiating a class whose capacity to betray it has experienced only too often:

"What I do I do alone," said Powell, "no help from you an' your lot, 'cause I learn, I learn how any playing 'bout with your lot bound to end. You know the rules too good, an' it too late, it too late for me to learn what rules you have for murderin' me. So is me go murder first. Otherwise is you what will murder me, or make me murder myself." (328)

The reader has to become accustomed to responding at the same time to the fullness of each relationship and to its being part of a larger web, to its realistic particularity and its symbolic representativeness. A further source of difficulty is that although Fola is given the most exposure in the novel, each of the other characters (whether Belinda the prostitute or Piggott, one of the new exploiters of the people) becomes a center of interest.

The author's compassion for his characters in the toils of a pressing set of social and political circumstances never permits the reader to rest on a selective principle in the way it is possible to rest with one character in V. S. Naipaul's *A House for Mr. Biswas,* for example. In an "Author's Note" at the end of chapter 14 of *Season of Adventure,* Lamming says: "Powell still resides somewhere in my heart, with a dubious love, some strange nameless shadow of regret; and yet with the deepest, deepest nostalgia. For I have never felt myself to be an honest part of anything since the world of his childhood deserted me" (332). This autobiographical strain, although not operating as explicitly as in the case of Powell, gives intensity to the presentation of yet another character—Chiki, the painter with four works behind him but now suffering a block to his creativity, as the confusing implications of his double cultural heritage begin to work themselves out in his consciousness. The reader approaching *Season of Adventure* with set principles about what the art of the novel is, or ought to be, will find many of the work's best effects achieved at times when those principles are most blatantly flouted.

Fola's process of self-discovery, which begins with her experience at the voodoo ceremony, thus takes place in a difficult and ambitiously crowded novel. The process is at once an example of "every man's backward glance" and a representation of the middle-class West Indian's relationship to the peasantry. The social cleavage with which Lamming begins is best expressed in the conversation between Crim and Powell, two Drum Boys who notice Fola in the crowd at the tonelle during the meeting:

"Is what my eyes seein'?" Powell said. "Over there, first row." They both looked at the girl whose elegance was no less conspicuous than the solitary white face beside her.

"Look at her good," said Powell, "education an' class just twist that girl mouth right out o' shape. Like all the rest she learn fast how to talk two ways."

Crim couldn't resist admiring the novelty which her presence had created in the tonelle. (21)

The tonelle, where the West African serpent cult has persisted, though undergoing change over three hundred years, is a stark reminder of Africa and the slave migration. In exploring Fola's attitude to the tonelle, Lamming is also writing about the West Indian Black's attitude to Africa. This becomes obvious in the novel when Fola, after her "awakening" experiences at the ceremony, suddenly realizes why her visit to the tonelle is more problematic than the visit of American tourists to European monuments. Lamming presents the middle-class West Indian's denial of the masses and his shame of Africa as obstacles to the fulfillment of the person, and the unauthentic existence of the unfulfilled person as a kind of death. Fola is imagined as a dead person, and the creative task of the novel is to probe this condition and to explore the problems and possibilities of rebirth.

The ceremony for the resurrection of the dead is projected both as a symbolic occasion and as an actual experience shocking Fola into her journey of self-discovery. Lamming insinuates the idea of Fola's "hidden parallel of feeling" with the "coarse exuberant faces" at the tonelle through the European's words. Charlot makes the observation that Fola responds to rhythm like the worshipers:

"You couldn't do your dancing without those women. It's from being so near to them that you have learnt how to move your body."
. . . "Near?" she said subtly.
"In feeling you are" said Charlot, "you can deny them anything except the way you feel when the same rhythm holds you." (28)

At this point the writer has to create, in the reader, an expectation that something is about to happen to Fola, and that the something has to do with a special relationship that exists between Fola and the cultists, but not between the cultists and Charlot. At the same time, the specialness of Fola's relationship with the cultists must not preclude the possibility of a more remote but equally valid kinship between the cultists and Charlot. By associating the voodoo drums with the more familiar and persuasive music of the steel band, Lamming gives an air of truth to Charlot's initial observation. If Charlot's insistence upon his lack of affinity with the cultists strikes the reader as too glib, however, Fola's strenuous denials only serve to confirm that she is aware of more than she cares to admit.

The detailed and spectacular ceremony described in *Season of Adventure* is subservient to a process of dissolution in the observing character. The episode is divided into omniscient authorial description of the ceremony, subjective impressions from Charlot and Fola, snatches of conversation between Crim and Powell, and a continuing argument between Fola and Charlot. Expectations are early set up with regard to Fola, and because each return to her consciousness finds her closer to a crisis of "conversion," each retreat to another perspective becomes charged either with suspense or with its indirect bearing on her subjective state. "The atmosphere of the tonelle had increased in its effect upon her. There was something intimidating about the women. The dance had become more feverish. Fola recognised what they were doing, but there was too much tension in their bodies" (24–25).

In *Season of Adventure,* the view of the dark continent is located in a character who is to be disburdened; the sensational aspects of the ceremony are used as a corrosive force, mesmerizing Fola into participating in the rites at the tonelle. Lamming does not try to present Fola's actions as arising from anything more than fear, shock, and a confusion of the senses. Fola does not come to share the faith of the cultists. But when she later reflects on her experience, she recognizes that her fear and ignorance in the tonelle are closely related to her revulsion for the peasant masses. From this point, she starts to free herself from shame, seeking desperately to add to the known "Fola" the "other than Fola" that her education and privileged upbringing have conspired to bury.

Since the ceremony is one for the resurrection of the dead, it lends itself symbolically: the "dead" Fola finds the opportunity to break out of her purgatory and hope for a new future. Expanding in her season of adventure, Fola sees the privileged families of the republic as forever locked in water, "decrepit skeletons near Federal Drive polluting the live air with their corpse breathing" (253). But while Lamming uses the cult and the cultists to image lost meanings and to shock Fola into "her season of adventure," he deliberately refuses to take a sentimental view of the tonelle. At the end of the novel, the meeting place is destroyed by fire, and the *houngan,* the ceremonial leader, has lost command of it and self.

This novel cannot be discussed without considering the mother's role in Fola's life. Agnes, Fola's mother, is of the privileged mulatto middle class in the West Indies, which Zora Neale Hurston describes with emphasis:

> The upper class women in the Caribbean have an assurance that no woman in the United States possesses. The men of her class are going to marry inside their class. They will have their love affairs and their families whenever they will or may. But seldom does one contract a marriage outside his class. Here in the United States, a man is liable to marry when he falls in love. The two things are tied together in his mind. But in the Caribbean it is different. Love and marriage need not be related at all. What is shocking to an American mind is that the man has no obligation to a girl outside of his class. She has no rights which he is bound to respect. What is worse, the community would be shocked if he did respect them. Fatherhood gives no upper class man the license to trample down conventions and crash lines, nor shades-of-color lines, by marrying outside his class.[11]

In the West Indies, despite a mixed heredity, it is one's class that confers distinct social advantages or disadvantages. Fola, unlike her mother, does not know her paternal parentage; neither does it seem important to know it early in the novel. One is led to believe that the mother purposely hides this crucial information from her daughter. At age seven, when Fola contemplates her childhood, and looks at her light-skinned mother, she has memories of a fat white rat attacking her throat and images of an old Black woman, whom she thinks may be her grandmother. She learns that when Agnes became pregnant

11. *Tell My Horse,* 75–76.

she was put out of the house by her mother. These facts, flashbacks, and images provide the reader with enough information to try to resolve the puzzle, so reader and protagonist begin the search together. The mother–daughter relationship therefore hinges on the effort to identify Fola's heritage. Although the absence of fathers does not seem to harm or cripple G and Francis in the previously discussed novels, "in Fola's world, however, to be 'normal' is to have a father as well as a mother; children born 'without fathers' are 'bastards,' and unmanned women who have children are 'whores.'" It is not clear why this is important to Fola because the literature of the West Indies has shown that men are conspicuously absent from the lives of most women and children. But as Leota Lawrence further suggests, "theirs can be considered to be a problem of the Middle Class West Indian."[12]

Agnes's function in Fola's life is nebulous. As was the case with Silla and Selina in *Brown Girl, Brownstones,* they are so similar that they alienate each other. Fola distrusts and hates Agnes because as a mother she denies her the one thing that is all important for her to function fully—a father. She thought "her mother was a whore, a whore, nothing but a whore. . . . condemned to this woman by the fact of birth, she felt entirely severed from her, by the meaning of her past. Fola would see no point of contact between the nature of a whore, and the accident which had entitled this woman to call herself a mother . . . she thought of Agnes simply as that woman" (153).

The harsh feeling toward "that woman," however, is momentary, as the reader discovers the reason for the mystery or silence about Fola's father. Agnes, as a young woman, was raped twice in the same day, by a White man, the Bishop's son, and a Black man; in essence, neither woman knows who Fola's father is. "And so Fola became that beauty and cherished burden which Agnes has always borne! Fola, now fugitive as the double fatherhood, no certainty can separate. . . . And Agnes reflects that her conscience is clean. Only justice can say what happened that afternoon" (343).

When the novel ends one possible father is Chiki's older brother, who had left for the United States. Therefore, the answers or solutions for both women are not available. Agnes, by denying Fola a "real" father and providing a substitute father in Piggott, carries on

12. "Mother–Child Relationships," 14.

the West Indian tradition that despite one's paternity life goes on and we do the best we can. Studies of West Indian family life continue to tell us that fathers are not truly important to a child's development; in this respect, Fola should bear no scars by not having this missing male family member. It is Agnes, however, whom Fola wishes for at a crucial point in her search when she adopts the culture's custom. "She had no other prayer but to be with Agnes. She wanted to coil herself to an infant's size, and nestle calm and forgetful in her mother's arms. . . . She was whispering through a salt, white froth of spit and tears: 'Aggie . . . Aggie . . . Aggie . . .'" (282). This scene, similar to that between Silla and Selina in *Brown Girl* upon realizing their special "love," demonstrates the close mother–daughter bond that exists despite anger, rebellion, and perhaps hate. It is not only mothers and daughters, however, who do this; it is also mothers and sons. Consider the floggings given to G by his mother and the untouched, priceless closeness between them. It must be understood, also, that dislike seems a lot more frequent in these novels with female–female relationships at their core.

While Fola's "season of adventure" and knowledge of her true self *begin* at the ceremony of the souls, Bita's mesmerization occurs at the end of her particular process of discovering her true being and cultural connections. Fola is involved in a process of self-discovery, but with McKay's heroine, it is possible to see more clearly, by comparison, a process of self-assertion.

■   ■

The year 1970 was an important marker for the West Indian woman's bildungsroman. That year Trinidadian author Merle Hodge published her first novel, *Crick Crack, Monkey,* a work that explored issues not dealt with in prior works by male or female Caribbean authors. She highlighted such issues as economic class consciousness within the Black community, new postcolonial idiosyncracies, extensions of the meaning of family and mothering, family crises, estrangement, orphaned children, the joy of folk culture and manners, and the Black girl's relationship to this world.

Hodge's *Crick Crack, Monkey* came eleven years after Paule Marshall's *Brown Girl, Brownstones* and seventeen years after White

Caribbean writer Phyllis Alfrey's *The Orchid House;* all three works have distinctive character portrayals and themes. George Lamming in his novel *Season of Adventure* created a special kind of West Indian heroine in Fola Piggott, but it is Tee Davis whose voice is newest, freshest, and easiest to comprehend as she takes us through the early years of her life. This novel, like many other bildungsromane, is a veiled autobiography, and at times the author, Hodge, steps outside Tee's narrative to comment on an experience or scene. This stylistic device is used so cleverly that the reader is forced to return to the action before and after these passages to see, if indeed, this narration is first person rather than third. In a scene with Tee and her grandmother in which the narrator, Tee, speaks directly to us, the sentences quickly change: "But Tee was growing into her grandmother again, her spirit was in me. They'd never bent down her spirit and she would come back and come back and come back; if only she could live to see Tee grow into her tall straight grandmother."[13] Here the inner stream of narration blends with the outer *expected* voice, to create a new way of telling.

The reader meets Cynthia Davis, who is fondly called Tee by her Aunt Tantie and is alternately called Cynthia or Cynthie by others at different times. Tee is significantly younger than the other protagonists in this study—perhaps six years old. Since Hodge's biography does parallel the story, there is validity, authority, and believability as the experiences unfold; at the same time, she also manages stylistically to make us feel that this is a fictive work. In contrast to Michael Anthony's *The Year in San Fernando,* Hodge makes us hear Tee and those around her through the use of appropriate dialogue in the Trinidadian patois of her Aunt Tantie's community, as well as the more proper English of her Aunt Beatrice and the "better off" rising Black middle class.

Tee's world is vast because it is made up of several communities, and all of them raise her, teach her, nurture her, and awaken her to the idyllic and the real in the village and country. In a way she is blessed even more than the sheltered, protected Annie John in Kincaid's work of the same name. The first community that affects

13. *Crick Crack, Monkey,* 19. Further references to this work will be made parenthetically in the text.

her life is that of her Aunt Tantie, where Tee and her younger brother, Toddan, have resided since her mother's death in childbirth and her father's subsequent emigration to England. Each day for Tee in this household is "loud and hilarious and the intermittent squawk and flurry of mirth made me think of the fowl-run" (4). Noisy, childless, husbandless, earthy Tantie is also raising another child—a relative, Mikey, who also plays a significant role not only in the younger children's lives but for Tantie as well. It is Tantie and Mikey and Toddan who make up Tee's first family. Tee tells us: "Then Papa went to *sea*. I concluded that what he had gone to *see* was whether he could find my Mammy and the baby" (3). This allusion establishes not only the child's acceptance of the spoken word/sound/meaning of "sea/see," but also a complete trust and belief in the adults around her.

Mikey's world is extremely important in this novel because of the roles of Black men in West Indian society and in the lives of their women and the ways in which they are portrayed in the early bildungsromane. Mikey's presence in the children's lives is one of the more positive depictions of Black men in Black women's contemporary fiction. Hodge's Mikey, like Paule Marshall's Deighton in *Brown Girl,* is a very likable, nonexploitative character. We are made to believe that the reason this eighteen year old "hangs out" instead of working is that the economic conditions are so poor in Carioca, and his education so inadequate, that he cannot find regular or respectable work. The "older" Mikey is a partner and caretaker of the children and Tantie. Tee and Toddan obey him and are silent about his not so circumspect behavior at times, as well as his friendships. He exposes them to another facet of life that exists in their town—a place and community where he is comfortable and respected as an "almos' man."

> Life was wonderful when he was out of a job, and in a good mood, which was less predictable. There were days when we would be as quiet as mice from morning till night, or kept out of his range altogether. But we would rather die than report to Tantie that he had delivered one of us a sound back-hand slap for vexing him. The rest of the time we were strutting in his shadow, off to raid the Estate or down to the Savannah to fly our kites that he made us. . . .

Often we went down with him to the steelband shed where Santa Clara Syncos practiced, and sometimes he beat a second-pan. At the shed there was usually a fringe of children hanging about, and they let us shake the chac-chac; there were some little boys who were regular pan-men and who even got to beat a pan on the road at Carnival. . . .

Mikey took us down to the bridge from time to time, always reminding us in no uncertain terms before we set out of what would befall us at his hands if we breathed a word to Tantie for he wasn't having that settin'-hen takin a turn in his arse. . . .

Manhatt'n was an individual who at some obscure date had "gone away." . . . When the fellows were in a tolerant mood they would let Manhatt'n tell of his encounter with the sheriff in Dodge City and how he outdrew him; or of the blonde chick in Manhattan who wouldn't leave him alone, kept coming to his apartment when there was this red-head thing he was working at (Martinis, yer know, and a lil' caviar on the side). And when the fellows screamed with laughter Manhatt'n looked imbecilically happy. But when one day someone maliciously murmured "Crick-crack"! at the end of one of these accounts in perfect Western drawl, Manhatt'n in his rage forgot to screw his mouth to one side before starting to speak.

"Crick-crack yu mother! Is true whe ah tell yu—yu only blasted jealous it ain't you! Crick-crack! Ah go crick-crack yu stones gi' yu!" (5–7)

Through Mikey, Tee and Toddan experience other facets of the West Indian culture, as well as the West Indian fascination with "America." This is reminiscent of Lamming's Trumper and Boy Blue, as well as Clarke's Willy-Willy. From the reverse viewpoint, Selina in *Brown Girl, Brownstones* was enamored with her mother and father's discussions of youth in Barbados, as well as those lively stories of "back home," a place to which Selina eventually goes. Mikey's friends have names like Audie Murphy, Rock Hudson, and Gary Cooper and rename themselves after places like Manhattan and Texas. These scenes enlarge the children's world without them ever having to read a book or go to a movie.

The fact that Mikey also fights with a young man who made negative comments about his "Nennen"—grandmother/mother—is an important cultural marker. Within the Black culture one should never speak ill of the Black mother figure. The children will come to realize the importance of this event later. The importance of Mikey to Tantie as the husband /male figure in her life is evidenced when he tells her later in the novel that he has an opportunity to go abroad to perhaps better economic opportunities. She responds: "Yu ain't have twenty-one years yet. Is yesterday I put yu on mih back and bring yu here. And we come till we live like two man-rat in the same hole; but that ain' say yu have to pic up and go from me now before I even see you grow" (65). In a last effort to deter his decision to leave, Tantie says, "they dun much like black-people up-there yu know" (62). These scenes show this loyal, loving woman's anger, dismay, futility, and loss. Mikey does leave, and the household changes for everyone; one has a sense of Tantie's world getting smaller and crumbling.

Tee's grandmother, Ma, is the third community—one that, as with many children, is remembered fondly. Ma is "a strong bony woman who did not smile unnecessarily" (13). Each summer Tee goes to her grandmother's place in the country, the often idyllic place of many childhoods.

> Ma brought with her a wooden box and a stick. While we splashed about in the water she sat immobile and straight-backed on her box, her hands resting together on the stick which she held upright in front of her. When someone started to venture too far out she rapped sharply on the box with the stick. And when it was time to go she rapped again: "Awright. Come-out that water now!" . . .
> Ma's land was to us an enchanted country, dipping into valley after valley, hills thickly covered with every conceivable kind of foliage, cool green darknesses, sudden little streams that must surely have been squabbling past in the days when Brar Anancy and Brar Leopard and all the others roamed the earth outsmarting each other. . . .
> Ma had a spot in the market on Sunday mornings, and she spent a great part of the week stewing cashews, pommes-cythères, cerises, making guava-cheese and guava jelly, sugar-cake, nut-cake, bennay-balls, toolum, shaddock-peel candy, chilibibi. . . . On these days we hung slyly about the kitchen, if only to feed on the smells; we were never afforded the opportunity of gorging ourselves—we partook of these delicacies when Ma saw fit, and not when we desired. She was full of maxims for our edification, of which the most baffling and maddening was:

> > Who ask
> > don't get
> > Who don't ask
> > don't want
> > Who don't want
> > don't get

Who don't get
don't care

For her one of the cardinal sins of childhood was gluttony: 'Stuff yu guts today an' eat the stones of the wilderness tomorrow.' (Ma's sayings often began on a note of familiarity only to rise into an impressive incomprehensibility, or vice versa, as in 'Them that walketh in the paths of corruption will live to ketch dey arse.')
She was equal to all the vagaries of childhood. (14–15)

Before Ma dies, her wish is "to see Tee grow into her [Ma's] tall proud straight grandmother" (19); when she dies during Tee's absence, Ma leaves a wish for Tee to rename herself her great-grandmother's "true-true name," which she remembers as being "Euphemia or Euph-something" (19). Tee had learned from her much folk wisdom and had observed her speech, manner, and body language and the sounds like "cheups" with which she greeted the day and "expressed her essential attitude before the whole of existence" (16).

The other women's community in which Tee spends a significant part of her childhood is her Aunt Beatrice's home. Beatrice's and Tantie's frames of reference for child rearing and economic uplift seem worlds apart. The only thing they seem to share is their interest in Tee and Toddan's upbringing. Aunt B is referred to by Tantie as "The Bitch," while Aunt B to the children was "only a blurred distant lady in our memory, grew horns and a djablesse-face and a thousand attributes of female terrifyingness" (10). Tee's relationship with this aunt is unique. While Tantie is her father's sister, Aunt B is her mother's sister. This situation of having relatives from both sides of the family with concerns about and personal interest in the protagonist brings about conflict for the aunts and feelings of ambivalence for Tee. Although it seems that Tantie had original foster care of the two children, there are constant battles as to who is better fit to bring them up.

At Aunt B's middle-class home, in Pointe d' Espair, are three cousins—Jessica, Carol, and Bernadette. They become the major antagonists in Tee's life. It is there that Tee feels for the first time completely out of place after being in Tantie's care for so long. The cousins have their proper clothes, hair, friends, school, car, books, and boys. Also, within the household, Tee is called, formally, Cynthia, and Toddan, Codrington. Aunt B does not seem to be "loved" by anyone; her girls are openly hostile and rude to her, and her husband, Norman McNeil, has "retreated permanently . . . was either absent or unnoticeable." Aunt B, therefore, "had to resign herself to his abdication, even to be in favor of it" (82). At points during Tee's story one feels sorrow for this driven woman who tries so hard to be something "more"; although she succeeds economically and socially, she ends up alienating her family and others. "You see the family I got! Spend my life teaching my children to be decent, teaching them what is important and then they forget who it was that got them where they are" (92).

Aunt Beatrice points out to Tee all the things that would be proper and improper in a new class consciousness. Unacceptable are such things as "niggery-looking dresses"; weddings that are "coolie affair"; peppersauce, which is "nastiness"; annual carnivals, which are unmistakable "niggerness"; and the lowest personages of all, the "ordnry-market people" and "riff-raff." Acceptable are such things as dance classes, proper clothes, etiquette, good books, and good English—not the "bad English of Grenadians." Obviously this is quite overwhelming for Tee, so that even though "it was the first time in my life, too, that I was to sleep in a bed by myself" (72), she wishes to be rescued from all of this smothering and says: "Tantie had said that Aunt B had no right at all over me, for my father had sent a paper and they had been to court and any day I wanted to leave that bitch's house she couldn't stop me" (79).

She longs for the people of Tantie's community: Ling, the crooked shopkeeper; MR. Braithwaite, the "whitey-cockroach"; "Mrs. Hinds' high stiff bottom and spectacles and stockings"; Miss Terry hauling drunk Mr. Christopher home singing "Gimme piece o' you dumplin mae-dou-dou." She misses the nonsuffocating life of flying kites, fishing, and natural laughter.

Overcome with sorrow, Tee, like most protagonists at this stage, decides to seek shelter, to go underground or run away to sort things out. This she does, but it is only for a few hours, which she spends in a thicket of bushes contemplating, poignantly, her family origins— from her grandmother who was a market woman to Tantie and her father and mother—in order to come to some understanding of her situation, draw conclusions, or make changes. This also suggests the beginning of a sensitive, adolescent maturing. She learns through this contemplation that Aunt Beatrice is not really a bad person but is basically unhappy. B and Tee are left together quite a bit, and a special bond and relationship develops between them. "I must have forgotten that I was walking beside Auntie Beatrice but that could not have been. . . . Perhaps I had been walking straight *into the group*, and she had only wanted to draw me aside, *out of their way* . . . a ragged, dirtyish light. . . lay on her features, but I wished that it were pitch dark so that I would never have seen the devastation in her eyes and around her mouth" (93). This marks the beginning of a strong connection between these two; at this point one wonders which way Tee will go yet feels that a change is quite imminent. Tee adds: "Our camaraderie remained *almost* intact when the other three were about, but I knew that the air had changed. Everything seemed to be a different colour from before" (94).

There are many instances in the novel of development in which the protagonists feel pity or understanding for their well-meaning benefactors. Bita Plant felt some remorse for the Craigs who had made her "their Bita"; Fola, for her mother who could not explain the riddle of her fatherhood; Selina Boyce, for Silla "the mother"; and Francis, for bedridden Mrs. Chandles.

The fifth community in which Tee will spend much of her formative years is school or, broadly stated, the world of education. This takes up a significant portion of the novel, and at no time is this young girl allowed to forget school—the West Indian passport to success.

She attends three schools from the time we meet her to the novel's end. The first is the most personal, the school of Mr. and Mrs. Hinds in her town, with its two tables, one for boys and one for girls. Mr. Hinds is headmaster; Mrs. Hinds seems to spend most of her time knitting while the children memorize Little Boy Blue, Little Miss Muffet, and other stories from their readers. Mr. Hinds berates their inability to learn by calling them "little Black nincompoops" and "picaninnies," with his ever present ruler hitting knuckles for punishment. This is a school familiar to many West Indian children who never forget the intimacy of small classes, individual attention (no matter how alarming), wonderful friendships, and, quite possibly, strict teachers and cruel headmasters.

The second school Tee attends is Santa Clara Elementary, where Sir and his whip reign supreme, where even the young teacher Gloria wilts in his presence and looks "up at him as though he was the Governor" (45). Hodge's many vivid scenes of these days are full of humor and descriptively accurate. "He [Sir] sat in state upon a chair with his legs crossed and a tamarind whip resting delicately across his knees . . . , read us stories of exemplary children who quailed not at the call of duty and were loth to tell a lie . . . up and down the school Third Standard was viewed as a minor Valley of the Shadow" (46), while on the blackboard a permanent inscription reads: "The Disciple Is Not Greater Than The Master" (54).

When Tee wins a scholarship, she is quickly bailed out and sent to St. Ann School with Aunt Beatrice's three daughters. Not only is her education there more formal but she also realizes unquestionably that books can transport you abroad. It is here that many other changes take place for Tee. Helen, a student, becomes her model of ladyhood, and she fancies that "Helen was the Proper Me. And me, I was her shadow hovering about in incompleteness" (62).

Tee, after being in these various communities, again steps out of herself to try to establish some objectivity about her fate and place from this point on, but we also learn that she is quite distraught:

> I wanted to shrink, to disappear. Sometimes I thought I would gladly live under the back steps with Dash, rather than cross their paths all day long. I felt that the very sight of me was an affront to common decency. I wished that my body could shrivel up and fall away, that I could step out new and acceptable.
>   At times I resented Tantie bitterly for not having let Auntie Beatrice get us in the first place and bring us up properly. (97)

Feeling a sense of distance and separation because of the journey from Tantie's community to Aunt Beatrice's, a visit from Tantie with her native foods, talk, and laughter reminds Tee of her past and establishes what she *does not* want to be any more. Tantie is aware of the gulf between them and does not visit for long. "Everything was changing, unrecognizable, pushing me out, this was as it should be since I had moved up and no longer had any place here. But it was awful and I longed all the more to be on my way" (110–11). Tee will realize in retrospect, as Margaret Mead suggests in *Coming of Age in Samoa,* that preadolescent turmoil is less a function of biology and more one of culture.[14]

Crick Crack, Monkey is a sort of altered "great expectations" in that Tee's early development does not follow the usual structure with which readers would have been familiar prior to 1970. It does not fit the formula of the European bildungsroman, nor is it consonant with stereotypical roles in the African American or West Indian coming-of-age novels. Tee, like Selina in *Brown Girl, Brownstones,* however, has a multicultural experience in her aunts' two households, Mikey, Ma, and the various educational communities. So her wish to return to Tantie's home is a token of fear and insecurity. As her journey into adulthood continues, she will have benefited from all five communities and like, her sister protagonists, become more conscious of life's choices.

■   ■

Antiguan writer Jamaica Kincaid is one of the younger writers from the Caribbean. Through her wonderful and poetic novel *Annie John,* she has developed new techniques to explore the beauty of a specific West Indian girlhood. This story also has very close parallels with the author's life. In several interviews and talks, she has outlined her Antiguan childhood, her struggles with her mother, and her resolve to not return "home." Those struggles and ambivalent feelings are still with her.[15]

The main character in *Annie John* travels through her childhood essentially alone. Although surrounded by the lush, exotic world of the island of Antigua, Annie is isolated from all around her including her parents, most males, her schoolmates, and the culture of the island itself. Her rebellion and dissatisfaction eventually lead to her abandonment of her family and her desertion of the culture it includes.

It is only near the end of the novel that Annie gives us her biography, poignantly.

14. White, *Growing Up Female,* 10.
15. Jamaica Kincaid, address given at Multicultural Conference, Washington University, St. Louis, fall 1991.

If someone had asked me for a little summing up of my life at that moment as I lay in bed, I would have said, "My name is Annie John. I was born on the fifteenth of September, seventeen years ago, at Holberton Hospital, at five o'clock in the morning. At the time I was born, the moon was going down at one end of the sky and the sun was coming up at the other. My mother's name is Annie also. My father's name is Alexander, and he is thirty-five years older than my mother. Two of his children are four and six years older than she is. Looking at how sickly he has become and looking at the way my mother now has to run up and down for him, gathering the herbs and barks that he boils in water, which he drinks instead of the medicine the doctor has ordered for him, I plan not only never to marry an old man but certainly never to marry at all. The house we live in my father built with his own hands. The bed I am lying in my father built with his own hands. If I get up and sit on a chair, it is a chair my father built with his own hands. When my mother uses a large wooden spoon to stir the porridge we sometimes eat as part of our breakfast, it will be a spoon that my father has carved with his own hands. The sheets on my bed my mother made with her own hands. The curtains hanging at my window my mother made with her own hands. The nightie I am wearing, with scalloped neck and hem and sleeves, my mother made with her own hands. When I look at things in a certain way, I suppose I should say that the two of them made me with their own hands. For most of my life, when the three of us went anywhere together I stood between the two of them or sat between the two of them. But then I got too big, and there I was, shoulder to shoulder with them more or less, and it became not very comfortable to walk down the street together. And so now there they are together and here I am apart. I don't see them now the way I used to, and I don't love them now the way I used to. The bitter thing about it is that they are just the same and it is I who have changed, so all the things I used to be and all the things I used to feel are as false as the teeth in my father's head. Why, I wonder, didn't I see the hypocrite in my mother when, over the years, she said that she loved me and could hardly live without me, while at the same time proposing and arranging separation after separation, including this one, which, unbeknownst to her, *I* have arranged to be permanent? So now I, too, have hypocrisy, and breasts (small ones), and hair growing in the appropriate places, and sharp eyes, and I have made a vow never to be fooled again." (132–33)

The first and most important separation Annie feels is from her mother. Although the text is scattered with pleasant childhood memories, a deeper theme is Annie's hatred toward her mother, which begins during the summer of her twelfth year. It is the harsh reality of growing up that causes much of Annie's dislike for her mother. When her mother blatantly tells Annie that they cannot continue to dress alike, for "You are getting too old for that. It's time you had your own clothes. You just cannot go around the rest of your life looking like a little me,"[16] Annie is crushed. This conversation changes Annie's relationship with her mother. From this point on, her mother focuses on preparing her daughter to be a proper young lady who will carry on the traditions of wifehood and motherhood, lifestyles in which Annie has little interest. She says of her mother: "She said that she loved me and could hardly live without me, while at the same time proposing and arranging separation."

Annie, however, cherishes the "closeness" that she shared with her mother, the safety, warmth, and love that were present in their relationship. At the same time, she craves the intimacy that is shared by young girls of the same age and culture. This urge to seek out the company of peers instead of parents seems to be common to both American and West Indian girls. When young, friends are a source of entertainment, but with the approach of adolescence, they become an intimate part of the girls' lives. Young women's experiences are woven together at an early age, from the rituals of playing "house" to the wonderful discovery of budding breasts; as everlasting friendships develop, the weaving never stops.

Kincaid excellently illustrates the intimacy between two girls, Annie and the Red Girl. To an American, conditioned against blatant displays of intimacy, the behavior of Annie and her friends—similar to the friendship Selina shares with Beryl in Marshall's *Brown Girl—* might imply a degree of abnormality, almost a borderline lesbianism. About Gwen, her best friend in school, Annie says:

My own special happiness was, of course, with Gwen. She would stand in front of me trying to see into my murky black eyes—a way, she said, to tell exactly what I was thinking. After a short while, she would give up saying, "I can't make out a thing—only my same old face." I would then laugh at her and kiss her on the neck, sending her into a fit of shivers, as if someone had exposed her to a cold draft when she had a fever. (50–51)

16. *Annie John*, 26. Further references to this work will be made parenthetically in the text.

On the evidence of these novels, openness and intimacy seem to be quite different in female relationships in the West Indies than in the United States. Women from the West Indies seem to be uninhibited with each other yet somewhat reserved when it comes to handling their children, while those in the United States are more inhibited with their friendships and less restrictive in the raising of their children.

Later in the novel, Annie befriends the Red Girl and briefly falls "in love." The Red Girl is a mysterious character who gives the illusion of a male lover. She and Annie build a confidential, possessive friendship that is broken up by Annie's mother, further adding to Annie's resentment for her. The mother manages to keep them apart while Annie dreams of their reunion. At the reunion, she is surprised at the reception she receives from the Red Girl.

> Then, without saying a word, the Red Girl began to pinch me. She pinched hard, picking up pieces of my nonexistent flesh and twisting it around. At first, I vowed not to cry, but it went on for so long that tears I could not control streamed down my face. I cried so much that my chest began to heave, and then, as if my heaving chest caused her to have some pity on me, she stopped pinching and began to kiss me on the same spots where shortly before I had felt the pain of her pinch. Oh, the sensation was delicious—the combination of pinches and kisses. (63)

This remembrance shows the feeling of love and warmth between two friends. One senses complicity in Annie, but the Red Girl's character implies a jealous male lover.

Kincaid illustrates the shift in dependency from mother and daughter to daughter and friend as Annie reaches pubescence. She begins to see her mother in a different light as she becomes aware of her own sexuality, femininity, and the power she possesses over her peers, who haven't progressed physically as much as she.

> At recess, among the tombstones, I of course had to exhibit and demonstrate. None of the others were menstruating yet. I showed everything without the least bit of flourish since my heart wasn't in it. I wished instead that one of the other girls were in my place and that I were just sitting there in amazement. How nice they all were, though, rallying to

my side, offering shoulders on which to lean, laps in which to rest my weary, aching head, and kisses that really did soothe. (52)

This supremacy that Annie feels among her peers even during her time of distress is very real. She is saddened because there is a certain finality in menstruating that only she, so far, has experienced.

Kincaid presents a very strong character whom the reader finds intriguing; yet Annie's strength seems to have turned her into a cold human being, even with the influence of a complete family and attentive friends. That influence was most important in her growth as a young, Black West Indian woman. Vivian Gornick, who discusses childhood struggles and mother–daughter relationships, mentions an important concept in Annie's separation from her mother. "Our necessity, it seems is not so much to kill our fathers as it is to separate from our mothers," says Gornick. "It is the daughters who must do the separating."[17] Annie's separation from her mother stems from her rebellion. She encourages her mother's withdrawal from affection by displeasing and publicly embarrassing her. After mortifying her mother with her "sluttish" behavior in front of four boys at the local store, Annie announces that she is only behaving like her mother. Although she contemplates apologizing for her rude comment, she realizes that that is impossible and says, "when I looked down it was as if the ground had opened up between us, making a deep and wide split" (103).

Another split between Annie and her mother is a result of Annie's jealousy of her parents' relationship. To begin with, Annie feels resentment toward her father because of his previous relationships. She also feels separate from the continuing conversations in which her parents engage, conversations that leave them laughing and her unamused. In one episode, Annie longs for her mother's attention after suffering punishment at school and becomes outraged when both parents fail to notice how miserable she is. "I could not believe how she laughed at everything he said, and how bitter it made me feel to see how much she liked him" (83). After coming home from Sunday school and discovering her parents having sexual intercourse, Annie is both appalled and disgusted. She pledges, "I was sure I could

17. "The World of Our Mothers."

never let those hands [of her mother] touch me again; I was sure I could never let her kiss me again. All that was finished" (31–32). Parental sex and rejection are among the lessons of life that Annie cannot accept.

Annie is detached from males besides her father. By attending an all-girls school, she is physically separated from boys her own age. The boys she does come in contact with leave her little more than bad memories. Mineau, a childhood friend, disappoints Annie by tricking her into lying naked on an anthill. "Soon the angry ants were all over me, stinging me in my private parts . . . and as I cried and scratched, trying to get the ants off me, he fell down on the ground laughing, his feet kicking the air with happiness" (100). When she encounters Mineau as a teenager, Annie fears that he and the group of boys he is with are laughing in amusement at her. When Gwen mentions that Annie could marry Gwen's brother Rowan, Annie realizes that even her best friend does not understand her and says, "suddenly I felt so sorry for myself that I was about to sit down on the sidewalk and weep" (95). Perhaps her detachment is best summed up when she announces to her parents, "I plan . . . never to marry at all."

At her all-girls school, Annie is isolated not only from males but from her classmates as well. Because she is usually the brightest student in the class, she finds herself segregated from the rest of the students, but she admits that she is accustomed "to being singled out and held up in a special way" (115). Although at first she finds herself befriending her classmates, her heart is not in it. Even Gwen, whom she at one point pledges eternal love to, becomes boring. At the age of fifteen, she realizes that they "no longer live on the same plane" and occupies herself with daydreams. Later in the novel, Annie distances herself even further by choosing a uniform with a long skirt, by wearing a too-large hat, and by speaking in a strange accent. "I created such a picture that apparently everyone talked about me" (128), she proudly states.

It is Annie's serious separation from her parents and friends that causes her to leave Antigua forever. Although it is her parents' sug- gestion that she study nursing in England, subconsciously she knows all along that she cannot remain on the island and follow its traditions. Her abandonment of her mother's trunk not only distances her from her mother but also foreshadows her departure. She forms a deep resentment when her mother tells her that they no longer have time to reexamine her trunk filled with Annie's childhood belongings. It is while kicking the trunk that Annie announces, "At that moment I missed my mother more than I had ever imagined possible . . . but also at that same moment I wanted to see her lying dead" (105–6). It is the mother of her childhood that Annie misses. When she realizes that she and her mother can never regain that relationship, Annie chooses to abandon her family forever. Her departure from the family is also foreshadowed by her "washing" herself from a photograph during her illness and removing others from the remaining pictures also. This idea of erasing the past is a temporary act for which she feels guilt and anger later; not only has she ruined the pictures, she has also removed herself from these family records.

For Annie there is little choice but to leave the island and her family, since her dislike of all that surrounds her is clear when she states, "I never wanted to see a boy climb a coconut tree again, how much I never wanted to see the sun shine day in, day out again, how much I never wanted to see my mother bent over a pot cooking me something that she felt would do me good when I ate it" (127). Despite her mother's declaration that "it doesn't matter what you do or where you go, I'll always be your mother and this will always be your home" (147), the reader is left believing that England will become Annie's new home and that she will probably never return to the island to visit her parents.

For Annie John, then, growing up is a series of disappointments and struggles. In her mid-teenage years she finds herself deeply isolated from her parents, from most men, from her classmates, and from the culture of the island itself. For Annie, who has no interest in the typical lifestyle of wife and mother, there are few choices but to leave Antigua forever. It seems that, despite her mother's claims, she will never accept Antigua as her home or forgive her mother for her emotional remoteness. To the reader, it seems that Annie will always isolate herself from these first seventeen years of her life and begin a new journey of personal choices.

Like her Caribbean and African American sister-writers, Jamaica Kincaid is notable for her presentation of women's experience. Jean Rhys was the first woman writer from the Caribbean to present the mother–daughter matrix as part of the full range of women's experiences. Like Rhys, Kincaid employs a wide range of modernist and postmodernist strategies, such as the use of dreams and associative thinking, as part of the narrator's strategies for resisting the dominant culture.[18] In *Lucy,* her *New Yorker* stories, *Annie John,* and *A Small Place,* Kincaid puts very little distance between herself and a narrator who recounts a portion of her life and analyzes its trajectories. The one exception to this is *At the Bottom of the River,* which also treats mother–daughter relationships, but always through the literary mediation of dream associations and language.

Like Rhys, Kincaid's greatest contribution to the full presentation of female life is her exploration of the mother–daughter bond, specifically the effects of the loss of the maternal matrix. In both *Annie John* and *Lucy,* alienation from the mother becomes a metaphor for a young woman's alienation from an island culture that has been completely dominated by the imperialistic power of England. In *Lucy* this point is carried through the narrator's very name. She feels that her mother's teasing explanation of "Lucy" as a diminutive of "Lucifer" is accurate because it represents Lucy's sense of herself as fallen away from a relationship with a kind of god. And at several points in the novel she refers to her vision of her mother as godlike. As in Rhys's work, Kincaid's narrators perceive and present their early, preoedipal relationships with their mothers as Edens from which they have irretrievably fallen.

Kincaid focuses intensely in all her works on the relationship between the narrator and her mother. There is always a correlation between the political difficulties afflicting the relationship between the island and the "mother" country and the problems affecting the relationship between the mother and the daughter. The characters' separation from the mother, or the "mother" country, evokes extreme anxiety that appears as a cultural and psychic alienation. The absence of the once-affirming mother, or an affirming "mother" country, causes dislocation and ultimately speaks to the importance of such bonds.

In both *Annie John* and *Lucy,* the narrators, Annie and Lucy, experience great tensions in their relationships with their mothers

18. Molly Hite, *The Other Side of the Story,* argues that for Rhys, as for other modernist writers, narrative strategies mark the sites of feminist discourse.

because of the early intensity of the bond and its later complete severance. For Annie, the separation is from her mother and occurs before she leaves the island. For Lucy, the separation is from Lucy herself and is represented in her habit of not opening the nineteen or so letters that arrive from her mother. In both novels the importance of female interaction is central and focused on the narrator's relationship with her mother. In both texts, the characters' personal alienation is explored directly and then as a metaphor for the alienation of the "daughter"-island from the "mother"-country. This metaphorical exploration offers a criticism of the neocolonial situation that inhibits the lives of Annie and Lucy. Both women are victims of their environments and both are in states of extreme anger because of this situation. Yet, at the end of *Annie John,* Annie can find her own identity, signaled through the calling of her name. She is able to achieve this end through her identification with her mother and her grandmother, Ma Chess, who fills the maternal role when Annie's mother can no longer cope with Annie's psychological breakdown and illness.

In *Lucy,* the narrator is much older, nineteen rather than fifteen— illustrating again that contemporary authors of the bildungsroman do not "obey" the traditional age limits for the protagonists. In addition, her relationship with her mother is less clear to her than is the case with Annie. Because Lucy is in the United States working as an au pair, she has no female relatives who can form a support group for her. In fact, she seems to long for total anonymity because those who knew her evaluated her harshly and judged each of her actions. She also exhibits a tremendous amount of anger toward her mother. Again, Lucy feels that the closeness she experienced with her mother was a kind of trap set by their very biological connection. As her mother says to her, "You can run away, but you cannot escape the fact that I am your mother, my blood runs in you, I carried you for nine months inside me."[19]

Lucy's source of anger is different from Annie's. For Annie, the anger comes from her mother's lack of faith in her abilities and talents. Although Mariah, Lucy's employer, points out to her that

19. *Lucy,* 90. Further references to this work will be made parenthetically in the text.

part of her mother's attitude comes from cultural conditioning, that is something Lucy is unwilling to accept. At this point, and indeed even at the end of the novel, the mother is not an individual, partly conditioned by history, culture, and class. Instead, the mother remains the "god" she is referred to as so often or a monster, as often happens also in the stories collected in *At the Bottom of the River*. This is one of the novel's major problems since the narrator never moves away from a childlike view of her mother as both super- and subhuman. In fact, her response is melodramatic and fixated at the preoedipal level: "For ten of my twenty years, half of my life, I had been mourning the end of a love affair, perhaps the only true love in my whole life I would ever know" (132). This statement, made by a twenty-year-old narrator who has also claimed that she is breaking the bond with her mother, is an unusual pronouncement for a West Indian woman.

The intensity of Lucy's bond with her mother is remarkable, although its sources are not revealed in the text. However, Lucy also displays a great deal of anger toward her father, a man thirty-five years older than her mother, and a man who engendered and abandoned almost thirty children. In a situation in which the parental focus is so asymmetrical, it is only natural that the bond between the mother and the daughter would attain great importance.

In both *Annie John* and *Lucy*, the process of leaving the mother is complicated by a parallel process of leaving the island. There is a great deal of anger stored in Lucy as a result of growing up in Antigua under the cultural domination of a British imperialistic empire. In *Lucy* and in Kincaid's other works, there is a concern with how and why these conflicts are situated in a West Indian island recently liberated from British rule. Lucy's anger at British cultural imperialism is best seen in her reaction to reading a poem about daffodils—probably Wordsworth's. The flower, which does not grow at all in the Caribbean, acquires a tremendous amount of psychic power as symbolic of the many ways in which British culture has been forced on the young women of Antigua and other islands. Lucy is herself surprised when the mention of daffodils unleashes such emotion: "I had forgotten all of this until Mariah mentioned daffodils, and now I told it to her with such an amount of anger I surprised both of us" (18–19). This motif occurs in three conversations in the novel. In each of them Lucy abhors daffodils for what they represent—the imposition of the British Victorian ideology on the conquered peoples of the West Indies. Even her relationship with Mariah, whom she loves, is affected by her feelings of anger and resentment. Despite her affection for her surrogate family in the United States, Lucy is still the "visitor" and questions the basis of the family's comfortable life as linked to the oppression of West Indians. Lucy wonders if Mariah's concern with an endangered species is not related to the type of work her lawyer-husband, Lewis, conducts with his stockbroker. And Lucy is offended when Mariah tells her that she was "looking forward" to telling Lucy that Mariah had some Indian blood in her. "How do you get to be the sort of victor who can claim to be the vanquished also?" Lucy asks (41).

Much of Kincaid's distrust of the postcolonial environment went unnoticed by the reviewers of *Annie John*. In *Lucy,* the narrator's resentment of her Victorian upbringing results in her relishing of open sexual behavior as well as her resentment of the wealth and comfort in Lewis and Mariah's life. That comfort, she believes, must be the indirect result of the oppression of people like herself.

Although Kincaid shows an overtly political allegiance, there is a close connection between her anti-colonialist essays in *A Small Place* and the feelings ascribed to the young narrators of *Annie John* and *Lucy.* The attitudes expressed explicitly in *A Small Place* are implicit in *Annie John* and *Lucy.* Kincaid's fiction, and that of Janice Shinebourne, Michelle Cliff, Olive Senior, Merle Hodge, Paule Marshall, and Rosa Guy, all deals with a grounded experience. Rosa Guy, for example, has explained the process as speaking a language that for Europeans was humorous and making it into West Indian poetry: "Their humor," she has said, "has become our poetry."[20] For Kincaid, however, it is a poetry grounded in an ongoing remembrance of West Indian childhood, which for her has its beautiful/ugly sides. Perhaps it has also become her *Kunstlerroman.*

■   ■

20. Address to the Second International Conference on Caribbean Women Writers, Port of Spain, Trinidad, April 1990.

Since the 1980s, other women writers have provided welcome additions to the West Indian bildungsroman as a canon. Erna Brodber in her *Jane and Louisa Will Soon Come Home* and Jamaica Kincaid in her work present prose poems of the female child maturing. In *Beka Lamb,* set in Belize, Zee Edgell moves away from the first-person point of view, used by her predecessors, to utilize the third-person omniscient point of view. We witness the concern and cooperation of an extended family in the growth and development of girl children. Beka, the fourteen-year-old daughter of Lilla and Bill Lamb, struggles to concentrate on schoolwork after failing her first year of high school. Her concentration is hampered by her deep concern for the seventeen-year-old Toycie, a friend and neighbor, who, after becoming pregnant and being abandoned by her lover, slips into a depression that culminates in suicide. While Edgell addresses a common conflict facing the protagonist, education versus sexuality, she focuses on the marginal achiever as her heroine.

Brodber's *Jane and Louisa Will Soon Come Home* takes its title and form from an imaginative re-creation of the Jamaican children's song that goes: "My dear, will you allow me to waltz with you into this beautiful garden? Jane and Louisa will soon come home." The novel is lyrical and, as Pamela Mordecai has noted, "In *Jane and Louisa* the balance between artful tale and crafted telling is tipped in favor of the telling."[21] This work shows the vast change and experimentation in form that has taken place in Black women's telling of their stories.

The novel, which many readers will find difficult because of its folkloric qualities, Broder's use of stream of consciousness, and the various frames used, is set in an isolated Jamaican rural community in which everyone is related. The author employs voices from the ancestral past of the protagonist, Nellie, to tell folk stories of the family and community. The characters in the novel as well as the author view themselves as mediums, or conjurers of folk wisdom. Broder's approach in writing *Jane and Louisa* is similar to Alice Walker's experience in writing *The Color Purple,* which Walker describes as a vital communication with her ancestors: "I gathered up the historical

21. Pamela Mordecai, "Into This Beautiful Garden," 44.

and psychological threads of the life my ancestors lived, and in the writing of it I felt joy and strength in my own continuity . . . that wonderful feeling writers get sometimes, not very often, of being with great people . . . acknowledging them . . . [and] through the joy of their presence that indeed, I am not alone."[22]

While the form of *Jane and Louisa* is clearly based on the circular image of the ring game, the book's theme is carefully worked out on three levels. The first, most apparent, level is the story of Nellie's emergence from childhood safety in the community into maturity and a new understanding of family and community traditions. The second level involves the cultural history of five generations of a rural Jamaican family. The third is the story of African folk traditions transported and transformed in the New World. The many uses of community, or "Kumbla," are central to this story of Nellie's coming of age.

There are also three sections indicating the steps necessary to become whole. In the first section, "My Dear Will You Allow Me," Broder employs ancestral voices to tell folk stories of the family and community. Through the verbal art of riddles, proverbs, folktales, and myths, the characters, past and present, speak to Nellie and to the reader. The second section, "To Waltz with You," deals with Nellie living in government housing and meeting weekly with childhood friends, Egbert, Errol, and Barry, to discuss such issues as "people coming into their own"[23] at the millennium and the second coming. These conversations are reminiscent of the pseudo-intellectual conversations G and his friends in Lamming's *Castle* held periodically near the seawall and elsewhere.

In the third section, "Into This Beautiful Garden," Nellie realizes that she can only enter "the garden" or come to a sense of harmony with the universe once she knows all her relatives and no longer attempts to live in the world as a stranger. The relatives and friends that she remembers and gives voice to in this section include her maternal grandmother, Granny Tucker, who prays for the entire community. Because of her spoken prayers, much is revealed about

22. *In Search of Our Mothers' Gardens: Womanist Prose*, 453.
23. *Jane and Louisa Will Soon Come Home*, 66. Further references to this work will be made parenthetically in the text.

the family to her granddaughters Jane, Louisa, and Aunt Becca, the relatives who most affect Nellie's development. The last section, "Jane and Louisa Will Soon Come Home," reflects the beginning in tone and voice, as Nellie remembers the pain of growing up and having to leave the safety of the family. Puberty has changed her relationship to all those around her, and she finally realizes that she has to leave the protective, yet hidden, Kumbla and find her direction from *within* herself. Aunt Alice leads Nellie to a greater understanding of Aunt Becca but, after a point, leaves her to converse with her ancestors alone. In this last section, as Nellie comes to terms with five generations of family history, she remembers "the place still lovely with coconut trees and fine banana trees shifting their shoulders like rag effigies of our politicians, like dying swans, dancing with quiet controlled conviction, trees growing out of our kin planted in the soil . . . no paths lay before us. We would have to make them" (146).

A central motif in this unusual bildungsroman is the onset of "IT"—menstruation. This motif is set up early in the novel, and the author creates a distinct female-centered story with references to "getting it" (15) and how "it" began (21) or injunctions such as "Don't let boys get near you for they can tell just by looking at your fingernails that you have 'IT'" (24). Also there are the lessons to be learned early in life; for example, that "girls should stick to girls so that nothing will happen . . . and make men your brothers" (18). There are many other images of sexuality: a cousin being "spoiled" by a man; "hands going where nobody else's had been" (28). All of these are a bit humorous and real, so that despite the intricate use of folkloric voices, flashbacks, and other effects, there is a narrator who tells everybody *the story* of growing up, realistically, in a believable child's voice.

Broder's achievement is admirable in that it is political, cultural, and experimental and points the way to a new direction for the West Indian novel. Some of the things she does are reminiscent of the work of another writer, Ntozake Shange, who creates Black women's culture from the pieces of her world—myth, folklore, music, poetry, food, dance, lyrics, and history. The narrator describes the setting and community where Nellie grows up as a "mossy covert, dim and cool and very dark. . . . Mountains ring us round and cover us, banana leaves shelter us and sustain us, boiled, chips, porridge, three times a day" (9). This community is probably Woodside in St. Mary, a mountainous region in Jamaica where Broder grew up. This then suggests a veiled autobiography, an inherent feature of the bildungsroman.

Nellie, like most of the West Indian protagonists in this study, is held in a warm place, protected by the family. Unfortunately, however, childhood joys have to end. She notices that Egbert and Errol have stopped playing with her as they once had. Her father, coming back from a trip, notices for the first time how tall she has gotten. She is told that something strange will happen to her soon and she must hide her shame. Her Aunt Becca sends her a straw bag for Easter, which seems to symbolize that she has entered another phase of her passage into adolescence. And she is soon sent to live in the city with Aunt Becca and her husband, who is a teacher.

The novel ends before Jane and Louisa do come home and before Nellie is ready to enter the "beautiful garden." But Nellie has listened to the wisdom of her ancestors; she has visited them and knows that she is not alone. It is this knowledge that sustains her, giving her optimism and a clear understanding of her place in the family and the Kumbla. As the novels ends she tells us, "we are getting ready" (147). *Jane and Louisa Will Soon Come Home* can be read over and over and interpreted on many levels. With patience and appreciation it is possible to understand the very intricately written story of a girl from the Caribbean experiencing a fortunate, rich, and blessed upbringing, even though she does not recognize it until adulthood and distance highlight it.

■   ■

Since the mid-1980s there has been a major outpouring of Caribbean texts in the genre of the bildungsroman, and all are worthy of detailed examination. Michelle Cliff's *ABENG* examines the coming of age of Clare Savage "in mango time," which indicates a ripening of the protagonist who is ready for the picking. Clare's world is a loving one, especially her relationship with her father. Paralleling Clare's journey and initiation into womanhood is the story of dual cultures,

English history, color and class differences, and religion. It is what Cliff calls "a carefully contrived mythology."[24] For the first time, the reader of West Indian literature gets a suggestion of a taboo subject—homosexuality. Cliff takes lots of chances and explores many themes, including heritage, aging, and passing. This novel is a fine example of how a writer of color has rearranged the bildungsroman to a specific intent.

The Unbelonging by Jean Riley shows the protagonist, Hyacinth, brought from Jamaica to London, where she experiences her "differentness." Her highly anticipated reunion with her father, whom she thought would be "a cross between Sidney Poitier and Richard Roundtree," turns out to be a disappointment. Her journey, from her early life of freedom and love, soon becomes one of despair. She finds that she "doesn't belong" and longs to return to Jamaica to lie back in the "sweet smelling grass."[25] The novel addresses the issues of physical and emotional abuse as well as that of incest. Again these are topics seldom dealt with in Caribbean novels published before the 1980s. It is a depressing book; each step of the protagonist's development is negative, as she is thwarted in her home, community, city, school, and family. In retrospect she sees these occurrences as motivators for her eventual successes. Hyacinth begins to heal and become whole only when she returns home to Jamaica and her origins. Some elements of this novel are reminiscent of Fola's and Bita Plant's renewals when they reenter the native community.

Marlene Nourbese Philip's Harriet's Daughter offers a fresh look at the West Indian expatriate experience previously examined in the novels of Paule Marshall and Rosa Guy, who used the United States for their setting. Philip chose Canada as the backdrop for her first work. The central plot, focusing on inter- and intra-generational female bonding, concerns Margaret Cruickshank, a Canadian-born fourteen-year-old living in Toronto with Barbadian-born parents and two older siblings. In her story of being faced with dual cultures, she somewhat resembles Selina Boyce in Brown Girl. Margaret's angst is caused, on the one hand, by her inability to fit the model for daughter that her older sister Jo-Ann has seemingly impressed

24. ABENG, 29.
25. The Unbelonging, 14, 143.

upon her parents. On the other hand, she is unable to change her sex so that, like her brother Jonathan, she can be prized for being male. However, Margaret's problems are temporarily shelved when she meets Zulma, newly arrived in Toronto from Tobago and suffering a case of acute homesickness. Until Zulma's arrival, Margaret had shown her differentness from her family and her resistance to full assimilation into Canadian culture by wearing ethnic clothing, sporting an Afro, and enjoying West Indian music while everyone else in her family publicly displays their love for everything Canadian.

Although Philip creates a fine portrait of the tensions of a West Indian expatriate family, she employs a thin subplot that gives rise to the novel's title, *Harriet's Daughter*. The name *Harriet* first surfaces when Margaret asks her mother, Tina, to cash "baby bonus checks" given to Margaret by her godmother, Harriet Blewchamp, a White Canadian for whom Tina worked after emigrating from Barbados. Margaret wants to use the money to buy Zulma a ticket to Tobago. When her mother turns down the request, Margaret draws on her knowledge of another Harriet, Harriet Tubman, to distract herself from the problem of Zulma's airplane fare. The author trivializes the events of the historic Underground Railroad conducted by Tubman, however. Obviously an exploration of that subject is not the novel's intent. The narrator tells us that Margaret decides after reading a report that she wants to be called Harriet after this heroine and convinces her school friends to spend their Saturdays playing a game dubbed the Underground Railroad Game. As she organizes children to play the roles of slaves, dogs, slave-owners, and owners of safe houses, Margaret's intent is not consciousness-raising among the predominantly White school community. She makes no attempt to educate her classmates about African American history. Rather, Margaret explains her impulse to invent the game thus: "It was because my life was dull, dull, dull. . . . It was because I admired Harriet Tubman and wanted to change my name to Harriet."[26]

While the game itself is pointless, Margaret's interest in history and Miss Tubman does provide the framework for Zulma's safe passage to Tobago and later for Margaret's own journey there. As is typical of the bildungsroman, this departure marks the end of her

26. *Harriet's Daughter*, 61.

childhood and the beginning of her interest in writing books. The resolution of *Harriet's Daughter*, as in other bildungsromane of the African diaspora, leaves the protagonist poised for new challenges. Philip attempts, in this novel, to bring together the dual Commonwealth experience—Canadian and West Indian—with token homage to the strength of historic African American heroines. Her novel indicates the desire and inventiveness of the contemporary postcolonial woman writer to create bridges to understand the growing-up experience of Black children of the diaspora. The women of the West Indies clearly have voices raised in affirmation and celebration of their identity, and recent female texts complement the previously male-dominated canon of the West Indian bildungsroman.

■   ■

Claude McKay's *Banana Bottom* and Merle Hodge's *Crick Crack, Monkey* show what can happen to a young girl when the natural initiation process is complicated by an imported metropolitan culture. The two protagonists handle the "foreign" intrusion differently; Bita's story ends happily and Tee's unhappily because success or happiness depends on the emotional involvement of the individual. As seen in *Season of Adventure,* in which Fola is the African-anchored protagonist, the "search for a father" is also a search for one's origins. The question "Who am I" is different for a member of the White population than it is for Blacks because the quality of cultures is always the focal point of the Blacks' search, and all the searches are painful. Some Blacks like Bita are forced to function within the White society, in order to form images of themselves under its influence. Consequently, they must incorporate what is of value to them in White Western culture into their Black consciousnesses. This is true for both African Americans and West Indians, but for West Indian women the problem is compounded by issues of gender, race, class, color, a long colonial history, and biculturality.

Bita, Fola, Tee, Annie, and Lucy are given opportunities to escape their environments. But even before Tee's physical departure we have witnessed her emotional and cultural alienation from her own people. Unlike Pecola, in Morrison's novel, who must fend for herself in a hostile world, Tee, Bita, and Annie experience the basic richness and security of rural West Indian culture, and later all three are given an opportunity to take part in a more sophisticated culture. However, while Bita is able to absorb the subtlety of this new experience, many of the values she considered positive must be discarded, and for Tee there seems to be no middle ground. Fola is similar to Bita only in this respect. Tee, once having caught a glimpse of how "the other half" lives, totally discards the values of her former life and becomes obsessed with being accepted into her new environment.

As much as one is tempted to applaud McKay for his treatment of his heroine and question Hodge for hers, anyone familiar with the West Indian culture would agree that McKay's Bita is a romanticized version of West Indian womanhood and that Lamming's Fola and Tee are more reasonable renderings of those blessed by opportunity. Annie John is a balance between the two. She has a compact family unit, experiences "normal love," and has no highly charged outside experiences. In Lucy, Kincaid further extends the mother–daughter matrix of the other works. The writers have shown that human feelings are universal despite geography or culture.

An inevitable part of growing up, for both males and females, is coming to terms with racial conflict. Closely connected with race issues is the question of identity. In Brown Girl, for example, the racist attitude of White America looms large in the background. Selina's cry of anguish voices the feelings of all minority people. Her desire for violence, "to grab the cane and rush into some store on Fulton Street and avenge that wrong by bringing it smashing across the white face behind the counter" (216), is not uncommon. Selina comes closest to the African American girl child's concern about daily racial reminders that confront her from a White and racist society. Very early the Black girl child finds out that to be Black and female is a "double whammy," one that is quadrupled when she is also poor and "ugly."

The portrayals of the American protagonists by Brooks, Marshall, and Morrison are very real, believable, and unromantic. Their characters feel a dislike for themselves because they lack the power to shape their lives. In contrast, the West Indian female protagonists take positive actions to change their lives; West Indian girls act instead of being acted upon. The American girls' self-concept is based heavily on color and physical beauty, and it becomes a crippling factor in their lives. But for the West Indian girl, class and education are the vehicles that offer upward mobility with color being a secondary though important attribute. Tee, though inwardly torn and her dilemma unresolved, opts for the chance to "move up," while Annie and Lucy become expatriates. The West Indian's environment, unlike the African American's, is not so overwhelming that she relinquishes all control over it. It seems, therefore, that in growing up female into what one might consider normal adulthood, the West Indian has the edge over the African American to the extent that the West Indian lives in a less charged racial context—at least as their lives are presented in these novels.

CONCLUSION

TEN IS THE AGE OF DARKNESS

Listen child, said my mother
Whose hands had plundered photo albums
Of all black ancestors: Herein
Your ancestry, your imagery, your pride . . .
Listen child, said my father
From the quicksand of his life:
Study rivers. Learn everything.
Rivers may find beginnings
In the clefts of separate mountains
Yet all find their true homes
In the salt of one sea.
                    Olive Senior, "Talking of Trees"

Toward the end of Richard Wright's *Black Boy,* Richard says: "I was leaving the South to fling myself into the unknown, to meet other situations that would perhaps elicit from me other responses. And if I could meet enough of a different life, then, perhaps gradually and slowly I might learn who I was, what I might be. I was not leaving the South to forget the South, but so that someday I might understand it, might come to know what its rigors had done to me, to its children" (284). These words echo other literary voices, those of Joyce's Stephen Dedalus, Lamming's G, Kincaid's Annie, Hodge's Tee, who fling themselves into the world to "forge" their way through it. This same poignant voice is echoed by many of the other protagonists in this comparative study. At the end of each novel all are poised for travel to another life; the closure of their stories marks the start of their new lives. To have survived all their varying experiences is almost always a cause for celebration, even if a sense of celebration is not always felt in the novels explored.

Two that come to mind immediately are *The Bluest Eye,* with Pecola Breedlove's mad demise, and *Amongst Thistles and Thorns,* which ends with Milton Sobers laboring at a stone quarry. All of them, nevertheless, experience, as Annie John says, their "never-to-see-this-again feelings." Often at the end of their initiations they are leaving parents, country, community, and, in every case, either childhood, adolescence, or some concrete step in their lives. Their journeys have, however, been important for their development and journey. Despite the fact that Western initiation seems to have been created for White boys, the development and expansion of the bildungsroman shows that writers and children of the Black diaspora do vividly experience their individual childhoods—similarly to and differently from their peers elsewhere. That there are certain signposts and markers along the way to universalize the experience is not surprising. The Black writers in these works stress the importance of the racial, cultural, historical, as well as gender and class identity of each character. This is very important in assessing the uniqueness of their journeys, whether in Africa, the Caribbean, the United States, or elsewhere.

Women writers, of any color, have expanded the contemporary bildungsroman to include older protagonists, as a result of feminist and womanist studies and the Civil Rights movements of the last thirty years. The knowledge gained by disenfranchised people here and abroad, especially women, during this period has been eye-opening. It is not only in prose fiction that this is being expressed, but in drama, poetry, and film as well. Pieces like Paule Marshall's *Daughters,* Bebe Moore Campbell's *Sweet Summer: Growing Up with and without My Dad,* Audre Lorde's *Zami: A New Spelling of My Name,* Tina McElroy Ansa's *Baby of the Family,* Joan Cambridge's *Clarise Cumberbatch Wants to Go Home,* Opal Palmer Adisa's *Bake-Face and Other Guava Stories,* Mark Mathabane's *Kaffir Boy,* playwright Geina Mhlophe's *Have You Seen Zandile?,* and cinematographer Julie Dash's *Daughters of the Dust* are compelling in their depictions. Since some of these writers have a socialist/feminist bent, their works develop the themes of what happens to women of any age whose roles are predetermined in a patriarchal culture. In these works, the protagonists can express sorrow or be rebellious. Toni Morrison's and Terry McMillan's women come to mind. Women as "old" and "new" mothers are also essential to these analyses, as has been seen in selected works discussed in this study. Womanist writers such as Gloria Naylor and Michelle Cliff are exploring other parental relationships besides mother–daughter ones. "Other mothers," as well as mother–son and father–daughter pairings, are also important in the investigation of bonding, power, and other same-sex relationships as they relate to the theme of "pre-adult" development.

It is certain that the impetus of these movements has led women to discover themselves, their potential to be fulfilled and whole, and enabled them to move toward a "more viable existence free from predetermined roles."[1] Other books, such as *Surfacing* (1973) by Margaret Atwood and a novel written "befo' its time" by Paule Marshall, *The Chosen Place, the Timeless People,* portray the older, mature heroine striking out for another frontier, becoming self-asserting, knowledge-seeking, independent. Even Ann Petry's novel of the 1940s, *The Street,* shows a maturing journeying protagonist deciding what is best for her. What these "new" novels reveal is that age and experience are two different things. Often the protagonist of the bildungsroman is too young to question traditional values and concepts of the larger society, but somehow Black writers have managed to make their characters do so because they, like the authors, are born into their own histories.

Each of the writers in this study has made radical changes to the traditional form. Some of the most obvious and memorable are Ralph Ellison's use of parody, satire, abstraction, and impressionism; Langston Hughes's use of Black folk forms, folk language, history, "slice of life," music, and notions of rural life; Baldwin's protest against the values of the church in Black life and his careful synchronology of the autobiographical mode; and Richard Wright's use of fact and fiction to paint the plight of the Black boy/man, lost without his history. Since all initiations are supposed to lead to manhood or womanhood, one wonders in some cases how the miniature adult of ages past has not become the "voiceless, helpless" child of today.

Toni Morrison continues to surprise us since creating *The Bluest Eye* by telling us hidden stories and having us read about things we never before imagined. Who ever heard of a Black girl with blue eyes

1. White, *Growing Up Female,* 194.

or, for that matter, Black people flying or being born without navels. Gwendolyn Brooks's and Paule Marshall's early works show young Black girls as intelligent and probing, with critical and brilliant perceptions of their various colonialisms that they have deeded to their younger literary sisters, such as Ntozake Shange, Jamaica Kincaid, and Michelle Cliff.

Very important in this study is the use of memory and voice. Writers of the bildungsroman seem almost required to be faithful to the past in reliving it for their readers, who must then accept the voice as authentic. Trinidadian Michael Anthony, Barbadian George Lamming, Antiguan Jamaica Kincaid, and Jamaican Erna Brodber have had exceptional success in this respect. It is not surprising that their texts have been adopted for use in Caribbean public schools more than some of the others. What child living through a childhood between the ages of eight and fourteen, a typical range for the protagonists, would not like to hear his or her feelings of despair, hope, confusion, shyness, or joy expressed by another:

> Girls were there to be liked. Some of them were very beautiful. Some of them with the long plaits. And with nice shy smiles. I liked girls.[2]

> On the morning of the first day I started to menstruate, I felt strange in a new way—hot and cold at the same time, with horrible pains running down my legs.[3]

These are secret feelings that many young children feel and are afraid to voice to adults or peers but would relish reading about. Since youth and age are often denigrated in our society, it is primarily through texts like these that the young get a voice.

Many of the scenes in these novels have similarities and yet reflect reality in striking ways, illustrating a "peculiar psychology" on each author's part. For example, the voices of Maud Martha, Selina, John, Richard, or Milton are similar, yet each has different intentions.

The concepts that children are asked to grasp despite their young age or inexperience are amazing. They are supposed to know why

2. Anthony, *The Year in San Fernando,* 49.
3. Kincaid, *Annie John,* 51.

Blacks are somehow different from other people and that there are different kinds of Black people and why that is. Richard's almost White grandmother is a case in point, as is the wondering about class differences by Tee and Tantie in Merle Hodge's *Crick Crack, Monkey* or Pecola's wanting to know "when and how do you know someone loves you." These children are supposed to understand early the concept of inequality in their neighborhoods, schools, workplaces, and homes, and that one culture is less important than another, or that class lines are clearly drawn between these groups. They are to know that the color white is special and that at the top of the list are White people. Pecola's drinking of "white" milk, not the chocolate milk that most children love, her love for White Shirley Temple dolls, and her discovery that pale versions of herself are better than ugly and Black ones, are overwhelming concepts for a developing child. For these children, understanding that "having a past to hold onto" is a gift and a right must be very confusing, when all of the symbols of success and access to it do not look like him or her.

Within these stories, Black writers of the Caribbean and the United States have extended the use of Afro-World history into their bildungsromane to instruct us. The boys in George Lamming's *In the Castle of My Skin* are led into discussions of British history and colonialism after reading the Michael John Readers and singing "Rule Britannia." They ponder the role of their elders, Ma and Pa, in that history, as well as the slave history of Barbados. Similarly, Milton and Willy appraise the value of their Black hero Marcus Garvey; Selina Boyce is confused by her bicultural heritage; and Sandy's grandmother wishes him to be another Frederick Douglass. The past is also represented by the immediate past. Black history and culture are passed on to another generation in many ways: the home that Betsey Brown's father creates with its Black poetry, music, and song of the 1940s and 1950s; the past that Hilda Effania wills to her children through Black foods and arts; and the "befo-time" stories told by various grandmothers in these texts. In the early bildungsromane, by European, male, traditionalist writers, these concerns and content were absent.

The various motifs used by these authors to tell their stories are also taken from the Black experience. The motif of beating is repeated in many ways and in different instances. "Ugly" Pecola is beaten by her mother for embarrassing her; John Grimes, by his father for being a bastard child; Richard, by his father for standing up to him; and Milton and G's friend, by cruel headmasters in a strict West Indian school without sufficient and apparent reason. The overriding emphasis of the beatings, however, is that these children don't get "strapped" or "whipped" but mercilessly *beaten* in the old slave tradition. They are also metaphorically "beaten up" in their lives. These bildungsromane are the most depressing to read; they are also the same ones that exhibit a master–slave relationship in their protagonists' lives. On another level is Francis's "little slave" status in the white Chandles household; Pecola's mother's role as a domestic in the White household; and Richard in his various menial jobs for Whites. The motif of color and its importance is also pervasive in this genre, from Baldwin's emphasis on blackness and its many meanings, Shange's glorification of it, Brooks's and Wright's examination of it, to Lamming's exploration of its rootedness in Africa.

Sexual awareness, inherent in all its forms, is a part of all bildungsromane, yet in the Black novels of a people who are supposed to be stereotypically "oversexed," the subject is handled dexterously and is tastefully controlled by the writers. In the works considered here, including the rapes of Bita and Pecola, the theme is not overdone or overworked. Critic Leslie Fiedler suggests that some characters in the bildungsroman have a boy/girl blend and that male writers have a "homosexual sensibility."[4] If this includes Black writers, it may be worth considering in another study—one of Baldwin and Hughes perhaps. Because a particular society's definition of manhood and womanhood often encompasses that group's view of sexuality and nature, the novels are explorations of cultural and mythical beliefs based on these standards.

The recent publication of many anthologies of African American and West Indian writers, as well as single texts, clearly indicates the explosion of interest in Black writing, especially writing done by Black women. They are the carriers of the tradition and the experimenters with the form. Anthologies like Pamela Mordecai and Betty Wilson's *Her True-True Name,* Carole Boyce Davies and Elaine

4. *No! in Thunder,* 2d ed. (New York: Stem and Day, 1972).

Savory Fido's *Out of the Kumbla,* Patricia Bell Scott et al.'s *Double-Stitch: Black Women Write about Mothers and Daughters,* and others, prove that women have used the tradition as a vehicle for their multiple voices and variousness. These works also demonstrate their bonding and sisterhood—be they African, Caribbean, African American, or some combination thereof. We must watch to see if the current emphases on Afrocentrism, womanism, and multiculturalism will affect the directions of these and newer texts. For White women the "*bildungsroman* is the most salient form of literature,"[5] but will it be the same for other women of color? Also, will the call for multicultural curricula see these texts included on more reading lists, as Doris Lessing suggests? The scholarship on the form is growing, and we can hope there will be many more examinations of the Black bildungsroman, because irrespective of place, it is that population's rites of passage that need more attention. This is not to say that the male tradition has "died." The books of Trey Ellis and Charles Johnson, for example, deserve more attention as well.

Growing up is indeed "a pain." But the universality of the experience enriches us, especially when the experience is somebody else's. If only we could be like Indigo rescuing her dolls from growing up, what a blessing or pity that would be: then, in discussing our growing-up experiences we could tell our children that they don't "haveta" because we "can save them."[6]

5. Helen Morgan, "Human Becoming: Form and Focus in the New Feminist Novel," 185.

6. Shange, *Sassafrass, Cypress, and Indigo,* 52.

CHRONOLOGY OF THE AFRICAN AMERICAN BILDUNGSROMAN

The following works are selected as bildungsromane based on my use and definition of the category.

1853	William Wells Brown	*Clothel or the President's Daughter*
1859	Harriet Wilson	*Our Nig*
1861	Harriet Jacobs	*Incidents in the Life of a Slave Girl*
1929	Jesse Faucet	*Plum Bun*
	Wallace Thurman	*The Blacker the Berry*
1930	Langston Hughes	*Not without Laughter*
1937	Zora Neale Hurston	*Their Eyes Were Watching God*
1945	Richard Wright	*Black Boy*
1946	Ann Petry	*The Street*
1948	Dorothy West	*The Living Is Easy*
1950	William Demby	*Beetlecreek*
1952	Ralph Ellison	*Invisible Man*
1953	James Baldwin	*Go Tell It on the Mountain*
	Gwendolyn Brooks	*Maud Martha*
1959	Paule Marshall	*Brown Girl, Brownstones*
1962	George Wylie Henderson	*Ollie Miss*
1963	Gordon Parks	*The Learning Tree*
1965	Claude Brown	*Manchild in the Promised Land*
	Gordon Parks	*A Choice of Weapons*
1968	Kristin Hunter	*The Soul Brothers and Sister Lou*
	Anne Moody	*Coming of Age in Mississippi*

1970	Maya Angelou	*I Know Why the Caged Bird Sings*
	Louise Merriwether	*Daddy Was a Number Runner*
	Toni Morrison	*The Bluest Eye*
1973	Nikki Giovanni	*Gemini*
	Toni Morrison	*Sula*
1976	Alice Walker	*Meridian*
1977	Ntozake Shange	*For Colored Girls Who Have Considered Suicide When the Rainbow Is ENUF*
1982	Audre Lorde	*Zami: A New Spelling of My Name*
	Ntozake Shange	*Sassafrass, Cypress, and Indigo*
1985	Ntozake Shange	*Betsey Brown*
1986	Sherley Anne Williams	*Dessa Rose*
1987	Toni Morrison	*Beloved*
1988	Gloria Naylor	*Mama Day*
1989	Tina McElroy Ansa	*Baby of the Family*
	Bebe Moore Campbell	*Sweet Summer: Growing Up with and without My Dad*
1991	Paule Marshall	*Daughters*

CHRONOLOGY OF THE AFRICAN WEST INDIAN BILDUNGSROMAN

The country indicates the author's birthplace and/or chosen association and nationality.

1903	Tom Redcam	*Becka's Buckra Baby*	Jamaica
1909	Tom Redcam	*One Brown Girl and . . .*	Jamaica
1913	Herbert G. De Lisser	*Jane*	Jamaica
1914	Herbert G. De Lisser	*Jane's Career*	Jamaica
1915	Herbert G. De Lisser	*Susan Proudleigh*	Jamaica
1933	Claude McKay	*Banana Bottom*	Jamaica
1936	C. L. R. James	*Minty Alley*	Trinidad
1939	Alice Durie	*One Jamaica Gal*	Jamaica
1941	Edward Mittelholzer	*Corentyne Thunder*	Guyana
1949	Victor Reid	*New Day*	Jamaica
1952	Samuel Selvon	*A Brighter Sun*	Trinidad
1953	Phyllis Allfrey	*The Orchid House*	Dominica
	Herbert G. De Lisser	*Morgan's Daughter*	Jamaica
	George Lamming	*In the Castle of My Skin*	Barbados
	Edward Mittelholzer	*The Life and Death of Sylvia*	Guyana
1958	Jan Carew	*Black Midas*	Jamaica
	V. S. Naipaul	*The Suffrage of Elvira*	Trinidad
1959	Geoffrey Drayton	*Christopher*	Barbados
	Paule Marshall	*Brown Girl, Brown-stones*	Barbados
	V. S. Naipaul	*Miguel Street*	Trinidad
1960	Neville Dawes	*The Last Enchantment*	Jamaica
	Peter Kempadoo	*Guyana Boy*	Guyana
	George Lamming	*Season of Adventure*	Barbados

1961	Geoffrey Drayton	*Zohara*	Barbados
	Ismith Khan	*The Jumbie Bird*	Trinidad
	V. S. Naipaul	*A House for Mr. Biswas*	Trinidad
	Namba Roy	*Black Albino*	Jamaica
1963	Michael Anthony	*The Games Were Coming*	Trinidad
1964	Orlando Patterson	*The Children of Sisyphus*	Jamaica
	Garth St. Omer	*Syrop*	St. Lucia
	Denis Williams	*Other Leopards*	Jamaica
1965	Michael Anthony	*The Year in San Fernando*	Trinidad
	Austin Clarke	*Amongst Thistles and Thorns*	Barbados
1966	Rosa Guy	*Bird at My Window*	Trinidad
1967	Michael Anthony	*Green Days by the River*	Trinidad
1968	Earl Lovelace	*The School Master*	Trinidad
1969	Earl Lovelace	*The Adventures of Catullus Kelly*	Trinidad
	Ian McDonald	*The Hummingbird Tree*	Trinidad
1970	Merle Hodge	*Crick Crack, Monkey*	Trinidad
1978	Albert Gomes	*All Papa's Children*	Trinidad
1979	Hazel Campbell	*The Ragdoll and Other Stories*	Jamaica
1980	Michael Anthony	*All That Glitters*	Trinidad
	Erna Brodber	*Jane and Louisa Will Soon Come Home*	Jamaica
	Austin Clarke	*Growing Up Stupid under the Union Jack*	Barbados
	Michael Thelwell	*The Harder They Come*	Jamaica
	Joseph Zobel	*Black Shack Alley*	Martinique
1982	Zee Edgell	*Beka Lamb*	Belize
1983	Jamaica Kincaid	*At the Bottom of the River*	Antigua
1984	Michelle Cliff	*ABENG*	Jamaica
1985	Rosa Guy	*My Love, My Love or the Peasant Girl*	Trinidad
	Jean Riley	*The Unbelonging*	Jamaica

1986	Opal Palmer Adisa	*Bake-Face and Other Guava Stories*	Jamaica
	Grace Nichols	*Whole of a Morning Sky*	Guyana
	Elizabeth Nunez-Harrell	*When Rocks Dance*	Trinidad
1987	Joan Cambridge	*Clarise Cumberbatch Wants to Go Home*	Jamaica
1988	Marlene Nourbese Philip	*Harriet's Daughter*	Tobago
	Sybil Seaforth	*Growing Up with Miss Milly*	Jamaica

BIBLIOGRAPHY

Primary Sources

Abrahams, Peter. *Mine Boy*. London: Faber, 1946.

Achebe, Chinua. *Things Fall Apart*. Greenwich, Conn.: Fawcett, 1969.

Adisa, Opal Palmer. *Bake-Face and Other Guava Stories*. Berkeley: Kelsey Street Press, 1986.

Angelou, Maya. *I Know Why the Caged Bird Sings*. New York: Bantam, 1970.

Ansa, Tina McElroy. *Baby of the Family*. New York: Harcourt, Brace & Co., 1989.

Anthony, Michael. *The Games Were Coming*. London: André Deutsch, 1963.

———. *Green Days by the River*. Boston: Houghton Mifflin, 1967.

———. *The Year in San Fernando*. London: Heinemann Educational Books, 1965.

Baldwin, James. *Go Tell It on the Mountain*. New York: Dell Publishing, 1953.

———. *Notes of a Native Son*. Boston: Beacon, 1955.

Brodber, Erna. *Jane and Louisa Will Soon Come Home*. London: Heinemann, 1980.

Brooks, Gwendolyn. *Maud Martha*. New York: Harper, 1953.

———. *Report from Part One*. Detroit: Broadside Press, 1972.

Brown, Claude. *Manchild in the Promised Land*. New York: Macmillan, 1965.

Cambridge, Joan. *Clarise Cumberbatch Wants to Go Home*. New York: Ticknor and Fields, 1987.

Campbell, Bebe Moore. *Sweet Summer: Growing Up with and without My Dad*. New York: Ballantine Books, 1989.

Carew, Jan. *Black Midas*. London: Secker and Warburg, 1958.

Clarke, Austin. *Amongst Thistles and Thorns.* London: Heinemann Books, 1965.

———. "The Endin' Up Is the Startin' Out." *BIM* 9 (July–December 1962): 181–83.

———. *Growing Up Stupid under the Union Jack.* Toronto: McClelland and Stewart, 1980.

Cliff, Michelle. *ABENG.* Trumansburg, N.Y.: Crossing Press Feminist Series, 1984.

———. *No Telephone to Heaven.* New York: Dutton, 1989.

Dash, Julie. *Daughters of the Dusk.* New York: New Press, 1992.

Dawes, Neville. *The Last Enchantment.* London: MacGibbon and Kee, 1960.

De Lisser, Herbert. *Jane's Career: A Story of Jamaica.* London: Methuen, 1914.

———. *Susan Proudleigh.* London: Methuen, 1915.

Demby, William. *Beetlecreek: A Novel.* New Jersey: Chatham Bookseller, 1950.

Dickens, Charles. *David Copperfield.* 1850. New York: Dodd, Mead, 1943.

———. *Great Expectations.* London: Chapman and Hall, 1864.

Douglass, Frederick, *Narrative of the Life of Frederick Douglass, an American Slave, Written by Himself.* 1845. Boston: Harvard University Press, 1960.

Drayton, Geoffrey. *Christopher.* London: Collins, 1959.

Edgell, Zee. *Beka Lamb.* London: Heinemann, 1982.

Ellison, Ralph. *Invisible Man.* New York: Signet, 1952.

———. *Shadow and Act.* New York: New American Library, 1966.

Esteves, Carmen C., and Paravisini-Gebeet eds., *Green Cane and Juicy Flotsam.* New Jersey: Rutgers University Press, 1991.

Faucet, Jesse Redmon. *Plum Bun.* New York: Frederick A. Stokes, Co., 1929.

Giovanni, Nikki. *Gemini.* New York: Viking Press, 1973.

Goethe, Johann Wolfgang von. *The Sufferings of Young Werther.* 1787. Translated by Bayard Quincy Morgan. New York: Frederick Ungar, 1983.

———. *Wilhelm Meisters Lehrjahre.* Weimar, Germany: Webe, 1795.

Gomes, Albert Maria. *All Papa's Children.* Surrey, England: KTA ODP, Cairi Publishing House, 1978.

Hansberry, Lorraine. *To Be Young, Gifted, and Black.* Englewood Cliffs, N.J.: Prentice Hall, 1969.

Hodge, Merle. *Crick Crack, Monkey.* London: André Deutsch, 1970.

Hughes, Langston. *The Big Sea.* Alfred A. Knopf, 1940.

———. *Not Without Laughter.* 1930. New York: New American Library, 1985.

Hunter, Kristin. *The Soul Brothers and Sister Lou.* New York: Avon Books, 1968.

Hurston, Zora Neale. *Their Eyes Were Watching God.* Philadelphia: J. B. Lippincott, 1937.

Jacobs, Harriet Brent. *Incidents in the Life of a Slave Girl.* 1861. New York: Harvest/HBJ Book, Harcourt Brace Jovanovich, 1973.

James, C. L. R. *Beyond a Boundary.* London: Hutchinson, 1963.

———. *Minty Alley.* London: Secker and Warburg, 1936.

Joyce, James. *A Portrait of the Artist as a Young Man.* 1916. New York: Viking Press, 1968.

———. *Stephen Hero.* Rev. ed. New York: New Dimensions, 1963.

Kempadoo, Peter [Lauchmonen, pseud.]. *Guyana Boy.* London: New Literature, 1960.

Kincaid, Jamaica. *Annie John.* New York: Farrar, Straus, Giroux, 1985.

———. *At the Bottom of the River.* New York: Vintage Books, 1983.

———. *Lucy.* New York: Farrar, Straus, Giroux, 1990.

———. *A Small Place.* New York: Farrar, 1988.

Kingston, Maxine Hong. *The Woman Warrior.* New York: Viking Books, 1975.

La Guma, Alex. *A Walk in the Night.* Chicago: Northwestern University Press, 1967.

Lamming, George. *In the Castle of My Skin.* New York: Schocken, 1953.

———. *Season of Adventure.* Great Britain: Allison and Busby, 1960.

Laye, Camara. *The African Child.* London: Collins, 1954.

Lorde, Audre. *Zami: A New Spelling of My Name.* Watertown, Mass.: Persephone Press, 1982.

Marshall, Paule. *Brown Girl, Brownstones.* 1959. Old Westbury, N.Y.: Feminist Press, 1981.

———. *Daughters.* New York: Penguin Books, 1991.

———. *Merle: A Novella and Other Stories.* London: Virago, 1985.

————. *Reena and Other Stories.* Old Westbury, N.Y.: Feminist Press, 1983.

————. "To Da-Duh in Memoriam." *New World Quarterly* 3:1–2 (1967): 97–101.

Mathabane, Mark. *Kaffir Boy.* New York: Penguin Books, 1986.

McDonald, Ian. *The Hummingbird Tree.* London: Heinemann, 1969.

McKay, Claude. *Banana Bottom.* New York: Harper and Row, 1933.

McMillan, Terry. *Mama.* Boston: Houghton Mifflin, 1987.

Merriwether, Louise. *Daddy Was a Number Runner.* New Jersey: Prentice Hall, 1970.

Mhlophe, G., T. Mtshali, and M. Vanrenneu. *Have You Seen Zandile?* Braanfontein, South Africa: Skotaville Publishers, 1988.

Mittelholzer, Edward. *The Life and Death of Sylvia.* New York: John Day Co., 1953.

Moody, Anne. *Coming of Age in Mississippi.* New York: Dial, 1968.

Mordecai, Pamela, and Betty Wilson. *Her True-True Name.* London: Heineman Educational Books, 1989.

Morrison, Toni. *Beloved.* New York: Alfred A. Knopf, 1987.

————. *The Bluest Eye.* New York: Washington Square Press, 1970.

————. *Sula.* New York: Alfred A. Knopf, 1973.

Naipaul, V. S. *Finding the Center: Two Narratives.* New York: Knopf, 1984.

————. *A House for Mr. Biswas.* London: André Deutsch, 1961.

————. *Miguel Street.* London: André Deutsch, 1959.

Naylor, Gloria. *Mama Day.* New York: Ticknor and Fields, 1988.

Ngugi, James. *Weep Not Child.* London: Heinemann, 1967.

Nichols, Grace. *Whole of a Morning Sky.* London: Virago, 1986.

Nwankwo, Nkem. *Danda.* London: André Deutsch, 1964.

Okoro, Anezi. *The Village School.* Lagos, Nigeria: Universities Press, 1966.

Oyono, Ferdinand. *Houseboy.* London: Heinemann Educational Books, 1966.

Parks, Gordon. *A Choice of Weapons.* New York: Harper and Row, 1965.

Petry, Ann. *The Street.* Boston: Houghton Mifflin, 1946.

Philip, Marlene Nourbese. *Harriet's Daughter.* London: Heinemann, 1988.

Redcam, Tom [Thomas H. McDermont]. *Becka's Buckra Baby.* Kingston: Jamaica Times Printery, 1903.

———. *One Brown Girl and . . . A Jamaican Story.* Kingston: Jamaican Times Printery, 1909.

Rhys, Jean. *Smile Please.* Berkeley: Creative Arts Book Co., 1979.

Riley, Jean. *The Unbelonging.* London: Women's Press, 1985.

Roy, Namba. *Black Albino.* London: New Literature, 1961.

St. Omer, Garth. *Syrop.* London: Faber and Faber, 1964.

Seacole, Mary. *The Wonderful Adventures of Mrs. Seacole in Many Lands.* London: Oxford University Press, 1858.

Seaforth, Sybil. *Growing Up with Miss Milly.* Ithaca, N.Y.: Calaloux, 1988.

Selvon, Samuel. *A Brighter Sun.* London: Allan Wingate, 1952.

Shange, Ntozake. *Betsey Brown.* New York: St. Martin's Press, 1985.

———. *For Colored Girls Who Have Considered Suicide When the Rainbow Is ENUF.* New York: Bantam, 1977.

———. *Sassafrass, Cypress, and Indigo.* New York: St. Martin's Press, 1982.

Smith, Betty. *A Tree Grows in Brooklyn.* New York: Harper Bros., 1943.

Teague, Bob. *Letters to a Black Boy.* New York: Lancer, 1969.

Thurman, Wallace. *The Blacker the Berry.* 1929. New York: Arno Press, 1981.

Walcott, Derek. *Another Life.* New York: Farrar, 1973.

Walker, Alice. *Meridian.* New York: Harcourt Brace Jovanovich, Washington Square Press, 1976.

Washington, Mary Helen, ed. *Black-Eyed Susans: Classic Stories by and about Black Women.* New York: Doubleday Anchor Books, 1975.

West, Dorothy. *The Living Is Easy.* Boston: Houghton, Mifflin, 1948.

Williams, Denis. *Other Leopards.* London: New Authors, 1964.

Williams, Sherley Anne. *Dessa Rose.* London: Futura, 1986.

Wilson, Harriet E. *Our Nig, or Sketches from the Life of a Free Black.* Boston: by the author, 1859; reprinted, New York: Random House, 1983.

Wright, Richard. *Black Boy: A Record of Childhood and Youth.* New York: Harper and Brothers, 1945.

———. *Native Son.* New York: Harper and Row, 1940.

Wright, Sarah. *This Child's Gonna Live.* New York: Seymour Lawrence, 1969.

Zobel, Joseph. *Black Shack Alley.* Translated by Keith Warner. Washington: Three Continents Press, 1980.

Secondary Sources

Abel, Elizabeth, Marianne Hirsch, and Elizabeth Langland, eds. *The Voyage In: Fictions of Female Development.* Hanover, N.H.: University Press of New England, 1983.

Abrahamson, Jane B. *Mothermaniá: A Psychological Study of Mother-Daughter Conflict.* Lexington, Mass.: Lexington Books, 1986.

Aidoo, Ama Ata. "Unwelcome Pals and Decorative Slaves—or Glimpses of Women as Writers and Characters in Contemporary African Literatures." In *Literature and Society: Selected Essays on African Literature,* edited by Ernest Emenyom. Oguta, Nigeria: Zim Pan African Publishers, 1989.

Andrews, William L., ed. *African American Autobiography: A Collection of Critical Essays.* New Jersey: Prentice Hall, 1993.

———. *Sisters of the Spirit: Three Black Women's Autobiographies of the Nineteenth Century.* Bloomington: Indiana University Press, 1986.

Anthony, Michael. "The Return of a West Indian: An Interview with Jan Munro and Reinhard Sander." *BIM* 14 (1977): 212–18.

Awkward, Michael. *Inspiriting Influences: Tradition Revision and Afro-American Women's Novels.* New York: Columbia University Press, 1989.

Bakerman, Jane S. "Failures of Love: Female Initiation in the Novels of Toni Morrison." *American Literature* 52 (1981): 541–63.

———. "The Seams Can't Show: An Interview with Toni Morrison." *Black American Literature Forum* 12 (1979): 60.

Baugh, Edward. "Cuckoo and Culture: *In the Castle of My Skin.*" *Ariel* 8, no. 3 (1977): 23–33.

Bell, Roseann P., Bettye J. Parker, and Beverly Guy Sheftall, eds. *Sturdy Black Bridges: Visions of Black Women in Literature.* Garden City, N.Y.: Anchor Books, 1979.

Bell-Scott, Patricia, et al., eds. *Double-Stitch: Black Women Write about Mothers and Daughters.* Boston: Beacon Press, 1991.

Berrian, Brenda F. "Snapshots of Childhood in Jamaica Kincaid's Fiction." Unpublished paper (nd).

Bischoff, Joan. "The Novels of Toni Morrison: Studies in Thwarted Sensitivity." *Studies in Black Literature* 6 (fall 1975): 21–23.

Bone, Robert. *The Negro Novel in America.* Rev. ed. New Haven: Yale University Press, 1965.

Braendlin, Bonnie Hoover. "*Bildung* in Ethnic Women Writers." *Denver Quarterly* 17 (winter 1983): 75–87.

Braithwaite, L. Edward. "The New West Indian Novelists." *BIM* 8, no. 32 (1961): 271–80.

Braxton, Joanne M. *Black Women Writing Autobiography.* Philadelphia: Temple University Press, 1989.

Bromley, Roger. "Reaching a Clearing: Gender and Politics in *Beka Lamb.*" *Wasafiri* 1 (spring 1985): 10–14.

Brown, Lloyd W. "The Crisis of Black Identity in the West Indian Novel." *Critique* 11, no. 3 (1969): 97–112.

————. "The West Indian Novel in North America: A Study of Austin Clarke." *Journal of Commonwealth Literature* 9 (1970): 89–103.

Buckley, Jerome. *Season of Youth: The Bildungsroman from Dickens to Golding.* Cambridge: Harvard University Press, 1974.

Buncombe, Marie H. "Androgyny as Metaphor in Alice Walker's Novels." *College Language Association Journal* 30 (June 1987): 419–27.

Butcher, Margaret. "From Maurice Guest to Martha Quest: The Female *Bildungsroman* in Commonwealth Literature." *World Literature Written in English* 21 (summer 1982): 254–62.

Campbell, Elaine. "Two West Indian Heroines: Bita Plant and Fola Piggott." *Caribbean Quarterly* 29 (June 1983): 22–29.

Carby, Hazel. *Reconstructing Womanhood: The Emergence of the Afro-American Woman Novelist.* Oxford: Oxford University Press, 1979.

Carpenter, Frederic I. "The Adolescent in American Fiction." *English Journal* 46 (1967): 313–19.

Christian, Barbara. *Black Feminist Criticism: Perspectives on Black Women Writers.* New York: Pergamon Press, 1985.

———. "Nuance and Novella: A Study of Gwendolyn Brooks' *Maud Martha.*" In her *Black Feminist Criticism: Perspectives on Black Women Writers,* 127–41. New York: Pergamon Press, 1985.

———. "Sculpture and Space: The Interdependency of Character and Culture in the Novels of Paule Marshall." In *Black Women Novelists: The Development of a Tradition, 1892–1976,* edited by Christian, 80–136. Westport, Conn.: Greenwood Press, 1980.

———, ed. *Black Women Novelists: The Development of a Tradition, 1892–1976.* Westport, Conn.: Greenwood Press, 1980.

Clarke, Austin C. "Harrison College and Me." *New World Quarterly* 3, nos. 1–2 (1967): 81–84.

———. "Some Speculations as to the Absence of Racialistic Vindictiveness in West Indian Literature." In *The Black Writer in Africa and the Americas,* edited by Lloyd W. Brown, 165–94. Los Angeles: Hennessee and Ingalls, 1973.

Clarke, Edith. *My Mother Who Fathered Me.* London: Allen and Unwin, 1957.

Cliff, Michelle. "Clare Savage as a Crossroads Character." In *Caribbean Women Writers: Essays from the First International Conference,* edited by Selwyn Cudjoe, 263–68. Wellesley, Mass.: Calaloux Publications, 1990.

Collier, Eugenia. "The Closing of the Circle: Movement from Division to Wholeness in Paule Marshall's Fiction." In *Black Women Writers, 1950–1980: A Critical Evaluation,* edited by Mari Evans, 295–315. New York: Anchor Press/Doubleday, 1984.

Collins, Patricia Hill. "The Meaning of Motherhood in Black Culture and Black Mother/Daughter Relationships." *Sage: A Scholarly Journal on Black Women* 2 (fall 1987): 3–9.

Cooper, Carolyn. "The Fertility of the Gardens of Women." Review essay on *Jane and Louisa Will Soon Come Home* by Erna Broder. *New Beacon Reviews* 2/3 (November 1986): 139–47.

Coulson, Sheila. "Politics and the Female Experience: An Examination of *Beka Lamb* and *Hérémakhônon.*" In *West Indian Litera-*

ture and Its Political Context, edited by Lowell Fiet, 92–105. Rio Piedras, Puerto Rico: University of Puerto Rico, 1988.

Courage, Richard A. "James Baldwin's *Go Tell It on the Mountain:* Voices of a People." *College Language Association Journal* 32 (June 1989): 410–25.

Cudjoe, Selwyn. "Jamaica Kincaid and the Modernist Project: An Interview." In *Caribbean Women Writers: Essays from the First International Conference,* edited by Cudjoe, 215–42. Wellesley: Calaloux Publications, 1990.

———, ed. *Caribbean Women Writers: Essays from the First International Conference.* Wellesley, Mass.: Calaloux Publications, 1990.

Dance, Daryl Cumber. *Fifty Caribbean Writers: A Bio-Bibliographical and Critical Source Book.* Westport, Conn.: Greenwood Press, 1986.

———. "Go Eena Kumbla: A Comparison of Erna Broder's *Jane and Louisa Will Soon Come Home* and Toni Cade Bambara's *The Salt Eaters.*" In *Caribbean Women Writers: Essays from the First International Conference,* edited by Selwyn Cudjoe, 169–83. Wellesley, Mass.: Calaloux Publications, 1990.

———. "An Interview with Paule Marshall." *Southern Review* 28 (winter 1992): 1–20.

Davidson, Cathy N., and E. M. Broner. *The Lost Tradition: Mothers and Daughters in Literature.* New York: Frederick Ungar, 1980.

Davies, Carole Boyce. "Black Woman's Journey into Self: A Womanist Reading of Paule Marshall's *Praisesong for the Widow.*" *Matatu* (West Germany) 1: 1 (1987).

———. "Wrapping One's Self in Mother's Akatado-Clothes: Mother–Daughter Relationships in the Works of African Women Writers" *Sage: A Scholarly Journal on Black Women* 4 (fall 1987): 11–19.

———. "Writing Home: Gender and Heritage in the Works of Afro-Caribbean/American Women Writers." In *Out of the Kumbla: Caribbean Women and Literature,* edited by Carol Boyce Davies and Elaine Savory Fido, 59–73. New Jersey: Africa World Press, 1990.

Davies, Carol Boyce, and Elaine Savory Fido, eds. *Out of the Kumbla: Caribbean Women and Literature.* New Jersey: Africa World Press, 1990.

Davis, Angela. *Women, Race and Class*. London: Women's Press, 1982.

Davis, Charles T. "From Experience to Eloquence: Richard Wright's *Black Boy* as Art." In *African American Biography*, edited by William Andrews, 138–50. New Jersey: Prentice Hall, 1990.

de Weever, Jacqueline. "The Inverted World of Toni Morrison's *The Bluest Eye* and *Sula*." *College Language Association Journal* 22 (June 1979): 402–14.

———. *Mythmaking and Metaphor in Black Women's Fiction*. New York: St. Martins Press, 1991.

Dill, Bonnie. "The Dialectics of Black Womanhood." *Signs* 4 (spring 1979): 543–55.

Down, Lorna. "Singing One's Own Song: Woman and Selfhood in Recent West Indian Fiction." M.A. thesis, University of the West Indies, 1985. Discusses *Beka Lamb, Crick Crack, Monkey*, and *Jane and Louisa Will Soon Come Home*.

Dudley, David L. *My Father's Shadow: Intergenerational Conflict in African-American Men's Autobiographies*. Philadelphia: University of Pennsylvania Press, 1991.

Eko, Ebele. "Beyond the Myth of Confrontation: A Comparative Study of African and African American Protagonists." *Ariel* 17 (October 1986): 139–52. Characters chosen include Selina Boyce from *Brown Girl, Brownstones*.

Ellison, Ralph. "The Art of Fiction: An Interview." In *Shadow and Act*. New York: New American Library, 1966.

Erickson, Erik. *Childhood and Society*. New York: W. W. Norton and Co., 1985.

Evans, Mari, ed. *Black Women Writers, 1950–1980: A Critical Evaluation*. Garden City, N.Y.: Doubleday Anchor Books, 1984.

Fabre, Michel. "Afterword" to *American Hunger*, by Richard Wright. New York: Harper and Row, 1977.

———. *The Unfinished Quest of Richard Wright*. New York: William Morrow, 1973.

Ferguson, Moira, ed. *The History of Mary Prince: A West Indian Slave, Related by Herself*. 1831. London: Pandora, 1987.

Fiedler, Leslie. *No! in Thunder*. New York: Stein and Day, 1972.

Foster, Frances Smith. "In Respect to Females: Differences in the Portrayals of Women by Male and Female Narrators." *Black American Literature Forum* 15 (summer 1981): 66–70.

French, Marilyn. *Her Mother's Daughter.* New York: Ballantine Books, 1988.

Friday, Nancy. *My Mother / My Self: The Daughter's Search for Identity.* New York: Delacorte, 1977.

Fuderer, Laura Sue. *The Female Bildungsroman in English: An Annotated Bibliography of Criticism.* New York: Modern Language Association, 1990.

Fullerton, Janet. "Women in Trinidadian Life and Literature." *New Voices* (Trinidad and Tobago) 5 (March 1977): 9–31.

Gilkes, Michael. *The West Indian Novel.* Boston: Twayne, 1981.

Ginsberg, Elaine. "The Female Initiation Theme in American Fiction." *Studies in American Fiction* 3 (spring 1975): 27–38.

Gonzalez-Berry, Erlinda, and Diana Rebolledo Tey. "Growing Up Chicano: Tomas Rivera and Sandra Cisneros." *Revista Chicana-Riquena* 13, nos. 3–4 (1985): 109–19.

Gornick, Vivian. "The World of Our Mothers." *New York Times Book Review,* November 19, 1987, 52.

Gross, Seymour. *Images of Blacks in American Literature.* Chicago: University of Chicago Press, 1966.

Guy-Sheftall, Beverly. "Mothers and Daughters: A Black Perspective." *Spelman Messenger* 98 (1982): 4–5.

Haisty, Donna B. "*The Bluest Eye.*" In *Masterplots,* edited by Frank McGill, 193. Englewood Cliffs, N.J.: Salem Press, 1986.

Hammer, Signe. *Daughters and Mothers, Mothers and Daughters.* New York: Quadrangle/New York Times, 1975.

Hardin, James N., ed. *Reflection and Action: Essays on the Bildungsroman.* Columbia: The University of South Carolina Press, 1991.

Harris, Trudier. *Black Women in the Fiction of James Baldwin.* Knoxville: University of Tennessee Press, 1985.

———. "Tiptoeing through Taboo: Incest in 'The Child Who Favored Daughter.'" *Modern Fiction Studies* 28 (autumn 1982): 495–505.

Hernton, Calvin C. *The Sexual Mountain and Black Women Writers.* New York: Anchor Books, 1987.

Hill, Errol. "An Interview with Olive Senior." *Kunapipi* 8:2 (1986): 11–20.

Hite, Molly. *The Other Side of the Story.* Ithaca, N.Y.: Cornell University Press, 1989.

Hodge, Merle. "Whither the Young Caribbean Women." *Women Speak,* Barbados (April 1985): 4–6.

———. "Young Women and the Development of a Stable Family Life in the Caribbean." *Savacou* 13 (October 1977).

Howe, Susan. *Wilhelm Meister and His English Kinsmen.* New York: Columbia University Press, 1930.

Huff, Linda. "Portrait of the Artist as a Young Woman: The Female *Kunstlerromane* in America." *DAI* 42 (1982): 3600A, University of Maryland.

Hunter, Charles. "Belize's First Novel, *Beka Lamb.*" *Belizean Studies* 10 (December 1982): 14–21.

Hurston, Zora Neale. *Tell My Horse.* New York: Lippincott Co., 1938.

Insally, Annette. "Sexual Politics in Contemporary Female Writing in the Caribbean." In *West Indian Literature and Its Political Context,* edited by Lowell Fiet, 79–91. Rio Piedras, Puerto Rico: University of Puerto Rico, 1988.

James, Louis. "The Sad Initiation of Lamming's 'G' and Other Caribbean Tales." In *Common Wealth,* edited by Anna Rutherford, 135–43. Aarhus: University of Aarhus, 1972.

Janheinz, John. *Neo-African Literature: A History of Black Writing.* New York: Grove Press, 1968.

Kapai, Leela. "Dominant Themes and Techniques in Paule Marshall's Fiction." *College Language Association Journal* 16 (September 1972): 49–59.

Kemp, Yakini. "Woman and Woman Child: Bonding and Selfhood in Three West Indian Novels by Women." *Sage: A Scholarly Journal on Black Women* 2 (spring 1985): 24–27.

Kent, George E. "Claude McCay's *Banana Bottom* Reappraisal." *College Language Association Journal* 18 (1974): 222–34.

———. "A Conversation with George Lamming." *Black World* 22 (March 1973): 430–51.

Klotman, Phyllis R. "Dick and Jane and the Shirley Temple Sensibility in *The Bluest Eye.*" *Black American Literature Forum* 13 (1979): 123–29.

Kom, Ambroise. "*In the Castle of My Skin:* George Lamming and the Colonial Situation." *World Literature Written in English* 18, no. 2 (1979): 406–20.

Koppleman, Susan, ed. *Between Mothers and Daughters: Stories across a Civilization.* New York: Feminist Press, 1984.

Kubitschek, Missy Dehn. "Paule Marshall's Women on Quest." *Black American Literature Forum* 21 (1987): 43–60.

Labovitz, Esther Klenord. *The Myth of the Heroine: The Female Bildungsroman in the 20th Century.* New York: Peter Lang, 1988.

Ladner, Joyce. *Tomorrow's Tomorrow: The Black Woman.* New York: Doubleday, 1971.

Lamming, George. *The Pleasures of Exile.* London: Michael Joseph, 1960.

Lawrence, Leota. "Mother-Child Relationships in British Caribbean Literature." *Western Journal of Black Studies* 5: 1 (1981): 10–17.

———. "Three West Indian Heroines: An Analysis." *College Language Association Journal* 21 (December 1977): 238–50. Discusses the work of Jean Rhys, Claude McKay, and Merle Hodge.

———. "Women in Caribbean Literature: The African Presence." *Phylon* 44 (spring 1983): 1–11.

LeSeur, Geta. "The Bildungsroman in Afro-American and Afro-Caribbean Fiction: An Integrated Consciousness." Ph.D. diss. Indiana University, 1982.

———. "*Brown Girl, Brownstones* as a Novel of Development." *Obsidian II* 1 (winter 1986): 119–29.

———. "From Nice Colored Girl to Womanist: An Exploration of Development in Ntozake Shange's Writings." In *Language and Literature in the African American Imagination,* edited by Carol Blackshire-Belay, 167–80. Westport, Conn.: Greenwood Press, 1992.

———. "Mothers and Sons: Androgynous Relationships in African-American and African–West Indian Novels of Youth." *Western Journal of Black Studies* 16:1 (1992): 21–26.

———. "One Mother, Two Daughters: The Afro-Caribbean Female Bildungsroman." *Black Scholar* 17 (March–April 1986): 26–33.

Lewis, Mary C. *Herstory: Black Female Rites of Passage.* Chicago: African American Images, 1988.

Luengo, Anthony. "Growing Up in San Fernando: Change and Growth in Michael Anthony's *The Year in San Fernando.*" *ARIEL* 6, no. 2 (1975): 81–95.

Lyons, Barbara. "Interview with Ntozake Shange." *Massachusetts Review* (winter 1987): 687–96.

Manley, Deborah. *Growing Up.* Lagos, Nigeria: African Universities Press, 1967.

Marcus, Mordecai. "What Is an Initiation Story?" *Journal of Aesthetic and Art Criticism* 19 (winter 1960): 222.

Marshall, Paule. "Poets in the Kitchen." In *Reena and Other Stories.* Old Westbury, N.Y.: Feminist Press, 1983.

———. "Shaping the World of My Art." *New Letters* 40 (1973–1974): 97–112.

Massiah, Joycelin. *Women as Heads of Households in the Caribbean: Family Structure and Feminine Status.* London: UNESCO, 1983.

McCluskey, Audrey T., ed. *New Perspectives on Gender, Race and Class in Society.* Bloomington, Ind.: Women Studies Program Occasional Papers, series 4 (1990): 125–41.

McCluskey, John Jr. "And Called Every Generation Blessed: Theme, Setting and Ritual in the Works of Paule Marshall." In *Black Women Writers, 1950–1980: A Critical Evaluation,* edited by Mari Evans, 316–34. New York: Anchor Press, 1984.

McColloh, Claire. "Look Homeward Bajan: A Look at the Work of Austin Clarke." *BIM* 14 (July–December 1972): 179–82.

McDowell, Deborah E. "The Self in Bloom: Alice Walker's *Meridian.*" *College Language Association Journal* 24 (March 1981): 262–75.

McDowell, Robert E. "Mothers and Sons: A View of Black Literature from South Africa, the West Indies, and America." *Prairie Schooner* 43 (1970): 356–68.

McPherson, Dolly A. *Order out of Chaos: The Autobiographical Works of Maya Angelou.* New York: Peter Lang, 1990.

McWatt, Mard, ed. *West Indian Literature and Its Social Context.* St. Michaels, Barbados: University of the West Indies, 1985.

Mead, Margaret. *Coming of Age in Samoa.* 1928. New York: American Museum of Natural History, 1973.

Memmi, Albert. *The Colonizer and the Colonized.* Translated by Howard Greenfield. Boston: Beacon Press, 1967.

Mordecai, Pamela. "Into This Beautiful Garden." *Caribbean Quarterly* 29 (June 1983): 44–53.

Morgan, Helen. "The Feminist Novel of Androgynous Fantasy." *Frontiers* 11 (fall 1977): 40–49.

———. "Human Becoming: Form and Focus in the New Feminist Novel." *Frontiers* 2 (fall 1977): 40.

Morrison, Toni. "Behind the Making of the Black Book." *Black World* (February 1974): 89.

Mullen, Harriette. "Daughters in Search of Mothers, or, a Girl Child in a Family of Men." *Catalyst* Premiere Issue, Fulton Public Library, Atlanta (1986): 45–49.

Munro, Ian. "George Lamming's *Season of Adventure:* A Failure in Creative Imagination." *Studies in Black Literature* 4 (spring 1973): 6–13.

Niesen de Abruna, Laura. "Twentieth Century Women Writers from the English-Speaking Caribbean." *Modern Fiction Studies* 34 (spring 1988): 85–96.

O'Neale, Sondra. "Race, Sex and Self: Aspects of *Bildung* in Selected Novels by Black American Women Novelists." *Multi Ethnic Literature of the United States* 9 (winter 1982): 25–35.

Paquet, Sandra Pouchet. *The Novels of George Lamming.* London: Heinemann, 1982.

———. "West Indian Autobiography." In *African American Autobiography,* edited by William L. Andrews, 196–211. New Jersey: Prentice Hall, 1993.

Perinbaum, Marie B. "The Parrot and the Phoenix: Franz Fanon's View of the West Indian and Algerian Woman." *Savacou* 13 (October 1977): 7–81.

Perry, Donna. "Initiation in Jamaica Kincaid's *Annie John.*" In *Caribbean Women Writers: Essays from the First International Conference,* edited by Selwyn Cudjoe, 245–53. Wellesley, Mass.: Calaloux Publications, 1990.

Pettis, Joyce. "Difficult Survival: Mothers and Daughters in *The Bluest Eye.*" *Sage: A Scholarly Journal on Black Women* 4 (fall 1987): 26–29.

Powell, Gloria. "Growing Up Black and Female." In *Becoming Female: Perspectives on Development,* edited by C. Kopp. New York: Plenum, 1979.

Pryse, M., and H. J. Spillers, ed. *Conjuring: Black Women, Fiction and Literary Tradition.* Bloomington: Indiana University Press, 1985.

Pyne, Timothy H. "Perceptions of the Black Woman in the Work of Claude McKay." *College Language Association Journal* 19, no. 2 (1975): 152–64.

Ramchand, Kenneth. *The West Indian Novel and Its Background.* London: Faber and Faber, 1970.

Ramchand, Kenneth, and Paul Edwards. "The Art of Memory in Michael Anthony's *The Year in San Fernando.*" *Journal of Commonwealth Literature* 7 (1969): 59–72.

Reagon, Bernice Johnson. "My Black Mothers and Sisters; or On Beginning a Cultural Autobiography." *Feminist Studies* 8 (spring 1982): 81–96.

Rich, Adrienne. *Of Woman Born: Motherhood as Experience and Institution.* New York: W. W. Norton, 1976.

Robinson, Jeff. "Mother and Child in Three Novels by George Lamming." *Release* 6–7 (1979): 75–83.

Rondon, Stewart. "Ralph Ellison's *Invisible Man*: Six Tentative Approaches." *College Language Association Journal* 12 (March 1969): 244–56.

Russell, Sandi. *Render Me My Song: African American Women Writers from Slavery to the Present.* New York: St. Martins Press, 1990.

Sadoff, Diane F. "Black Matrilineage: The Case of Alice Walker and Zora Neale Hurston." *Signs* 11 (1985): 4–26.

Saunders, Ellen. "My Daughter Listens to Me Sometimes, But I Listened to My Mother All the Time." In *Drylongso: A Self Portrait of Black America,* edited by John Langston Gnaltney. New York: Random House, 1980.

Scruggs, Charles. "The Tale of Two Cities in James Baldwin's *Go Tell It on the Mountain.*" *American Literature* 52 (March 1980): 1–17.

Shands, Annette. "Gwendolyn Brooks as Novelist." *Black World* 22 (June 1973): 22–30.

Smith, Sidonie, and Julie Watson, eds. *De/Colonizing the Subject:*

The Politics of Gender in Women's Autobiography. Minneapolis: University of Minnesota Press, 1992.

Spacks, Patricia Meyer. *The Female Imagination.* New York: Alfred A. Knopf, 1975.

Staples, Robert, ed. *The Black Family: Essays and Studies.* Belmont, Calif.: Wadsworth, 1971.

Steady, Filomena C., ed. *The Black Woman Cross-Culturally.* Cambridge, Mass.: Schenkman, 1981.

Thorpe, Marjorie. "The Problem of Cultural Identification in *Crick Crack Monkey.*" *Savacou* 13 (October 1977): 31–38.

Timothy, Helen Pyne. "Adolescent Rebellion and Gender Relations in *At the Bottom of the River* and *Annie John.*" In *Caribbean Women Writers: Essays from the First International Conference,* edited by Selwyn Cudjoe, 233–42. Wellesley, Mass.: Calaloux Publications, 1990.

Trescott, Jacqueline. "Jamaica Kincaid: Words and Silences." *International Herald Tribune,* April 29, 1984, 8.

Troester, Rosalie Riegle. "Turbulence and Tenderness: Mothers, Daughters and Other Mothers in Paule Marshall's *Brown Girl, Brownstones.*" *Sage: A Scholarly Journal on Black Women* 1 (fall 1984): 13–16.

Turner, Gordon Philip. "The Protagonist's Initiatory Experiences in the Canadian *Bildungsroman*: 1908–1971." *DAI* 40 (1979): 2057–58A, University of British Columbia.

Wade-Gayles, Gloria. *No Crystal Stair: Visions of Race and Sex in Black Women's Fiction.* New York: Pilgrim Press, 1984.

———. "The Truths of Our Mothers' Lives: Mother–Daughter Relationships in Black Women's Fiction." *Sage: A Scholarly Journal on Black Women* 2 (fall 1984): 8–12.

Walker, Alice. *In Search of Our Mothers' Gardens: Womanist Prose.* New York: Harcourt Brace Jovanovich, 1983.

Walker-Johnson, Joyce. "Autobiography, History and the Novel: Erna Broder's *Jane and Louisa Will Soon Come Home.*" *Journal of West Indian Literature* 3 (January 1989): 47–59.

Ward, Catherine. "Self-Realization in the Fiction of Paule Marshall." Paper given at the Midwest Modern Language Association Conference, Western Kentucky University, 1991.

Washington, Mary Helen. "I Sign My Mother's Name: Alice Walker, Dorothy West, Paule Marshall." In *Mothering the Mind: Twelve Studies of Writers and Their Silent Partners,* edited by Ruth Perry and Marture Watson Brownley. New York: Holmes and Meier, 1984.

————. "Plain Talk, and Decently Wild: The Heroic Possibilities of Maud Martha." In *The Voyage In: Fictions of Female Development,* edited by Elizabeth Abel, Marianne Hirsch, and Elizabeth Langland, 270–86. Hanover, N.H.: University Press of New England, 1983.

————. "'Taming All That Anger Down': Rage and Silence in *Maud Martha.*" In *Black Literature and Literary Theory,* edited by Henry Louis Gates Jr. London/New York: Methuen, 1984.

White, Barbara. *Growing Up Female: Adolescent Girlhood in American Fiction.* Westport, Conn.: Greenwood Press, 1985.

Williams, John, trans. "Return of a Native Daughter: An Interview with Paule Marshall and Maryse Condé." *Sage: A Scholarly Journal on Black Women* 3 (fall 1986): 52–53.

Willis, Susan. *Specifying: Black Women Writing; The American Experience.* Madison: University of Wisconsin Press, 1987.

Wright, Richard. *American Hunger.* New York: Harper and Row, 1977.

INDEX

Survivors of the Crossing (A. Clarke), 61
Susan Proudleigh (De Lisser), 151
Sweet Summer: Growing Up with and without My Dad (B. Campbell), 195
Syrop (St. Omer), 50

"Talking of Trees" (Senior), 194
Tee *(Crick Crack, Monkey)*, 5, 21, 23, 152, 166–74, 191, 193, 194, 198
Their Eyes Were Watching God (Hurston), 15, 102, 107, 156
Tobago, 190
Toronto, 24, 189, 190
Tradition, 39, 40, 81, 85, 106
Tree Grows in Brooklyn, A (Smith), 102
Trinidad, 23, 29*n11*, 38, 41, 42, 53, 69, 151, 152, 165, 166
Tubman, Harriet, 190
Twain, Mark, 8, 12, 19, 32

Unbelonging, The (Riley), 189
Uncle Tom, 76
Underground Railroad, 190
Unfinished Quest of Richard Wright, The (Fabre), 92
United States, 1, 12, 24, 39, 53, 153, 177, 182, 184, 189, 195
Unvanquished, The (Faulkner), 20

Vassa, Gustavas. *See* Equiano, Olaudah
Victorian era, 2*n1*, 12
Victorian ideology, 184
Village, 9, 33, 166. *See also* Community
Voice: 33, 74, 91, 92, 95, 166, 185, 186, 194, 197, 200; of children, 11, 42, 150*n2*, 187, 197; of oppressed peoples, 132
Voodoo, 51*n10*, 158, 159, 160, 162

Wain, John, 20
Walcott, Derek, 1, 16
Walker, Alice, 14, 102, 108, 133, 147, 185
Walker, Margaret, 52, 101
Walk in the Night, A (La Guma), 9
Walrond, Eric, 108
Washington, Booker T., 74, 82–85 *passim*
Weep Not Child (Ngugi), 9
Wells, Ida B., 26*n8*, 85
West Africa, 1, 161
Whiteness. *See* Identity
Wide Sargasso Sea (Rhys), 151
Wilby *(Growing Up with Miss Milly)*, 7
Wilhelm Meisters Lehrjahre (Goethe), 1*n1*, 21, 31
Wilson, Betty, 199
Wilson, Harriet, 12, 19, 20
Wolfe, Thomas, 20
Womanist, 101, 108, 133, 195, 196, 200
Woman Warrior, The (Kingston), 8, 107
Wonderful Adventures of Mrs. Seacole in Many Lands, The (Seacole), 150*n2*
Woolf, Virginia, 20
Wright, Richard, 6, 12, 13, 19, 24, 26, 26*nn7,8,* 73, 74, 85, 92, 95, 98, 99, 194, 196

Xuma *(Mine Boy)*, 9

Year in San Fernando, The (Anthony), 22, 23, 33, 41, 42, 63–69 *passim,* 73, 166

Zami: A New Spelling of My Name (Lorde), 195
Zobel, Joseph, 151

CREDITS

Acknowledgment is made as follows for permission to reproduce portions of my previously published work:

Passages from "*BrownGirl, Brownstones* as a Novel of Development" in *Obsidian II* 1:3 (Winter 1986).

Passages from "Mothers and Sons: Androgynous Relationships in African-American and AfricanWest Indian Novels of Youth" in *Western Journal of Black Studies* 16:1 (1992).

Passages from "From Nice Colored Girl to Womanist: An Exploration of Development in Ntozake Shange's Writings," first published in *Language and Literature in the African American Imagination,* edited by Carol Blackshire-Belay (Westport, Conn.: Greenwood Press, 1992).